MW00715785

Going Walkabout through the Suburbs

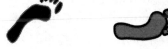

About the Author

Actively involved in working for the common good for over thirty years, Robbie Lloyd focuses on social justice for disadvantaged groups, and community cultural development for indigenous people. Combining social change with creating community, he works in reforming mental health and services for people living with intellectual disability. He also volunteers on community committees combining all age groups in sharing the task of 'people power' - for celebration, empowerment and giving voice to difference and diversity.

Robbie's emphasis is on person-centred, extended non-blood family models of community, and strategies to bring elders and young people together in shared development. With a focus on Action Research, he likes to encourage modelling new approaches to making a difference.

Starting out in the early 70s in school teaching, he got involved in alternative 'child centred' education, then became a university lecturer in education, then journalist on the same topic, before teaching that as well at university. National politics and communications then lured him away from education in the mid-80s, and he worked on organisational change in business and government, coupled with voluntary community work. Ten years ago he turned towards Aboriginal Reconciliation, and went on a journey of learning, which took him through a number of years among Aboriginal communities in western and south-western NSW, as well as supporting cultural renewal in Bali, New Zealand and South India. Work which continues, alongside addressing the needs of people living with the challenges of mental illness and/or intellectual disability, and celebrating their unique consciousness.

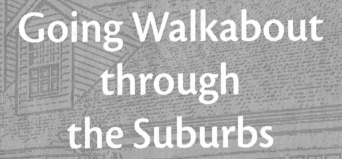

Going Walkabout
through
the Suburbs

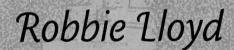

Robbie Lloyd

The author and publisher would like to thank copyright holders for permission to reproduce copyright material. Every effort has been made to trace the original source of all material in this book. Where the attempt has been unsuccessful, the editors would be pleased to hear from the author or publisher concerned to rectify any omission.

Published in Australia by
Temple House Pty Ltd,
T/A Sid Harta Publishers
ACN 092 197 192
Hartwell, Victoria

Telephone: 61 3 9560 9920
Facsimile: 61 3 9545 1742
E-mail: author@sidharta.com.au

First published in Australia 2005
Copyright © Robbie Lloyd, 2005
Cover design, typesetting: Chameleon Print Design

The right of Robbie Lloyd to be identified as the Author
of the Work has been asserted in accordance with the
Copyright, Designs and Patents Act 1988.

Lloyd, Robbie
Going Walkabout through the Suburbs
ISBN: 1-821030-01-1
pp376

In establishing our basic attitude toward the world around us, we might simply reflect on the awakening of consciousness in our earliest years. As soon as we awaken to consciousness, the universe comes to us, while we go out to the universe. This intimate presence of the universe to itself in each being is the deep excitement of existence…The word 'universe', 'universa' in Latin, indicates the turning of the grand diversity of things back towards their unit. I mention this tendency here because the purpose of this book on insects is simply to indicate the intimate presence that exists between ourselves and the insects. The immediate corollary is that we and the insects depend on each other in some profound manner. This was the primordial insight of the Taoists of ancient China: the movement of the Tao is 'to turn'. After differentiating, all things turn back to that primordial unity where each is fulfilled in the others. To go far is to come near. Such is the basic law of existence. We are at the moment of turning.

(Joanne Lauck, *The Voice of the Infinite in the Small*)

On our journey to understanding, the universe throws all kinds of opposition and enemies in our way. It is possible to learn and gain from this adversity, only if we have the humility to acknowledge that we are not always right, or in the right. This book clearly outlines the experience which young mental patients such as myself, and others living with Down Syndrome, go through in everyday life, and life itself, and also lends an ear to our suffering. May much good come to you in this reading. and may God be with you, in your travels through the heart.
(William Lloyd)

And some notes from William Lloyd on why Caring Engagement counts in Healing…
(Comments written in William's journal in 2004, on appreciating his psychotherapist Ludmilla Kopel Fields, Sydney, and being sceptical of 'case managers').

My Psychotherapist:
She listens.
Helps me with my emotions.
Strategies to help me manage my madness.
Opens my mind to things about myself I may never have discovered.

Doesn't scare me.
Is willing to accept my ideas and wants to, it's my
treatment.
Can be a provider of proof that my needs are actually
acceptable by medical professionals.
Gives me advice about avoiding nightmares, and it works.
Seems to have really helped with my madness – less
fear, better rationalisations; and things,
now that I see her, are heaps better.

Case Managers:
Scare me. Don't listen. Don't care. Don't have my needs and
best interests as important at all. Push me around. Push
me into treatment I don't want. Don't matter to me. Tell
lies. Want what they want, not what I want. Incarcerate me.
Don't understand me. Threaten my life. Say that details of
my treatment are up to them not me. Tell me I will (basically)
never win and it's their right to do what they want to me.
Bully me until I get annoyed, and then use that disruption
to call me unwell and I end up in hospital.

Selected verses from two songs performed by Christine Anu, 'Photograph' and 'Love That Heals'

<u>Photograph</u> *(by David Bridie)*

Old photograph on the wall
Making the past come alive
You've got this truth I can tell
From your iron gaze
From your cold stare
It's taking me back

Whose clothes are you wearing
I can see they're from the mission world
Why aren't you smiling
Did you know I'd be staring back
Right into your eyes

You're with me every step I take
You're like the roots in the ground
Passing love to our family
You're the knowledge
You're the strength
That I've found...

You're the old, you're the new
You're the past, you're the present
You're my brother, you're my sister
You're the future.

Love that heals (by Neil Murray)

I've been waiting for a thousand years
Waiting here just for you
I am the woman you've been searching for
I am the woman right next to you
With a love that heals

So much trouble in the world today
So much pain and misery
Oh yes I know that you're breaking down
And I know you're in desperate need

For a love that heals
For a love that heals

We sing the songs that turn the night into day
We sing to bring the joyous rain
We sing for children to come into our lives
We sing to take their pain away

With a love that heals
With a love that heals
With a love that heals
Only love can heal...

I've been singing for a thousand years
Can you hear me calling out to you
All I know is that we're breaking down
And I know that you're worried too...

For a love that heals.

Contents

Acknowledgements

This work is dedicated to William Lloyd and Tom Elenor

This work has resulted from many years of working and living with the groups of people it covers. The ideas expressed may not be shared by some of these individuals, but their contributions have been important and valued, in shaping a sense of the map for further walkabouts. I thank them all and maintain connection, even if separated by the illusion of time and distance.

Peter Beilharz, for introducing me to Bernard Smith's whole oeuvre, and James Clifford for goading me into embracing Raymond Williams.

Bernard Smith, for permission to use his works, and for patient acceptance of another way of seeing one's own work, in a debated exchange over style and emphasis.

James Cowan, and Brandl & Schlesinger, for permission to use his works, plus kind and generous support of an admiring follower.

Carmel Gold for rhyming a melody out of a cacophony, with kind, wise and inspired editing of my original mess. Thanks for your guidance and insight to the further horizons Carmel.

Susan Murphy has been a friend, fellow traveller, curious inquirer about the spaces being entered, and continues to be an inspiration with her own leadership in matters of antipodean spirited living. Lead on Susan.

Debbie Horsfall is like a wiser older sister, watching and suggesting ways to avoid mistakes and enhance opportunities to progress. Thanks for the partnership Debbie.

Virginia Kaufman Hall for wise guidance, teasing and stretching beyond my polemical corral.

David Bridie, for permission to use the words of the song "Photograph" in the opening section.

Neil Murray, for permission to use the words of the song "Love That Heals" in the opening section.

Indigenous: Mana Forbes, Hamilton NZ; Ian Woods and the Nari Nari, Hay NSW; Uncle Col and Aunty Fay Walker and the Yorta Yorta; Judith Davis; Barry Pearce; John Bugg; Rachel Carney; Bobby Merritt; R. Ashok, R. Arumugung, P. Elumalai in Pondicherry, India; Margot and Tony and Ariani Anwar, Bali; Janet and Ketut, Bali; Cambodya, Jakarta; Lola Forrester; Philippa McDermott; Lloyd McDermott (Mullanjaiwukka); Sister Pat Linnane, and Sister Michelle Farrugia, Bathurst; Tony McAvoy; Josslyn Fairey; Trevor Maranda; Joy Kirby, and Jeannette Cupitt.

The Dharug, Wiradjuri and Gandangarra Aboriginal nations of central and western New South Wales.

Addiction: Ben 'Benson' Lloyd; P. 'Santosh' Subramanian and the Pondicherry AA Family; Gibb, Neil and the St Stephens AA Family, Macquarie St Sydney; Stella Maris AA Family, Stanley St Sydney; Margherita Tracanelli.

Mental Illness: William 'Big' Lloyd; Hiltrud Kivelitz;

David Millikan; Pioneer Clubhouse Family, Balgowlah, Sydney; Athma Shakti Vidyalaya Family Bangalore, India; Fr Hank Nunn; Bruce Watson; Heather and Lai Yin Gibb; Kim Bagot; David Duval; Allison Nunn; Nicole Tillotson; Ben Ladd; David Webb; Meg Smith.

Intellectual Disability: Tom 'Hit Man' Elenor; Paula Rix; Chris Elenor; Rohan Fullwood; Barbara Nance; Saday Special School Family, Pondicherry, India; Mr & Mrs Sukumar Pondicherry; Chitra Amit, Pondicherry, India; Margot Elliffe; Helena O'Connell

Love and The Common Good: John Poulos; Max Taylor; Ian Lloyd; Peter Lloyd; Gai Lloyd; Heather 'FJ' Lloyd; Maggie 'Boo' Lloyd; Suze Morris; Toni Boyd; Virginia Winley; Jane McLean; Brett Neilson; Johnny Allen, Auroville, India; Prof. P. Marudanayagam Pondicherry, India; Sally Gray; Carl and Gurdive Webster; Jenny Melville; David Woods; Rachel Morley; Ann Walsh; Cristina Ricci.

Spirit of Place: Blue Mountains North Katoomba Valley Dreaming, Capertee Valley Dreaming, Goolooinboin; James Cowan; Bernard Smith.

Balancing Body, Energy, Mind, Spirit and Consciousness, and Addressing Our Resistance: Craig Sharp, Yoga Teacher; Peter Tumminello, Homoeopath; Helen Meekosha.

While all these people have been contributors to the content and spirit of this work, only one person has ultimately made the process possible. My partner Margaret Bailitis, without whose forgiving and accepting, caring and providing support in trying circumstances, it would not have reached this stage, with strong hopes of going further walkabout. Thanks darling.

Chapter One

Introduction

Not long after the ravages of the Second World War (1939-45), the historian, Arnold Toynbee, was thinking about human history. He expressed what I believe is true for all of us:

If my individual view of history is to be made at all illuminating, or indeed intelligible, it must be presented in its origin, growth, and social and personal setting. There are many angles of vision from which human minds peer at the universe. (1)

The 'angle of vision' for this work refers to 'the others', those human beings who are not identified in the mainstream of Western society, at least in the way humanity currently organises itself in the new millennium:

- People living with mental illness and intellectual disability, who are part of the publicly unacceptable face of society where image and form seem to take precedence over content.
- Indigenous peoples are increasingly neglected and exploited, their lands are being overtaken by the rapacious search for profits from natural resources. Yet, they maintain, in both urban and outback environments, a practical connection with the numinous which can inform all of humanity.

- Addicts, those individuals who have given in to the desire to seek oblivion, away from 'normal life', through insatiable pursuit of escape behaviours, or 'fixes' which allegedly help them to achieve relief from the discomfort of living in that 'normal' world. In fact, they only receive temporary relief from their dis-ease with life. Increasingly, this way of life is becoming an allegory about modern life. People feel trapped in lives they do not enjoy, earning money to survive, or searching hopelessly for work that no longer exists in a world they find de-spirited and meaningless.

Although we all share aspects of these universal human perspectives, most people are uncomfortable with facing them. Toynbee knew this. After the atom bomb was dropped on Hiroshima, he witnessed the 'outbreak of a third Western technological revolution':

Technology is, of course, only a Greek name for a bag of tools; and we have to ask ourselves: What are the tools that count in this competition in the use of tools as means to power?…all tools are not of the material kind; there are spiritual tools as well, and these are the most potent man has made. (2)

Humanity is depleted, it is not exercising its spiritual muscle, which enables us to fully value our lives and embrace difference among human beings. Our collective soul is sick and in need of repair.

In the Australian Aboriginal sense of choosing to reconnect with the transcendent, 'to go walkabout' is a way of communing with the greater soul of the universe. This faculty of human awareness is available to all people in several dimensions. It seems to me that many people would benefit from going walkabout.

Humanity, in late capitalism, can restore its communion of souls and community of lifeworld (Lebenswelt) by valuing universal aspects of the higher good: in earth's spirit of place; in sharing our consciousness of the numinous; in our practical expression of mercy and compassion for one another; and in holding to the common good. The way humanity chooses to run the world of politics, economics, the market and our responsibilities for the earth and one another, can be integrated with these values.

The 'others' among us are also our teachers who can help us replenish our 'bag of tools' so that we can exercise our spiritual muscle. These teachers can offer alternative and/or exaggerated perspectives that inform our understanding of ourselves. The way we feel and experience the same variations between love, fear, anxiety and joy, may provide us with clues about how we can better manage our world.

The underlying premise of this book is that we are all individuals living in a shared society. If we are to restore some value to human life, respecting each person's right to exist with dignity, safety, health and happiness, we need to re-learn ways of thinking and feeling. In this way, the late capitalist world can remember to value our humanness as the core of progress.

Understanding that life is a shared experience, more than a ruthless competition of winners and losers, will enable people to genuinely know each on the other's terms. This could lead to sharing of our inner lives as much as we share our material life concerns.

If the old individualism artificially isolated the 'bare human being', there is an equal danger in certain trends in the new sociology which isolates the group, society or culture as an absolute point of reference. If people are essentially learning, creating and communicating beings, the only social organisation adequate to our nature is a participating democracy in which all of us, as individuals, learn, communicate and control. Any lesser, restrictive system is wasteful of our true resources. By shutting individuals out from effective participation, our common process is damaged. (3)

One way to enable this participating democracy is through story. Others include dance, art, music, theatre and expressive forms of creative release. Such narrative forms can peacefully gather the rational and irrational, the known and unknown, the truth and the lies, the facts and the mysteries, in ways which can reconstruct information to reveal a new view of truth. This is the gift of the four groups being discussed as we follow them on the walkabout trail. They do not obey the rules and they do not remember their table manners, but they make a bloody good story.

Sources and Original Contribution

This book is based on Raymond Williams' and Bernard Smith's explorations of culture, society, art and ideas, as well as on my own experience with the four groups. It draws new interpretations of the possibilities in establishing a Structure of Feelings and Experience from the combined perspective of these two authors. I will examine the consciousness of people living with mental illness and intellectual disability, as well as the addicted and indigenous, by using the work of other authors as well as drawing on my experience of living and working with these people. My aim is to develop a guide to better on-ground practice of rehabilitation.

Finally, a model of human consciousness is suggested, developed from my own views, as a framework for indicators to balance Feelings and Experience (I equate this with human awareness). This model is proposed as an attempt to enable the system's authorities to engage more with people living with mental illness and intellectual disability, to get them to contribute to the design and delivery of the policies and programs that effectively create their lifeworld. The model proposed is not claimed to be comprehensive, just as good a place as any to start. The Action Research Life Journalling project will ascertain from these two groups specifically what their lived experience has to say.

Progress comes from addressing our inner lives, as much as the outer world of the material, organising and representative processes. But, like Marshall Berman, I am in favour of continuing with the project of modernism, with a critical eye: 'If everything must go, then let it go: modern people have the power to create a better world than the world they have lost'. (4)

As Bernard Smith likes to say, 'in the mix' of this process of change is a return to the conversation of life, the notion of 'working the culture' of soul as an applied aspect of human life. Not religion, not ideology, but shared human spirit, which informs daily decisions about values, priorities and bottom line issues, such as placing the common good before individual self interest. There is a need for more humility and less ego in the workings of humankind. I hope these issues will emerge as salient features of the new modernism, which replaces today's already old version with yesterday's echoes of spirit. Echo-logy in action.

So, what is the problem?

The needs of citizens are not effectively served because of the economic rational ideals and practices employed by health, rehabilitation and community services. (Throughout this book I will use the term citizen to emphasise the responsibility we all share to participate in community life to preserve the common good.)

There is a need to re-establish the indicators of human needs and aspirations which reflect people's Feelings and Experiences. Ultimately, this seems to be the role of those services which claim to be responding to people's needs with regard to their health and quality of life. The particular vulnerabilities of people living with mental illness and intellectual disability are exacerbated by this phenomenon of rationalisation that overwhelms the caring service sector. Care, as a societal process, has become a victim of economic logic. It is time to consider alternative ways of measuring efficiency and effectiveness by responding to what people need in their hearts, minds and souls.

This is not a romantic, idealistic notion. It is possible to be thoroughly bottom-line sensitive by valuing those aspects of human life which make us human. The emergence and practice of the ideologies of economic rationalism over the past fifty years has created a worldwide malaise. While managers pursue savings and downsizing, people are suffering from loss of services and loss of heart. My work with the indigenous, alcoholics, and people living with intellectual disability and mental illness, has shown me that these groups of 'others' have valuable things to teach us. The system is currently failing to meet their needs. By taking note of these alternative perspectives, managers of health, rehabilitation and community services can learn a great deal about how to serve their clients.

Scattered throughout this book are examples of where approaches such as these are working, as well as alternative ways of approaching a restructuring of these community services. The limitations of any proposed alternatives are also noted.

A framework for exploring feelings and experience

Humanity includes great diversity in consciousness, onto-diversity as well as shared or common attributes of Feeling and Experience. Feelings and Experience are taken to be the representations of consciousness lived out in people's daily lives. These aspects of consciousness are affective indicators of the basic humans needs of heart, mind and soul.

Therefore, by establishing a framework of Feelings and Experience, which reflects common consciousness among people living in Western society, I believe it is possible to achieve two objectives: to identify and better understand difference and diversity between people living with intellectual disability and mental illness, and ultimately what they represent that is part of all of us, and to identify useful parameters for practical application in public policy and programs serving the disadvantaged.

People living with mental illness and intellectual disability have special attributes of consciousness which are both challenges and opportunities for soul growth. Using the word 'soul' does not alienate this work from rational analysis and applied discussion of social issues. It is 'soul' in the sense that old and new writers, such as Carlyle,

D.H. Lawrence, David Tacey and John Caroll see 'soul' as the substance of humanity and culture — something people live within and work with every day, and which is shared between all humans.

The Feelings and Experience of people living with intellectual disability and mental illness, reveal attributes that exist in all humans, but they can be exaggerated and problematic. If policy makers, who are meant to serve the needs of these people, can adopt a rationale that views life in terms of the rich universality of their 'otherness and diversity', then these attributes of consciousness become a resource.

Indigenous people (both urban and outback dwellers) have inherited other levels of consciousness that link them closely to earth's rhythms and the 'dreaming' consciousness, which is more than logic and emotion alone. Without romanticising this as some halcyon return to the native, non-indigenous people can access skills for their inner lives, which are still available to all people, by sharing their territory of consciousness in urban and more natural locations.

Addictions (to all habits) can be exaggerated products of modernity, which leave the addict stuck in a dis-eased state, both bred and irritated by conditions of late capitalism. They use habitual fixes to try to avoid sitting with their discomfort of soul.

Going Walkabout through the Suburbs sets out to explore the human condition in Western society, and particularly that of some 'others' who show difference and diversity of consciousness. On this journey I have adopted (in the Aboriginal use of this term) several aunties and uncles. That is, elders who provide guidance and observing wisdom which can inform my own journey. Foremost among these are Raymond Williams and Bernard Smith. They are accompanied by, among others, Aunties Anne Wilson Schaef, Karen Horney and Marie Louise von Franz, and Uncles Jurgen Habermas and his colleague Michael Pusey, James Cowan, Peter Beilharz, Theodore Zeldin, and Michael Jackson.

In the following quotes, as part of his investigation into artistic inspiration, Uncle Raymond refers to a view of Sigmund Freud's account of the mind operating in layers of consciousness. And Williams quotes Herbert Read reflecting on how artists get their inspiration:

If we picture the regions of the mind as three superimposed strata…we can imagine in certain rare cases a phenomenon comparable to a 'fault' in geology, as a result of which in one part of the mind the layers become discontinuous, and exposed to each other at unusual levels…Some such hypothesis is necessary to explain that access, that lyrical intuition, which is known as inspiration and which in all ages has been the rare possession of those few individuals we recognise as artists of genius. (5)

Likewise, in society there are fault lines which reveal connections between people, knowledge, folklore, mysteries and archetypes. These fault lines are often to do with the people and places where differences gather. By entering into a conversation with those places and people, it is possible to learn a great deal about how to reintegrate humanity, and to better serve the needs of people living in marginalised circumstances of lifeworld.

Having identified a Structure of Feeling and Experience that forms a framework for 'normal' human consciousness, I then examine those areas highlighted by the different experiences of 'the others'. This leads to a set of parameters that can, hopefully, be used to better meet the needs of those living with mental illness and intellectual disability to be more integrated and valued in mainstream society. In addition, my hope is that it will empower them to express their Feelings and Experience in the program planning and delivery of the health, community and rehabilitation services they experience.

Modern lifeworld and the common good

The motivation behind this work is to create pathways towards walkabout, ways people can rediscover their existence as both social and numinous beings by protecting and exercising the common good. This is basic to the rights and needs of people, so they can live with dignity and treat each other decently, without prejudice, injustice, neglect or being taken advantage of. This value system has been eroded across late capitalist societies. Restoration starts among those in greatest need — such as the people who live with mental illness and intellectual disability. If Western society cannot help those most in need, it has little chance of helping those in the mainstream to engage with more integrated ways of being.

No utopian vision of society is held aloft in this work, this is no promise of some miraculous salvation for humankind. The lifeworld proposed for a 'normal', healthy human life is simply the kind of social democratic capitalist system that modernity was built on in the years following the Second World War — a lifeworld that supports individual enterprise and the process of 'doing business', but with an assumption of the maintenance of the public estate and a safety net of basic essential life supports, especially for those in need. We need an integration of our lifeworld systems that will incorporate more ways of valuing and exercising the Feelings and Experiences at the core of humanity, and to balance that with respect for, and protection of, natural and socio-cultural environments.

Like Jurgen Habermas, I hold to the value which joins the inner world of our shared subjectivity with the object world 'out there'. (6) I do not believe it is either romantic, nor in denial of real-politik, to argue for greater involvement of people who live with mental illness and intellectual disability in organising their lifeworld. Like Uncle Jurgen, I believe 'the inner motive we all share is the need to better understand our own lives so that we can live together more productively'. (7)

Community is the combination of people I share my life with – my partner, children, extended family, work mates, neighbourhood, and the wide network of acquaintances, whom I do not know well, but who contribute significantly to my lifeworld. Beyond those people is my wider society. The nation state's community, where traditions meet, values mix, and priorities for valuing aspects of shared humanity are continuously evolving and being debated.

Presently, a major debate in Western society is about the death of the common good — a value system shared across societies, which holds that each person has a basic right to quality of life, through freedom, justice, choices and opportunities. Until the last three decades of the twentieth century, choice about life circumstances seemed to be one of the hallmarks of the progress of modernism. But, choice has been removed from the lifeworld of many citizens, and this trend should be challenged and reversed in political, legislative and administrative ways.

Too many people's basic needs are not being met under economic rationalism, the dominant ethos of late capitalism. Things are so bad now, that talking about acknowledging difference and diversity, and seeking engagement of the disadvantaged in managing their life-world, could be seen by many as an idealistic dream. But like Uncle Jurgen, I argue it is now time that 'the limits set by the need for social reproduction and social integration' (8) were activated on the seesaw of modernism, 'pushing problems back and forth between state and market'. (9) Now is the time when people in Western societies are feeling 'the pain and the confusions that accrue from the side-effects of development (which) will both clear the way and at the same time lead the movement of reflection in a rational direction'. (10)

Acknowledging and servicing the needs identified by the affective indicators of the Structure of Feelings and Experience (SOFE), among those who live with mental disability and intellectual disability, may point the way for revaluing them within society. For if culture is our soul as a people (Tacey, Carroll), it will only stay healthy if people 'work it' (Jackson). Meaning, modern citizens need a balance in acknowledging the numinous, the imaginative, the celebratory and the reverent, alongside the rational, reasoned, logical and materialist.

We need our rituals to be more than the routine of listening for the state of the stock market on the morning news, which is not a 'return to the native'. People can share stories, celebrate beliefs, pass through stages of maturation in rites of passage, and acknowledge the human spirit, all in a late capitalist context. Not as a touchy-feely alternative lifestyle excursion, but as an ordinary everyday shared ritual in an evolving lifeworld. Such as the way other developing cultures I have lived with (Balinese, Maori, Tamil, and some Australian Aboriginals) combine modernity and tradition: through morning household puja offerings in tourism venues; daily staff gatherings to share reverent multi-faith prayers in large modern hospitals; stopping to value cultural celebrations in business places; and by making the spirit of place an honoured context for all who visit.

Progress is as much about the development of our inner lives as it is about material gain and technical invention. Empirical assessment and evaluation of life has assisted material development, but humanity needs to be more officially engaged with its affective and numinous sides. Not in the pursuit of some new version of 'Gemeinschaft' (11), but a more mature, and in fact indigenous sense of 'working the society and culture', by making social democracy work for everyone's shared needs. This includes integrating a new valuing of the spirit and the common good.

It means replacing the current domination by vested interest groups in representative politics and public administration with a rejuvenated democratic process. The neo-feudal, almost neo-fascist, theory and obsessions of economists and politicians have come to a dead end. They do not provide for more than an elite minority, and work against the interests of the majority, undermining basic notions and applied values of community and the common good.

We also need to challenge the trend of applying impression management (12) to the provision of a Wirthian 'ecological urbanism'. (13) In such versions of democratic social development, people who are lucky enough to score jobs in the new e-economy can also claim a neo-colonial, urban enclave life (Gibson), safe from the underclasses. This version of progress is nothing more than a game of virtual reality. It neglects the true needs of both the well-off and the poor, replacing them with images from *The Truman Show*. (14)

People can reclaim ordinary Western democracy by removing the corporate 'life-support' systems that have been catheterised into all areas of public provision. The life-streams would flow again to meet people's needs if the tax dollars went to the public estate, not privatised or out-sourced services. At the same time, the corporate world needs to pay the real price for doing business, by acknowledging its debt to the environment and to people all over the world who have been exploited in the interests of profit.

Rather than being tired Marxist talk, this approach applies responsible, respectful rejuvenation of the common good, and assertive declaration of the responsibility of representative social democratic processes to serve that higher good. So, business goes on, but it pays its way, and meets the human and ecological costs that go with profits.

Terms and assumptions in a 'grammar of forms of life'

Consciousness refers to the moment by moment awareness of mind that all people share, processing Feelings and Experience continuously and differently for each individual, while also sharing common perspectives and perceptions.

Humans are social beings with hearts, minds and souls.

Hearts refers to our affective experience of emotions, combined with thoughts to generate Feelings, which both create and respond to our Experiences. All people live their lives through a system of perception and projection, which means people 'see the movie of their lives' according to how their own consciousness is 'screening it' from moment to moment. A basic assumption beneath the optimism of this work is the fact that intention and action can move a democracy to shift its power structures.

Like Uncle Jurgen, I believe that 'Our own modern condition is a kind of tug-of-war between the lifeworld and the system (and)…Given the unyielding organizational principle of capitalist mediatized colonization by the economy and the state (money and market, power and bureaucracy, respectively)…The outcome of this dialectic between system and lifeworld cannot be predicted.' (15)

Nevertheless, people still have the choice to act on their inner values and beliefs. Responding to the common good is a precious reason to act. Focusing on the needs of deeply disadvantaged people creates a context of grounded urgency in maintaining the so-called advances of social democracy.

Culture is the 'soul of the people', and society is our combination of ideas, values, traditions, practical management systems and lifestyle choices which vary from group to group, and nation to nation. Culture and Society combine to form the matrix of our lives and they set the conditions for development of each individual born into human society. The way those individuals are treated by their immediate parents and siblings, extended families, community and wider society, creates the quality of life in each society. Western society is lacking in its exercise of values and practical life services that acknowledge our shared inner needs.

Jurgen Habermas says that the lifeworld (Lebenswelt) is: 'the background consensus of everyday life…the storehouse of knowledge that is passed from one generation to the next…(where) social and economic structures interpenetrate with action and consciousness'. (16) Late capitalism has become disconnected from the inherent lifeworld value system, at the same time as having invaded it. So, while it has lost touch with deeper human needs of heart, mind and soul, it occupies them with second-rate notions, of power, wealth, competitive self-interest and resulting aggression or powerlessness. This is due to 'Reification, the increasing penetration of exchange values and power into society, culture, and the lifeworld'. (17) Two groups who suffer in particular from this lack of valuing deeper human needs are those who live with mental illness and intellectual disability. They become lost through a preoccupation with efficiency and effectiveness that measures people in monetary terms. Their Feelings and Experiences are commonly shared by all of us, but are more easily noticed because of their differences.

Using the lifetime work of two theorists of Western culture and society, Raymond Williams and Bernard Smith, I will create a framework of the Structure of Feeling and Experience (SOFE) and attempt to show you where humanity's needs could be better met. I will look specifically at the two subject groups, who are positioned for a deeper study following completion of this work. More open and assertive conversations about the attributes of human consciousness, which we all share, are needed to counteract the mindless pursuit of an irrational 'economic rationalism', which has overtaken our lifeworld in the last forty years. The dismantling of the welfare state, firstly, by denigrating the very notion, and then, by privatising its infrastructure, has left humanity in a wasteland of neglect.

This book is based on a valuing of the common good via our elected representatives and public institutions. Administering the public estate in the interests of all, with guarantees for those in greatest need to be protected by their society, is the foundation for my view of humanity.

Further development can then be undertaken to explore the potential for growth by integrating the broader aspects of humanity into our lifeworld. This means taking a view of spirit that needs to be incorporated into mainstream life, and valuing its maintenance as much as people value income, food, shelter and safety. This is not about religion, which is a personal choice for all, but it is an acknowledgment of the numinous source of that desire to pursue meaning beyond the material elements of life.

Spirit is defined as that conscious life force and energy for life, linked with the numinous, which all humans possess. There is also the greater shared human spirit which crosses all cultural boundaries and makes the human connection with all forms of life in the universe. Western society is severely de-spirited, and it needs some rejuvenation to fight back and heal this wound by acknowledging the Structure of Feelings and Experience (SOFE) across all societies as a pragmatic applied aspect of daily life and societal maintenance. This battlefield of values and practices is embroiled in a conflict 'not sparked by problems of distribution, but concern(ing) the grammar of forms of life'. (18)

There are limitations to this goal of rejuvenating public

involvement in restoring and implementing the common good. One is the predominant influence of self-interest as a sales tool of late capitalism. Cynics argue the case is already lost where powerful elites run the world according to a process that is detached from the people. The only answer I can imagine, is that while people can communicate with one another, there is still a chance of restoring values which represent the interests of the majority without preventing the on-going function of capitalism, but adjusting it to a more responsible version of 'the customer is always right'.

We need to find the means to give voice to the disadvantaged, help them speak for the betterment of their own lives, and ultimately contribute to the return of valuing the common good across Western society: 'The universal means in which speech is used to create and sustain social relationships…universal skills of communication. We are born with the potential to use them to create a better society.' (19)

Method

Feelings and Experience contribute to human consciousness, but many of these aspects have been ignored by modernity, to its cost. People who live with mental illness and intellectual disability, indigenous people and addicts, experience variations in the intensity of these Feelings and Experiences which are like the boundary posts for human consciousness. Identifying a framework for Feelings and Experience is the first task: exploring how the 'others' experience life from moment to moment, processing Feelings and Experiences in a myriad of ways which represents their individuality — the solo journey of ego coupled with spirit which connects us to each other and the universe.

Because the subjects of this work are people living in Western society, the territory of Western culture and society is the natural ground to place this exploration of consciousness. By analysing the recurring themes in the work of Raymond Williams and Bernard Smith, it is possible to identify some of the key aspects of consciousness which these two cultural researchers have discovered.

The initial set of affective indicators of human Feelings and Experiences is called the Structure Of Feeling and Experience (SOFE). This book combines an exploration of the last few centuries in Western culture, art and society, plus the Antipodean or 'other' vision of the world and what it reveals about Western perspectives. Uncles Raymond and Bernard provide rich ground for thinking about consciousness, followed by an exploration of the four subject groups. Their stories come from two main sources: the stories written about these four groups by many members of the groups, and those who work with them (the uncles and aunties); and from my direct experience of living and working with them.

My focus is not on collecting stories about marginalised people, but to illustrate aspects of Feelings and Experience in action which reveal general trends. These examples, both positive and negative, can be applied to current community settings, among the groups themselves and to wider humanity.

Ultimately, my aim is to find a set of parameters for the Structure of Feelings and Experience directly drawn up by the disadvantaged themselves, which can be used to help indicate how to better meet their needs and aspirations. People with mental illness and intellectual disability can then record, in an Action Research project, an assessment of their own Feelings and Experiences. Their input and feedback can be used to better inform the system about how it can engage them in planning the design and delivery of health, rehabilitation and community services. As well as this it can be used to inform society about meeting their needs for inclusion, respect and equal engagement in life.

Along the walkabout path, examination of late capitalism's processes, along with the perspectives and practices offered as alternatives, will be tested against Uncle Jurgen's four way values criteria: truth, truthfulness, rightness and comprehensibility. Do they value the lifeworld, not ideology? Do they responsibly work for the common good? Are they just and equitable, wise and compassionate? Do they make sense for improving humanity's condition?

Aspects drawn from the four subject groups are then compared with the SOFE work by 'uncles' Raymond and Bernard, to create a Mandorla, Venn Diagram-style, overlapping the patterns that emerge from these perspectives. This will be used to make observations about the modern condition, and possible ways of helping to restore a more balanced, integrated way of living among Western citizens. But, especially for people who live with mental illness and intellectual disability, there is a need to improve living conditions, which under current circumstances are largely determined outside of their will.

Seeking a perspective on walking about this suburban lifeworld

Breaking out of Occupied Territory

Human consciousness is a daily workplace, playground and potentially a prison for the mind. If people experience thoughts and feelings that create dis-ease, and they cannot find a way out, this field of awareness and perception becomes a cage occupied by captive minds. Like Weber's 'Iron Cage', the mind can be overtaken by negative rationalisation. (20) Add to that, Durkheim's 'social facts' (21), where money and power 'coordinate action "from outside in", with obligatory force' (22) and injustice and marginalisation are made into an occupied lifeworld, it becomes a miserable place. Increasingly, this is where much of humanity lives.

According to Jurgen Habermas, 'lifeworld is the substratum of our conscious worldviews (Weltanschauungen) and of all social action'.(23) Roughly speaking, worldviews share the same relationship to the lifeworld for Habermas as the conscious does to the unconscious for Freud.

The ego lives in our consciousness, it is that self-determining source of identity which worries about its survival above all else. Surrounding the ego is a greater awareness transcending the level of perception into the universal world of spirit. Shared human spirit is where people can return to their common humanity, motivated by love and determining universal values of truth, justice, compassion and forgiveness. Not by power, money, competition or status.

If one accepts that for the majority of people, economic rationalism has successfully appealed to the ego by arguing for greater efficiency and effectiveness in how late capitalism works, then they have agreed to its progress on the basis that everyone can benefit. The apparent success of this logic becoming the dominant ideology of the last two decades is in its appeal to people's desire to participate in growth and profits. Such a view, now influencing all business, public administration, policy development and legislation, has reached the point where the Western lifeworld has been radically changed. Its former core commitment to the common good is being threatened with extinction. Whether citizens intended it or not. This commitment needs to be restored through sharing more Feelings and Experience as respected parts of daily human interchange.

'In phenomenological terms the lifeworld comprises that vast stock of taken-for-granted definitions and understandings of the world, that give coherence and direction to our everyday actions and interactions'. (24) The common good has been removed from this taken-for-granted status, precisely because it has been taken for granted, gazumped by the economic rationalists. Since Milton Friedman won his battle for world powers' embrace in the Reagan/ Thatcher shadow years of the eighties, what were previously assumed to be the natural underpinnings of civilised democratic societies, have been largely removed.

The lifeworld is, as Habermas reminds us, 'so unproblematic that we are simply incapable of making ourselves conscious of this or that part of it at will'. (25) The evidence reveals, that this lack of consciousness about people's basic needs and how they are met, has led to their protective web being removed. The common good has been replaced by self-interest as a defining basis of democracies such as the United States, Britain and Australia, who employ the practices of economic rationalism. A strong rearguard action is needed to restore consciousness to its rightful place at the foundation of our culture, society and lifeworld. Like Marshall Berman, I believe that the process of modernism which created many of these problems, also holds the hope for reversing them.

Maya Ying Lin's Vietnam Veterans Memorial in Washington, dedicated in 1982, shows how the idioms of the modernist movement…may be uniquely qualified to tell the truth about contemporary history…This memorial tells us virtually nothing but the names and dates…(yet)everybody who goes through this space, cries. (It) shows how modernism can help a culture look the negative in the face and live with it. If Americans can learn to examine the wounds we have inflicted on others, along with those we have inflicted on ourselves, maybe we can begin to heal. (26)

For people with mental illness or intellectual disability, separation from mainstream society has been exacerbated by the demise of the common good. Not only do fewer people have time to think about them, but they often miss out where previously it was to such marginalised groups that this notion would be first applied. However, it may be that a new light is coming from this darkness – a light that will shine onto the doctors, psychologists, social workers, health and rehabilitation administrators, and researchers who, for the most part, are having to work to a drug-based, materialist, behaviourist, symptom-suppressing model of human life and healing.

A framework of consciousness that relates to

neurotransmitters has been placed over the lives of people who live with mental illness and intellectual disability as well as the rest of us. They are basically treated as machines that need to be garaged and have the occasional grease and oil change. The state of their hearts, minds and souls is not seen as relevant, beyond nominal impression management in policy paperwork. I have worked with these realities over the past five years and seen this rationale expand over wider and wider territory. I have felt the same way that many of the clients and workers in this system feel, that it has gone awry. The Americans knew in their hearts that the Vietnam War was a mistake and Maya Ying Lin gave them a space within which they could cry and express their grief.

Just as Lin's memorial was fought over to the last by a conservative, sexist, racist backlash, there are always going to be forces of resistance against the processes of opening awareness to growth. I will follow the yogic maxim of 'address your resistance' to explore and celebrate the Feelings and Experience of these disadvantaged groups. They have lessons to teach us, if we can only envisage and illustrate the existing practical and celebratory expressions of their connection and integration with all of humanity.

Restoring Spirit to the Public Estate

The proposition behind this journey is that human beings are spirit beings who share a community of spirit that goes beyond individual consciousness. Many indigenous people can still access this way of being. However, most Westerners have been separated from engaging with this dimension of their inheritance. Now there is a need to find the way back. People who live with mental illness and intellectual disability both exemplify that separation, and are victims of its widening gap. I also see these groups as potential guides to some return trails.

Indigenous people, who are still in touch with their culture and belief system, have a continuing connection with the spirit of place and access to alternative states of consciousness taught in traditional rites of passage. Acknowledging these levels of awareness may be part of the restoration of more holistic lifeworlds for all of humanity. Not in some 'return to the native', but in a contemporary acknowledgement of the nature of human consciousness and shared social spirit, which needs to be 'worked' to keep it alive and contributing to human wellness.

Addicts are those people who seek to ease the suffering from dis-ease in their daily lives by engaging in activities that help them get out of it, releasing them from the usual run of life by escaping into another state of mind. Many observers of Western culture believe this has become chronic within society. They see people becoming stuck in dependent cycles of consumption, power broking or being manipulated, escaping from material meaninglessness through substance abuse, co-dependency and many other habits.

The positives and negatives that show up in the groups of 'others' offer perspectives on modernity that can point to areas in need of improvement, healing and restoration. The first task is to reclaim the common good, while also redefining basic human needs and aspirations to incorporate a wider view of the shared lifeworld and worldview (Lebenswelt and Weltanschauungen). (27)

Further, suburban life is a paradoxical mix of lifeworld

dreams and the potential nightmare of enclaves. All over the Westernised world, suburbs are springing up where people live separated from each other behind security-guarded walls. Due to the revolution in information technology, some people are rocketed to unforseen wealth, while others are falling into poverty at an alarming rate. The prevailing value system of politics and business seems to assume this is OK. The underclasses grow, while at the same time becoming more invisible, in a bizarre sort of 'virtual unreality'.

While the people who live with mental illness and intellectual disability are already on the lower end of society's success scale, they actually hold up hope for many submerged under this suburban virtual reality-scape now unfolding across the world. They reflect the state of mainstream humanity by the way they are seen, treated and understood. It would seem that humanity is in a pretty sick state. Effort needs to be made to maintain some sense of valuing, not only difference and diversity in consciousness, but standards of moral behaviour. Behaviour which acknowledges and respects those worse off than the rich and powerful, who, at the expense of everything else, seem to have become the new gods for many societies. People even comply with their own degradation by continuing to agree with the dismantling of what used to underpin their lifeworld.

Humanity will return to principles and practices that value the common good and apply it through the public estate, firstly, because it represents the universal foundation of values for human life. Secondly, because provision for those marginalised by disability, disempowered by health problems, and suffering through adversity, is a bottom-line standard in all traditional human value systems. And thirdly, because we need to remain vigilant against ideologies of any kind which can threaten the lifeworld that is the basis of our shared humanity.

That is not to say it is a given. The circumstances prevailing in contemporary modernity are dire. Many regard that something akin to a miracle is required to reverse the lemming-like trend still being pursued by most Western political leaders and their corporate masters. Yet, as South Africa and Eastern Europe proved towards the end of last century, it is often those who are at the bottom who end up succeeding in changing the world. Jean Vanier reflects that those who live with intellectual disability are the most representative group of the meek, those about whom Jesus spoke of as the inheritors of God's kingdom. I believe there can be no better point to begin the work on behalf of all humanity than by advancing the interests of these people and calling for a return to love and valuing the common good. If this happens, there is some hope of rejuvenating our shared responsibility for one another.

A word about words
Inventing language

One of the concepts arising from this exploration of consciousness, is that human experience mixes with the rest of the energy in the universe in a sort of 'sensational soup'. We sense things. We sense ideas. We use common sense to try to grope our way forward, sideways and across the gaps in our knowledge and awareness.

This book is not an academic 'pursuit of excellence' or competition for learnedness. It is the lived experience of feelings, ideas and wisdom passing around in the ether.

Language helps capture some of that stuff, giving it form to help us see, and hopefully understand, some more of the mystery and wonder in life. Never capturing all of it — it is meant to keep swirling and changing.

My way of honouring this phenomenon, is to sometimes allow words to invent themselves, out of the sensational alphabet soup of consciousness. I hope you will share in this playful acknowledgment of how meaning and purpose can be refined and strengthened by staying open to the echo-logy of our shared awareness in the universe.

Montages in the mind – building a story picture with quotes

I am not identified as a visual person. I do not easily remember scenes, colours, room designs, or space layouts in buildings. But I do paint pictures in my mind by building montages with words, to form streams of ideas, in order to tell stories. Hence, you will find sections in this book which contain lots of quotes.

This is not because I am too lazy to think how to say something in my own words, but because I appreciate the beauty in the expression already achieved by others – and I want to share and celebrate that with you, in the combined company of others whose ideas I feel form a natural connection. This 'montage of ideas' is what I am aiming at when I use larger quotes in sequence. I hope you can see the murals of the mind.

Diamonds and dust

There is a circular meditation that surrounds this text. It begins in the dirt. 'Dust to dust, ashes to ashes' is one of our funeral descants, and it captures the energy cycle nicely — to celebrate renewal. Earth recycles organic matter and chelated molecules (from chlorophyll and haemoglobin in plants and animals) into humus. This fertilises new life. And we build to the point of consciousness — the six-pointed diamond shape (see Chapter Ten) that I use to model the Structure of Feelings and Experience. It is just a picture, but still, it carries the energy of consciousness – which, for me, reverberates in all human endeavour and communication, including those country and western classic phrases about 'diamonds and dust'. Anyway, that is just my meditative mantra technique. What is yours?

Chapter Two

Community, consciousness and the common good

Reclaiming the spirit of community

Nearly a century ago, Tonnies coined the twin terms Gemeinschaft and Gesellschaft (1) (Giddens, Pusey) — for the opposing forms of social organisation that were being removed from community by industrialism (I call them 'the twin Gs'). Since then, there has been a debate among sceptics on both sides of the modernism fence.

The Gemeinschaft argument sees life harkening back to a glorious past when all was well in the shared village-like community. This was before industrialism took people away from their personal relationships and traditions into a structural association with one another which is impersonal and isolating (Gesellschaft). This book is based on neither concept. While I argue for a return to more caring, sharing and celebrating forms of community, I am not portraying those as ideal practices residing in an Arcadian past, nor a utopian future. Nor am I saying that modernism has resulted in a complete destruction of the possibility of a shared worldview (Weltanschauungen) (2), working for the common good.

Just as Max Weber saw the move from traditional 'magic' to modern 'rational progress' as a process of 'disenchantment' (3), contemporary writers are viewing the process of modernism since then as having created the need for 're-enchantment'. (4) Understanding more about the core elements of human consciousness should present humanity with its criteria for assessing the worth of the processes used to run our society.

The Structure of Feelings and Experience (SOFE)is a framework of consciousness which presents such a set of criteria. It is not claimed to be comprehensive or fully representative, but at least worth introducing 'into the mix' (as Uncle Bernard says) of values and processes currently dictating Western society. By taking advice from Uncle Jurgen Habermas, it is possible to collect a set of tools for thinking about these issues. I will introduce those after defining the territory through which this book 'goes walkabout'.

Community and the Common Good

The following concepts are meant as tools for individual and community life, to be applied in a modern democracy through personal behaviour and values, group processes, political decision-making and the public administration of health and community services. The focus is on empowering individuals through creating decision-making processes and therefore power over matters affecting creation of their lifeworld. The practical expression of these faculties creates a working community. This differs from the twin-Gs debate, in that active expression of feelings, communal celebrations, shared spirit, rituals, and people's stories about life can be valued in mainstream modern environments. This is based on the indigenous notion, best described by the Australian Aboriginal concept of 'working the culture' and 'doing the business' (of life). Nothing fancy or ideal, just daily life.

I am critical of modernism's influence on social or-ganisation, capitalism's trends towards de-humanising work and emphasising profit over basic moral values of 'share and share alike', and 'do unto others as you would have them do unto you'. People should have basic rights to work, have enough income to support themselves, and be able to share in a community life which values the common good. It does not need the return to a halcyon past for such values to be realised.

Community is the people who mix with one another, living and working through their shared lifeworld. The common good is what everyone can expect as a basic minimum in quality of life provision — being protected and supported by their community and the wider society. This is not the case in many Western societies, such as Australia.

Community Spirit

In the experience of Western modernism, it appears many people have made choices which have changed their whole way of life. As 'a whole way of life' is one of the definitions of 'culture' used in this book (5), it can be argued that Western culture has been changed. Not just by technological progress, or by economic develop-ment, or by socio-political evolution. It has been changed by people's conscious choices. They have reconstructed their lifeworld.

The flipside of the choice for modernity has been detachment of that lifeworld from people's control. Decisions on behalf of vulnerable people are made by the bureaucrats and, increasingly, by privatised care providers. An outcome of this has been the management of previously shared communal life experiences by institutions. This separates individuals from active participation in the group, the community and society as a whole. They become submerged in the fight for work, minimum standards of living, and succeeding or failing in the competition for wealth. Raymond Williams saw this trend emerging in the sixties and seventies. Now, forty years later, it is instructive to reflect on the creeping separation modernity has brought with it, ever widening the gaps between people:

He looked along the street: at the separate people passing, on so many different journeys; at the more distant crowd and traffic, the slow aggregation within which they stood, leaning close to each other and talking, close as always but close now in their separateness; a conscious separateness, within a crowd of strangers. (6)

Large numbers of people have not only become atomised, isolated and effectively left competing for place, space and opportunity in their lifeworld, they have also become effectively devoid of the capacity for decision-making within the system they have 'signed up with' and 'over to'. This version of democratic capitalism, where vested interest groups (elites) run the lifeworld, is what people who live with intellectual disability and mental illness have no choice but to accept. Other people seem to have elected to live in this more passive way of life, mainly because it has become so complex and demanding.

The effect of disempowerment, a result of handing over control of the lifeworld to business and bureaucracy, is a deep redefinition of the Western concept of community.

Community spirit is the way people decide for themselves, in groups of shared interest, with overall responsibility for the affairs of all. As well as this there is a practical sense of the common good, which informs individual and group behaviour to support those in need and look out for your neighbour.

This model of community does not rely on the nostalgia of an Arcadian era. It is available as soon as people decide to 'act local'. Then, when more people choose to do this and combine this with a sense of humanity's overall responsibility to the wider environment, Buckminster Fuller's 'think global, act local' (Fuller), moves into 'glocalisation', where there are many little cells breathing the same shared human spirit of community, expressing its full array of plurality, difference and diversity.

The message from this trend is that democracy needs people to be involved. Whether democracy is defined as 'government of the people, by the people, for the people', or, as Geoffrey Robertson points out (in Churchill's words): 'democracy is the worst form of government, except for all the others'. (7) If people want to see better processes used on their behalf they need to work at it, or it simply becomes impression management of a formerly representative process. The new virtual reality of political representation.

A scaffold to rebuild the lifeworld

Community spirit seems to be more vital among the weak than the strong. Because those with little to lose have always had to struggle, they appear to be better equipped to cope with the feelings of disempowerment which have been magnified under late capitalism and created a 'wear out factor' among voters. That is, modernism has weakened Western democracy, but hope may lie with its most disadvantaged.

While elite groups have taken over the representative and decision-making functions, because many people have dropped out of active political expression, marginalised groups represent a bottom-line which cannot be erased by impression management. The spin doctors cannot make a virtual paradise out of poverty and disability, so society's conscience remains alive in the space between, where the growing divisions between the 'haves' and the 'have nots' are exposed.

Among the members of mainstream society, the spirit of community is still latent, potent, close to the surface. I have seen this in environments of community welfare, cultural celebration, sporting clubs and people coming together in a crisis. Community spirit is one path back to active democracy.

The experience of the marginalised, who are even further detached from influencing their lifeworld conditions, is strangely equated with their fellow citizens. They have often made up for disadvantage by forming stronger group relationships and creating their own communities where self worth can be nurtured. In the absence of democracy realising its other definition, 'the absence of class distinctions or privileges in a society' (8), this aggregation of community spirit is a hopeful sign.

It may be possible to rebuild democratic societal process by building on such hopeful signs and revisiting the territory claimed by 'agents of the people'. Starting with the marginalised is not such a strategic mistake. Many of the bureaucrats working with them have good intentions to serve, even if their management restrictions and policy guidelines are strictly along the lines of economic rationalism. I was one of those bureaucrats when I worked for three years with Aboriginal people, and I know assistance can be made available in community-empowering ways. This is my version of community spirit — working for the common good with people with whom you develop relationship and mutual understanding.

Contrasted with that, is the value system of economic rationalism which has been proven to serve the interests of business and profit above all else. The way of business, as Raymond Williams saw it and portrayed it in his work, is to seek its own best interests, and where possible sell its own expansion to others on the basis of their self interest in the same process (see *The Fight for Manod*, Williams). This has been successfully completed now by most nations whose strategies are based on economic rationalism, where both the private and former public spheres have been commercialised. They have become profit centres for private agencies.

Testing the Argument for Change with Uncle Jurgen's Fourway Test

In order to avoid polemic, I have asked Uncle Jurgen for some advice. Using his early work on the Theory of Communicative Action (9), it is possible to identify four values tests for processes and phenomena which will crop up on this walkabout journey. Habermas 'tries to reconcile the two processes, of disenchantment and of rationalisation, into a single theory of modernisation and modernity'. (10)

His Theory of Communicative Action identified four ways of assessing the value of processes which he claimed could help reform the modern condition. They are: Truth, Truthfulness, Rightness and Comprehensibility. I will take these four categories and interpret them as criteria for assessing the current impacts and potential improvements of modern socio-economic processes on the lifeworld conditions of people who live with mental illness and intellectual disability. In practice, these four concepts pan out to mean:

- Truth — Does it reflect and value universal human feelings and experience? Is it relevant to the lifeworld, not a reflection of some ideology (such as economic rationalism)?
- Truthfulness — Does it responsibly act for the common good? Are its values right in terms of actually being of benefit to the people, not just impression managing?
- Rightness — Does it allow justice and equity with wisdom and compassion? Is it allowing individuals to be their full selves, and society to evolve in a healthy way?
- Comprehensibility — Does it make sense? Is it contributing to what most people would want in order for humanity to keep improving and expanding its awareness?

'Working the Culture' of Community

In Australian suburbs and country towns, as with many other Western nations, the growth of more economically rationalist commercial management processes, in the form of major regional shopping malls, has meant closure of the local stores, the small businesses where people knew each other, which has led to the demise of small towns. Aggregation of retail services into shopping malls has been justified as cheaper, more cost-effective and convenient. But until a new sense of community emerges from the people themselves, this process of rationalisation of our community life support processes seems to be still-born in the soul. Like cold-stored, genetically engineered foods — they might look like the real thing, but they taste like wax fruit.

Such moves may make sense in terms of efficiency and profitability for businesses managing these overtaking enterprises. However, they do not necessarily make long term sense for community. People do end up going to the shopping mall, using automatic teller machines for obtaining cash and eating at McDonald's. Nevertheless, many may have preferred to stay with the older, more personal connections if these had been transferred to the newer environments.

The evidence for this comes from initiatives to establish community banks across Australia. In a quiet, but powerful consumer movement, customer service has been redefined by a strong aggregation of community spirit. People who wanted to retain personal banking ended up taking their money out of the big banks which closed branches and even removed automatic teller machines because they said they were not busy enough. My own community bank, in suburban Sydney, was established because of community anger and disenchantment. This seems to me to be the sign of a return to community spirit, in places that could seem atomised and 'care less'.

The multinational banks clearly failed Uncle Jurgen's tests. That is, whether their services valued people's feelings, worked for the common good, provided an equitable service, and made sense. They did not. So they were dumped. This is the process of 'working the culture', that I believe can be revived in the modern context. It represents an Aboriginal, indigenous sense of the community spirit of the people acting in its own interest, which is the common good. As the Twelve Steppers say, 'it works if you work it' (Alcoholics Anonymous, Twelve Step speak, a modern tribal rejuvenation of spirit).

Where industry has aggregated into central and regional industrial parks, such as in the south-west of Sydney (Campbelltown) and the inner north-west (Baulkham Hills) and north-east (Terrey Hills), the decision by communities regarding the value of this trend is yet to be known. Jobs, workplaces, and surrounding homes exist there. People are joining the process, and social services are gradually being provided to these new industrial suburbs. But the broader issue, of redefining work and industry into discrete fields of grouped one-stop-shops serving major corporate industrial supply processes, is yet to be assessed. Global generic forms of business, such as Information Technology, Packaging and Distribution, Office Automation Services, Computer Aided Design and Manufacturing, and other generic categories, are still to be tested by citizens of the global village.

It is no wonder glocalisation is a concept growing in popularity. The Green movement's ethos has begun to show, both at local community level and in the ballot box. As more Green Party politicians replace the parliamentarians from traditional parties, the value of people's inner environment of soul and their connection with the larger environment of earth and humanity grows. This links a caring and sharing value system to an active living process within small groups and aggregating communities of spirit. This trend follows long-established Green Party practices directed at conservation and sustainability of ecosystems. They pass Uncle Jurgen's four-way test by reflecting the value system that supports people and nature over profit.

Inviting the moderns to remember their elders

The root of the trend to reclaim community is the core human reality — the indigenous 'us not me/ we not I' value system at work (Smith, Jackson). It applies as much to conditions of late capitalism as it does to native communities who live in both outback and urban environments. Taking responsibility for one's role in the group, and one's connections with community, is possible as much in K-Mart as the Kalahari. The neighbours are serving behind the counter, the kids are working in McDonald's, and people living with intellectual disability and mental illness, our brothers and sisters, should be there as well. In fact, in one inner city Sydney McDonald's store (in George Street near the major cinema complex), intellectually disabled young adults are on staff and doing well. They bring a particular joy to their work and they uplift those they serve and work alongside. Cynics may claim they work in front-of-house jobs to promote a good image for the company. But, the people I know on both sides of this equation, see it as a benefit for all concerned, specifically because the workers get to have maximum interaction with customers.

The idea of responsible capitalism is feasible. This may be criticised as nominalism, but things have to start somewhere. Giving back to the community it profits from, and taking responsibility for assisting those in need to find a place in the economy, answers Uncle Jurgen's criteria.

Such steps are not idealistic, they are practical and can be applied with a simple will to go beyond profit alone. Involvement of marginalised groups reminds customers of their shared humanity. It lifts the spirit by actively working the culture as a whole way of life. It is the stuff of community – those who serve our food fill our souls.

At the local swimming pool in Canterbury, in Sydney's south-western suburban belt, where intellectually disabled swimming teams practice and compete, pool staff have gained a deeper sense of compassion for humanity through interacting with these sports people. I have observed them joining in growing acceptance of, and engagement with, those who live with intellectual disability. Similarly, players, coaches and fitness back-up staff for the local inner western Sydney and nationally involved rugby league football team, the Wests Tigers, have adopted a Down Syndrome young adult as their motivator and mascot. This expands their engagement with wider humanity as more than just professional football, and gives everyone involved with the club a sense of 'we all share in this thing'.

People who live with intellectual disability, who have active and purposeful roles in the community, are included in the everyday affairs of the community. No longer isolated. Exchanging love as the substance of human intercourse, not money, or power, or status. They are acknowledged as valuable members of society. Refuelling everyone's lifeworld.

A musician who lives with mental illness, plays in a northern Sydney suburban community jazz band, joining in the joy making. His particular talent and brand of 'madness' adds to the colour of everyone's lives. A simple act of involving and respecting people of different consciousness opens a way for that consciousness to uplift all concerned. It is not lip service, patronising or nominal. Just basic work, play and sharing of 'normal' human activity. The stuff of life. Like the chef who lives with mental illness who cooks for people each day in a government Health building's Piaza Cafe, in Australia's national capital, Canberra. Or, the mature age women who live with mental illness, who organise catering services in a local RSL (Returned Services League) Club in Sydney's northern beaches suburb of Balgowlah.

These are instances where management is committed to supporting the introduction or reintroduction of people into workplaces where they would have formerly been shunned. The risk that they will under-perform is no greater than that of 'normal' workers, once their need for informed support by management and co-workers is agreed upon. This sort of measure is the reverse of what economic rationalism has brought to our society, and it needs to be continued if Western society is to restore and rebuild the heart and soul of the late capitalist lifeworld. These measures pass Uncle Jurgen's test of genuine good works for good reason.

It is possible to exercise initiative for compassionate decision-making, even from within management of multinationals like McDonald's. Now looms the job of returning the political, legislative and bureaucratic managers to the same kind of balanced human consideration. So far only a toe has been dipped in the water.

What went wrong in serving the people?

In his ground-breaking 1991 book, *Economic Rationalism in Canberra* (11), Michael Pusey showed the way Australia's nation state had changed its mind about governing for the people, and in keeping with the madness of economic rationalism, adopted management by an elitist class. A country that had led the world in many social reforms during the twentieth century was seen to have lost its way in what I call 'me, me, me-ism'. However, Pusey held the hope that the elements of youthful nationhood, and rejuvenation of a 'fair go' spirit among its people, would see Australians exercising their democratic rights to restore a more compassionate process of governing for the people.

There may yet be a way back to the other fork in the road that leads (along what were always assumed to be the 'natural' trend lines of Australia's development) to social democracy, of the kind enjoyed today by non-English-speaking nations: the Netherlands, Sweden, Finland, Denmark, and, in the next league, France, Austria, and perhaps Germany — among them, nations for whom Australia once used to be a distant lighthouse. (12)

Like Uncle Raymond, Pusey is a socialist of deep commitment to the common good. He believes Australia has unique opportunities to restore social democratic processes. Its treatment of the marginalised bears witness to how well that philosophy is being expressed. So far there has been a shift from engagement in their lives (the seventies 'warm and fuzzy' image) to management of their circumstances.

Generally, when social democratic regimes have

taken the political reins, their tactics have been to allow bureaucracy a strong say in determining how needs will be met. As a staff member of bureaucracy serving the disadvantaged, I have observed that this approach led to impression management of 'representative community interaction'. Marginalised groups were consulted, even involved on management committees, but the real decisions about priority setting, and allocation of vital public recurrent funds, came from the bureaucrats. Often they were contract workers, employed by agencies used by governments to avoid employing full-time public servants. So, due largely to managerialist surveillance, they nervously guarded the budget turf and rejected anything outside the box. Few chose to side with the community's wishes outside of policy guidelines, which in effect meant budget restrictions. This fits with evidence, such as in the McKinsey Report from the nineties, that showed how the Australian government increasingly off-loaded social responsibility to private providers. They failed Uncle Jurgen's tests of truthfulness and rightness.

Real involvement of people who live with intellectual disability and mental illness in the decisions that will affect their daily quality of life is not so common. It is given lip service in some agencies, but overall, it is not influential across the public sector. Cynics observe that this is not surprising, given the sort of rationality which condones continued use of medication alone to suppress symptoms of illness, while ignoring the need for addressing a patient's inner needs. The evidence was available twenty years ago that supported the involvement of people in their own life management to improve their attitudes, health and general hopefulness (I wrote many stories on this subject as a journalist for *The Daily Telegraph* in Sydney at the time, covering psychology, education, youth, welfare and disadvantage). This has not been kept in the corporate memory.

Linear thinking prefers linear solutions. The famous story of the British hospital that ran perfectly, but in fact had no patients, emphasises just how irrational, rational management can be. Many areas of social service management have slipped, under economic rationalism, into mechanistic Taylorist habits. It is up to the people, including the marginalised themselves, to demand a more responsive system — 'loonies in the lanes, and spazos in the streets' (borrowing the effective process of reclaiming language and redefining 'nigger and queer' labels, adopted since the sixties). By using the damning language itself to reclaim the naming rights, the patronising inherent prejudice in systems and services is disarmed before it gets going. Treating difference and diversity in human life as something to be managed into neat policy boxes is due for a spring clean.

In this model, 'the state emerges as the true independent variable, industrialisation being only an intervening variable in countries that are all capitalistic in structure' (Pierre Birnbaum). On that course, the ultimate resource for development is culture. Here, one speaks of culture not just as scientific, technological, or educational knowledge, nor even as tradition, but rather, as the social processes of identity formation. (13)

Sharing is survival — one in, all in

Raymond Williams was a mentor for many people who were seeking social justice. His work, as an academic and a creative artist, called for examination of modernity's problems. He asked questions, in this era of mesmeric change, about where modernity might be going in regard to notions of representative government, justice and equality. Will, his main character in the early novel *Border Country*, is a brilliant young social planner researching his native Wales, who hears from an old friend of his father, Harry, about how the young man's father dealt with change:

I learned something, Will. Something in general we all know about, but I learned it from him. He couldn't see life as chances. Everything with him was to settle. He took his own feelings and he built things from them. He lived direct, never by any other standard at all. (14)

This determination to 'take one's own feelings and to settle', to work things out in one's own mind, was a passion with Williams. He saw that people's life conditions were directly connected to their decisions about joining in community. We need to rebuild this sort of process among the disadvantaged by creating mechanisms which allow, encourage and inform self empowering processes of lifeworld design. And they can show the rest of us how to do it.

Services for those who live with mental illness and intellectual disability are the touchstones. If these two groups can be properly assisted to get out and spell out their needs and aspirations for better supported and integrated lives, then they can test the process. But, they need allies, and people prepared to go the long haul. Change may be moving at mesmeric speed across most of society, but resistance by the people running the system is likely to be strong, unless they agree there is an efficiency and effectiveness outcome inherent in it. I have observed improvements in health, lack of recidivism, improved rates of rehabilitation, and general uplift in individual and group spirit.

We're getting the result of our own denying. We're getting it all except the life…What we talk about, Will, he's lived. It all depends on a mind to it, a society or anything else…That's… why Harry's different. He changes a thing because he wants the new thing, and he settles to it because he wants it right through, not because the rejection is driving. (15)

Having 'a mind to it' is a starting point. The people who live with intellectual disability have expressed to me the desire to have more of a say in how their daily activities are designed and delivered. Certainly, the people who live with mental illness, with whom I live and work, show dissatisfaction with programs that do not help them recover or rehabilitate their skills for living in community and earning a living.

Something of what Williams saw in the modern era's change process is very telling in the predicament society has created for itself today. The generations from the first half of the twentieth century, who fought for what they saw as equal rights, have told me they have been dismayed by the reversal of much that had become taken for granted — in terms of wages, conditions, welfare provision, and stewardship of the public estate. Watching legislation reversed, public services removed or privatised, and the public estate sold off in the name of good financial management, has dismayed even Australian Liberal Party founding members (business-supporting people like my parents). Meanwhile, profits grew in the private sector, shareholders gained increased returns, and jobs began disappearing with the arrival of people-replacing technology, or by out-sourcing of previously permanent jobs in the public sphere. But things have been bad before:

September, 1938. What a time to be going away? Not really that the shouting mattered. You had to shout on your own to feel it as a cause. Not only indignation, but a training to indignation. History omits our particular occasions, as it weaves its spell of a date. (16)

As day-to-day life seems to accelerate, people do not seem to be able to remember why valuing certain basic levels of social provision is essential. Western society is still within memory of the gains that came from last century's fights for rights. Now many of those have been lost. However, they can be restored and redefined in terms that make the parameters of human experience much broader than simply material provision.

The needs of people who live with mental illness and intellectual disability go to the heart of the human condition — they need healing in their hearts, minds and souls — they need to share in the community of humankind. People with those needs are silenced in a world run by rationality and monetarism, where inner life is not valued or practised 'in communion' with one another. And these folks are barometers for everyone.

Belonging or dividing?

Changing for the Better

Change, pursuit of the new, impatience with tradition and restlessness in the company of old patterns of life, these are chapters in the story of modernity. Western societies have been swept up into their alluring winds over the past century. But, increasingly, members of those societies have been dumped, like Dorothy in *The Wizard of Oz* when the tornado stopped. These are people recovering from the shock of landing from modernity's tornado, such as redundant workers with many years of 'good working life ahead of them', along with people with skills who cannot get jobs, and small businesses overrun by corporations. Such victims of economic rationalism's 'friendly fire' have told me of their wounds, that they feel somehow emptier, unable to find their bearings to begin again.

But a father is more than a person, he's in fact a society, the thing you grow up into. For us, perhaps, that is the way to put it. We've been moved and grown into a different society. We keep the relationship, but we don't take over the work. We have, you might say, a personal father, but no social father. What they offer us, where we go, we reject. (17)

Isolation, lack of guidance, absence of mentors, and inability to remember inherited pathways, are all symptoms of modernity's loss. While those working to maintain the democratic, common good will empathise and express regret, it is now necessary for such supporters to 'just get on'. They need to rediscover the natural elements that can be applied for a healthy human life, like rites of passage, active reference to elders, non-sectarian rituals to teach reverence, and a way of reaching beyond the material concerns of life. These are some of the processes that I believe can, and are, able to be restored in contemporary settings. (Belhooks, Vindana Shiva) Such strategies are necessary for immediate re-spiriting, as well as supporting the long journey in using the democratic process to challenge socio-economic destruction for the majority. The marginalised have a key role in helping lead this debate.

Moves among some business and public sector managers to embrace a return to deeper values, such as the SLAM group (Spirited Leaders And Managers), show us that things are swinging back. I am arguing for more engagement with the intellectually disabled as a process for rebuilding empathy and engagement with human needs. This would help people regain a holistic sense of human purpose which serves the group experience of life, not just individual self-interest. In this way, by embracing progress we can also re-express the necessary Structures of Feeling and Experience that make us human. This encourages people to realise that life is not just about material survival, individual prosperity and financial success. It incorporates growth of personal spirit, social responsibility, celebration, shared communion in reverence for life, valuing of difference and diversity rather than worshipping 'the normal', and cooperative setting of priorities for the common good.

When the 'normal' spend time with those who live with intellectual disability, they see these individuals have none of the outward trappings of successful lives. Yet, they all share a common heartbeat. If it is beating off rhythm, everyone will know. The ability these people have to share such moments exposes 'normal' people's loss. Loss of the ability to open their lives to scrutiny by their community, and thus receive support.

Here is strength in weakness. The next step is to connect that need for commitment to active community process. The old maxim that an involved adolescent is a less suicidal adolescent applies to all of us. People who choose to mix with those who are intellectually disabled, and work towards their integration into the community, are rich.

Sharing the belonging, the effort towards equitable life, is enriching. It will help people who live with intellectual disability to secure jobs in mainstream circumstances and allow them to live in communities where they have enough practical and emotional support to live with independence and joy. This is something our whole society needs and desires, even if this attitude gets buried under self-interest. It is a return to love. Not a soppy Hollywood image, but an indigenous style human faculty, as expressed in the Maori and Hawaiian 'aroha', 'aloha'. You share it, you belong. Uncle Jurgen would approve.

Stuck in a Future with No Future?

The seeds of the current regime were sown out of good intention, among the generation of World War Two adults, who, like their parents, went on to try to make sure their children 'had a better life than us'.

People would rather see their children separated, going away from them into the rituals of another kind of life, than probe at all deeply into their own lives, where the important changes must come. (18)

Williams saw a malaise among the baby boomer generation, people like me, born after the World War Two explosion of modernism. For us there was the foot-in-both-camps experience, of seeing modernity's crazy products and feeling it drag us into the future. As this generation is now in charge, it is questionable how many are bothering to revalue the responsibility of leadership. The obsession our parents had with the future seems strangely nostalgic.

Change seemed so necessary after the Second World War, and education was deemed a major tool to ensure that the new generation would 'get away from what we went through'. Yet many previously held traditional values were discarded by that very decision to replace traditional patterns with an orientation towards the future. Not to be stuck, to move forward. I believe that is one reason the World War Two generation missed out on facing many of their internal issues. They had too big a job to do driving progress onwards after 'the big one'.

Although some, like my parents, may have regretted the very process they were driving forward so determinedly, they remembered being much happier when everyone was pulling their weight to fight against adversity throughout the war years. During those times of life and death, community for many was a moment-by-moment experience. Although, no consistency held across all societies, and self-interest still surfaced on a consistent basis during the war, there was a strong sense of community spirit and making sacrifices to help one another. They were moving themselves and their children away from the very thing that strengthened their own lives. On Jurgen's scale, this may have seemed a good idea at the time, but it was leading to dangerously compromised territory. Progress is not only measured by material achievement, status on the educational ladder, and how many 'old fashioned ways' can be discarded.

Those who live with intellectual disability represent

one of the groups still living in daily adversity. They are the least likely to 'get on', in terms of status, power and the material. Their very vulnerability and inability to perform in the achievement stakes means they are destined for second row status in the rush of modernity. I say, thank God, along with Jean Vanier and Henri Nouwen, because they can help the rest of us to see the importance of stopping, thinking and feeling a bit more about what people might decide is good for them as a species, a society, a community of souls.

And the people who live with mental illness also exemplify what many people fear — that the pace of change and its resulting stress will 'drive them crazy'. On the inside, many fear they are 'losing it', when in fact the best thing they could do _is_ to lose it — so that their lives might readjust, their hearts, souls and minds could slow down, and they could 'catch up' by stopping.

Williams felt the pain of change occurring in his home country of Wales, and across Britain and the Western world. Applying a similar view now, forty years later, to what remains a chronic problem in modern societies, it still feels painful — denial of the inner life. The pretence that material life is all that counts:

The directed self acted, and the other, the unknown, merely disturbed and compromised, in a widening area of misunderstanding and damage. At the very time when he saw beyond the limits of the settlement, he was still a child of the settlement...He could feel it now, every day, in the bodies of others. It came through as pain, and there was then no separation: the pain of others was quite literally his own. (19)

Protecting or denying?

Laws against Human Nature

In considering the path of legislative, regulatory and administrative progress, in serving the interests of vulnerable groups, like schoolchildren and people who live with intellectual disability and mental illness, it is interesting to reflect on where modern decision-making processes have ended up. The notion seems logical — that protecting people's rights means separating them from vulnerability to abuse. But when that same decision means denying the majority access to a healthy exchange of sharing, caring and affection, it seems to be out of hand.

Because of the rise in reported incidents of paedophilia in Western nations, rules have been introduced to prevent teachers and health workers from touching students and patients. They must have someone else present during any necessary procedural manoeuvres to protect the student or patient from potential abuse by an authority figure. Fear about a small minority of sick individuals, who act as paedophiles, has been allowed to steer a basic human communication process away from its healthy place in society. If the same value system put the exchange of love high on its register, along with the need all humans have for physical affection and reassurance, then such knee-jerk reactions would be reconsidered. People in professionally responsible positions would be trained and trusted to behave responsibly, not made the objects of suspicion because some particular individuals behave inappropriately.

Looking at the way those who live with intellectual disability seek affection, show affection, share feelings and explode with them when necessary, they seem to illustrate a healthy human process. My question to the current dominant decision-making system is: how have we 'advanced' to the point where humanity no longer trusts itself to naturally exchange what is its most needed commodity? And if evidence is needed, about what happens when this commodity is in low supply, you only need look to those who live with mental illness to see a group of individuals who have been left to 'cook in their own juices'.

Treating people like machines, or laboratory rats, as happens in drug-driven mental health treatments, demeans them. This was not the case when I worked in Bangalore, India, at the Athma Shakti Vidyalaya (Spirit Self Empowerment School - a therapeutic live-in community for people living with mental illness).In the West, these approaches have been down-graded. Are Western rates of recovery from mental illness improving? No. Are suicides increasing? Yes. Yet despite evidence that the current drug-based approach is not working, this is ignored in favour of continuing only with drug therapy and patient monitoring. They fail Uncle Jurgen's four tests. They are not serving humanity.

Anyone knowing the pressures, of course, also knew that the effort required, for the real changes, was almost beyond human strength. But there was no gaining of strength, there was only deliberate weakening, while this other pattern persisted. It was really as if, oppressed by an enemy, a people had conceived its own liberation as training its sons for the enemy service. (20)

Here, Williams is exploring the phenomenon of modernism — the changes wrought by 'progress', which create pain and separation, from each other and previous ways of being. He is both acknowledging its inevitability and questioning its worth. The emphasis is on the human experience, the feelings involved, and the way people silently comply. It is time to change the rules of compliance by illustrating the efficacy of ways which generate efficient and effective outcomes, but which use a value system based on Feelings and Experience.

Mutual celebration and wonder

What will you be reading Will? Books, sir? No, better not. History, sir. History from the Kestrel, where you sit and watch memory move, across the wide valley. That was the sense of it: to watch, to interpret, to try to get clear. Only the wind narrowing your eyes, and so much living in you, deciding what you will see and how you will see it. Never above, watching. You'll find what you're watching is yourself. (21)

Raymond Williams is such an appropriate uncle for our journey, because he felt for society. He knew change was inevitable, but that history had threads in it which were essential to humanity's manoeuvring through the future. 'Watching ourselves' is what people do when they work with people who live with intellectual disability and mental illness. By joining in with their lives, assisting in providing better quality experiences and integration into mainstream lifeworlds, they reciprocate by healing the sense of loss and uncertainty felt across society, about how to chart a course into the future.

Like the canary in the cage indicating a gas leak before it becomes too dangerous, there are indicators on humanity's side: 'Watch memory move, across the wide valley…(and) you'll find what you're watching is yourself'. (22) This is where the tribe of modernism is now. Life is crazy, things seem to be running amok. Some feel there are monkeys in charge of the ship. So what to do? Get involved and help steer a course that suits the human heart.

'Working the Mystery' and Healing

Two aspects that come from exploring Feelings and Experience stand out for special mention – mystery and wonder. I believe they are needed in the mainstream conversation about social progress. Not mumbo-jumbo, but actual acceptance of the fact that, just like imagination and creativity, feelings and dreams, fractals and holograms, we humans have these aspects to our lives. In our consciousness. They are part of people and culture, and therefore the thing people 'should be working', in the indigenous sense. To place them in context here, Uncle Raymond has some reflections on 'traffic':

There was an obvious strangeness in the fact of traffic. The approaching headlights, the amber indicator, the high bulk of a lorry: these were the facts with which consciousness had to deal. he remembered a definition of consciousness, in the report of an experiment: its elements were flashing light, reactions, learned signals, learned patterns. As in the traffic, most people were known in these isolated images, with a quick decision on relevance to oneself, in the rapidly changing series.

Peter wondered how deeply he had been formed by this world. (23)

This story serves to illustrate much about the modern condition. In the midst of the rush of modernity's traffic of change, people are uncertain, unfinished, inarticulate.

People need one another to help find the way through this era of post-industrial life.

Part of that journey is to revalue our indigenous heritage of numinous ways of being, and part of it is to learn from the meek. Williams was in a lifelong exploration of change and its impact on consciousness. His own version of 'the Structure of Feeling' was a version which combined 'culture' and 'real-politik'. Through literature, he examined what British writers had to say about how people felt when they lived through the rise of modernism. He looked at these indicators in the context of what was happening in their politico-economic world under capitalism. It did not wow him.

Now that the process has moved so far on from his vantage point, it pays to stop and reflect on what he was trying to call attention to, and illustrate possible ways to balance out the mad misalignment of values in so-called 'progress'. His allegory about traffic merges with Uncle Bernard's 'cultural traffic' allegory, in the echo-logical mixing of cultures in history. I believe that it is possible to respond to these processes with a healthy sense of mystery and wonder. Not denying any rational understanding of science and economics and their stories about life. But, with an added dimension of humility in the face of what comes up in the universe. The same sort of humility that acknowledges people who live with intellectual disability and mental illness as peers, brothers and sisters, with whom and from whom people can learn, share and grow.

In Freud's canon, which Uncle Raymond's era found so influential, 'ego' seems to me to be the best word for describing the predominant character of modernism. Its wilful, self-centred push for progress has lacked humility and sought its own ends before all else. Uncle Raymond felt for the boundary fences of modernism and what might be beyond. We need to return to that process and give it greater attention.

Like Jacques Lusseyran, 'touching the tomatoes' (24) in his blindness and energy-receiving, we can touch the edges of progress and find appropriate levels of mystery and wonder to help reclaim balance. Not out of control with egotistical certainty and rational bluster, but a quieter rationalism, based on responsibility for the common good informed by respect for the mysteries of life.

As Uncle Michael says: 'There is a potential for rationality already inherent in the culture to be released and to do its work in further 'domesticating' its once friendly political and administrative structures in the service of its own national population and its social and economic needs'. (25)

Chapter Three

*Travelling our Border Country
of the Structure of Feeling*

This book takes a wide view in exploring human consciousness through the doorway of Feelings and Experiences as uncovered by Raymond Williams and Bernard Smith. It scans the territory of consciousness where it is possible to reflect on the broad trends within humanity.

I will look at the trends arising from this exploration to refine a focus on the Structure of Feelings and Experience that can be applied to both mainstream humanity and the two groups which form the subject for follow-on work – people who live with intellectual disability and mental illness.

Comparative morphology of the soul

Emerging from 'the age of reason and irrationality', it pays to pause and reflect on what has transpired in humanity's love affair with evolution. Science has come full circle and now gathers in the corner with the alchemists exploring the ether and transmutation of energy, and even love. In the journey to explore alternative aspects of consciousness, there were distinguished forebears among those seekers of new knowledge in the eighteenth and nineteenth centuries, who wandered into territories occupied by the strange, even bizarre, on the way to the revolution of evolution.

The influence of the Pacific upon Darwin's other great friend, Thomas Henry Huxley, was not such that it led him directly to evolutionary theory. However, it did bring him into direct contact with most primitive forms of marine life which led him towards fundamental discoveries in comparative morphology. (1)

What these explorers of form and phyla discovered was a system for tracing patterns in creation. They showed humility and respect in the face of wonder and diversity. But it was rapidly replaced among their successors with a type of mechanical classification, which spread through all forms of knowledge – the confident assumption that naming something meant it was understood and under our control. Taxonomic despotism.

Confronted with a chaotic array of nondescript material, Huxley hit upon the notion of classifying according to an archetypal principle, that is, according to a fundamental structural plan revealed by a study of many individuals, rather than according to superficial resemblances in appearance or mode of life. (2)

In considering the shared attributes of consciousness, I believe it is also possible to trace an archetypal structural plan which indicates where many of the deepest links between humans lie. Two researchers of culture and society have plotted the traces of humanity's Structure of Feeling and Experience: 'Uncles' Raymond Williams and Bernard Smith. Williams explored Culture and Society. Smith, Art and Ideas. Like Darwin and Huxley, they make a good pair as guides for exploring consciousness.

To begin this exploration, it is advisable to apply one of Bernard Smith's major approaches. In sporting terminology it is called 'taking your eye off the ball' — in this way allowing natural instinct to find the target, and lateral vision and thought to influence the intuitive 'game'. It may then be possible to explore aspects of consciousness that show up through Feelings and Experience and are shared among all humans. This, combined with the meandering way of walkabout, the 'slow down' approach, is particularly important in considering the needs and aspirations of people who live with intellectual disability and mental illness. From my work with them, I have observed that the system does not consider their feelings as paramount to the way it sets its priorities. Thus, failing the tests of right and truthful realisation of their oft-stated departmental visions, goals, objectives and policies.

Furthermore, the study of zoological individuality became an important one for Huxley — he came to the conclusion that biological individuality was a process; that individuality was not to be expressed in static, but in dynamic terms. (3)

In the sense that this book explores consciousness, it is also understood as a process through which individuality is expressed in dynamic rather than static terms. (4) This is the territory of comparative morphology of the soul, a field that will hopefully lead to indicators for better understanding the human condition and finding ways to serve those whose needs are not clearly understood by 'the system' which is meant to serve them.

Framework for life experience

Raymond Williams established a way of thinking about human experience which changed the way people examined history. He believed that culture and society were built on a 'Structure of Feeling' shared in the consciousness of ordinary people. While he was a Marxist focused on applying dialectical materialism as a set of principles with which to understand the world, he actually wandered through the hearts, minds and souls of modern humanity in his work. Always taking the side of the underdog, principally the working class who were at the mercy of capitalism.

Williams said he used the work for his first book, 'as a way of finding a position from which I could hope to understand and act in contemporary society'. (5) I take that as my starting point, by examining the needs of people who live with intellectual disability and mental illness, and seeing how their Feelings and Experience can be more sensitively acknowledged.

Uncle Raymond had begun his work, 'in the post-1945 crisis of belief and affiliation'. (6) His efforts helped many people around the world find hope and belief in a better way for humanity to behave than the cruelty and pointlessness of war.

The aim in following his trail of thinking will be to find a Structure of Feeling which suits humanity today. In yogic wisdom, life operates best 'in balance', and that balance is shown in practice to be established through the exercise of tension between forces operating in opposing, but complementary directions. Not warring duality, but collaborating energies. I hope to expose some of the dynamic collaborative potential in aligning human needs and services informed by this understanding of consciousness.

A parallel principle applies to individual human lives and our group experience in society. It is the perspective on healing from homoeopathic teaching, that 'like cures like'. The work uncle Raymond did can possibly assist us in seeing where healing links can be made between Feelings, Experience and the services to meet their needs. His exploration of culture and society was based at the outset on 'the truths of his own experience', as his friend and biographer Fred Inglis put it: 'He kept up his faith in the moral content of ordinary life. He believed that people learned of necessity, and took to heart the lessons of solidarity and kindliness, peacefulness and an ecological good conscience'. (7) Williams came up with a basic set of life processes which can be used to see how we are going. His 'rider' message was the need to know that these things would always be changing:

The truth about a society, it would seem, is to be found in the actual relations, always exceptionally complicated, between the system of communication and learning, the system of maintenance and the system of generation and nurture. Our contemporary experience of work, love, thought, art, learning, decision and play is more fragmented than in any other recorded kind of society, yet still, necessarily, we try to make connections, to achieve integrity, and to gain control, and in part we succeed. (8)

He argued against the reduction of society 'to two spheres of interest, two kinds of thinking, two versions of social relationship: politics (the system of decision) and economics (the system of maintenance)'.(9) The lives of those who live with intellectual disability and mental illness fall into the gap which persists between these two remaining dominant forms of thinking. While Williams believed humanity needed to get beyond class and power determined versions of how the world operates, society remains stuck in that trap. I have experienced this in structures which are meant to serve human need. Those at the lower end of society's power hierarchy are unable to influence policies and programs directly affecting them. So it takes more of the general population to act on their behalf.

What uncle Raymond saw as unnatural and unhealthy, I believe is now directly degrading the lives of marginalised groups, such as people who live with intellectual disability and mental illness:

To limit a society to its systems of decision and maintenance is in fact ridiculous. The true nature of society — a human organisation for common needs — was in fact filtered through the interests in power and property, which were natural to ruling groups...the alternative society that is proposed must be in wider terms, if it is to generate the full energies necessary for its creation. The integration of work and life, and the inclusion of activities we call cultural in the ordinary social organisation are the basic terms of an alternative form of society. (10)

Here is a version of human organisation which bases social thinking on our 'general humanity', rather than on the needs of a 'received system'. (11) It argues for including the lived experience he used as a basis for discerning truth. The values uncle Raymond addressed need to be placed higher on the agenda if there is to be any improvement in the lifeworld of the marginalised. From English literature, he extracted patterns of human feeling and thought which he felt were valuable for understanding and improving the human condition. His work disclosed a series of contradictions in modern life which now dominate our lifeworld.

By exploring the experience of marginalised groups, he revealed aspects of all human lives, many of which were hidden beneath 'normal' behaviours and social structures. The need for more inclusion of heart and soul, for more communal expression of joy, grief and wonder, and for more shared engagement in the human connection with the rhythms of the earth, are suggested as just some of the areas needing to be brought back into regular human exchange. This is possible, through provision of public services, if the will of management is there to value such approaches. As Theodore Zeldin has said, the way back to healthy human affairs is through conversation. That activity unique to human beings, through which we can 'explore new territory to become an adventure'. (12)

In conversation feelings are handed back and forth until an intimacy develops, and the other person's concerns become one's own. Love ultimately means that another person's welfare, hopes and fears matter as much as one's own. We are entering a new age in the conversation of love. (13)

Perhaps the simplest analogy is that we are given the opportunity now to replace the currency of exchange in money and power with that of love, truth and responsibility for all life. Something akin to Uncle Jurgen's concepts, in his early work on the 'Theory of Communicative Action' (Habermas), that humanity needs to move towards achieving four expressions of our true nature: truth, truthfulness, rightness and comprehensibility. Raymond Williams spoke to and for 'everyman', yet despite wide acclaim and acknowledgment, the implications of his work have not been seen as an indicator of applied truth which could to be factored into social planning.

Zeldin's point, regarding conversation, reflects the process of indigenous life rhythms which are designed to 'celebrate the wonder of life' as a major process of human life. He put the practical survival processes into proper perspective alongside the greater acknowledgment of the two overarching values in human affairs: the common good and the higher power (of the mysterious universe, God, call it what you like). Put another way, as Chief Seattle told the world, 'all things are connected', (Schaef) and politics, economics, power and privilege are only one set of parameters with which to construct life.

Acknowledging the real lifeworld

Summing up Raymond Williams' main subjects, in relation to the Structure of Feelings and Experience, we can link them to a direct implication for the lifeworlds of the people who live with mental illness and intellectual disability. They can be aligned against Uncle Jurgen's four-way test. Williams expressed his interpretations in terms of both principles and life applications which can be extrapolated to the current Feelings and Experience of the two main subject groups we are exploring.

Knowledge is born of experience, not abstract ideas

Uncle Raymond believed that knowledge of life comes from experience more than abstract ideas. He saw that life driven by conceptual, mechanistic thoughts and values, placed above lived experience and intuition as paths to the truth, is separated from the world with which human beings are meant to be integrated. Life becomes (quoting Coleridge) 'translated into a dead language, for the purposes of memory, arrangement and general communication'. (14)

This concept of a 'dead language' could be used to describe the abstract, bureaucratic jargon and management processes overseeing the lifeworlds of people who live with intellectual disability and mental illness. For the former, there is basically an approach of corralling, treating people like sheep. For the latter, the system seems to need more directive, drug-based 'control' processes, as they view these people as being a possible 'danger to themselves and others'. In these instances, arrangements predominate over Feelings and Experience and, according to Uncle Jurgen's test of rightness and truthfulness to policy rhetoric, they do not pass.

Uncle Raymond pointed out that dualism in separating 'the mind' from 'feelings' is a mistake in human affairs. He showed it led to a split in values, which he claimed fuelled the destruction of essential human activities because they became regarded as peripheral. This is exactly what I have seen in a northern Sydney hospital's psychiatric unit, and in its community health services parallel operation, once patients are 'allowed out'. This has happened to my son, who meets with professionals who assess his condition for prescription drugs, but no respectful, person-engaging inquiry is made into his Feelings and Experience.

While legislation allegedly forced the removal of people who live with mental illness from institutional life many years ago, no provision was made for appropriate community support services to allow them to rebuild lives of dignity and independence. It is possible to return to responsive politics where voters can influence such inadequate public provision. They can do this by choosing political candidates who know the need for more person-centred, caring and hopeful development programs.

Political economy's concern is society's health

A bottom line belief of Raymond's was that political economy should be concerned with the general health of society. He felt that society was vulnerable to amoral behaviour when laissez-faire principles overruled all else. Quoting Carlyle he says: 'In came calculation and out went feeling'. (15) 'That there is an emptiness in the sort of society where the framework of relationships is built on money transactions, and that there are so many things which cash will not pay'. (16)

The dominance of monetaristic values in managing human environments, particularly for people who are not able to assertively demand their rights, has become chronic. Costs, efficiencies, balance sheets and budgets dominate health, education, housing, rehabilitation and community services. Consequently, people are subordinate, despite the rhetoric of eighties style business plans and vision statements for departments which sprout 'customer service' and 'learning organisation' as priorities. Without blaming any individual managers or even politicians, the system has become swamped in rhetoric, run by sphinctitis(the new street jargon for monetarist accounting), which cuts costs at the expense of services, staff and clients.

Uncle Raymond said industrial capitalism created a separation of people from one another, breeding a way of life where 'Recognition of evil was balanced by fear of becoming involved. Sympathy was transformed, not into action, but into withdrawal. We can all observe the extent to which this Structure of Feeling has persisted, into both the literature and the social thinking of our own time'. (17)

So it has become, among my own networks of self-help parent groups in Sydney and across Australia, that families and friends of those who live with mental illness cannot get changes in the way their loved ones are treated in the hospitals. Neither can they obtain better support for them when they come out of hospital and go into community group homes. The model of management requires medication, supervision and monitoring. Rehabilitation is a nominal gesture, which means little more than babysitting. And so an abstract idea about efficiency dominates over quality of life.

Coupled with this is the slavish following of mechanistic thought, discrediting the personal Feelings and Experience of all people involved in this situation. Uncle Raymond saw modernism ushering in 'One of the falsest maxims which ever pandered to human selfishness under the name of political wisdom. Forgetting that the very name of society implies that it shall not be a mere race, but that its object is to provide for the common good of all' (quoting Matthew Arnold). (18)

Detachment of the public sphere from responsibilities for either employees or customers, by out-sourcing personnel services and sub-contracting service delivery to private agencies, has seen the system sold out to business for the purposes of profit, rather than valuing people. This has been shown by research (McKinseys), but needs no further evidence than personal engagement with a system overtaken by financial considerations above all else. Families and patients have seen that arguments about greater efficiency and cost-effectiveness are not held up in practice. Costs have generally gone up. People would be forgiven for thinking the whole process has been one of privatising the public estate. This is a total failure of Uncle Jurgen's four point test.

It is not true to the spirit of what it is meant to be doing, not truthful, not right and does not make sense.

Human nature comes from the whole way of life of a culture

One of Uncle Raymond's key points is that human nature is the product of a whole way of life of a culture. (19) The sorts of services people are provided with in community care need to be holistic. I have worked in places where this is not the case. Overall, in Australia, this is not management policy. The concept that life 'is to be experienced in a way, which produces continuing and progressive civilisation' (20), is alien to today's prevailing conditions.

Instead of 'the harmonious development of those qualities and faculties that characterise our humanity' — ie. cultivation' (Coleridge) (21), we have mechanistic management of people's lives. 'A nation can never be a too cultivated, but may easily become an over-civilised, race'. (22) I observe this happening in the mental health and general rehabilitation system. Modern civilisation is run on mechanistic values where marginalised groups have lost all semblance of a quality of life which engages with the needs of their inner lives.

Raymond's view is that separating mind from feelings

produces a society of individuals who are denied acknowledgment of their full lives and effective relationships with one another. We only need to visit any mental hospital or community health centre to see the extent of this division in our society:

External attachment replaces inward claims to real experience. As Carlyle put it: 'Intellect, the power man has of knowing and believing, is now nearly synonymous with Logic, or the mere power of arranging and communicating. Its implement is not Meditation, but Argument'. (23)

In order to return from what I call this 'logical madness', we need a restoration of the sorts of people-valuing priorities that uncle Raymond believed in. It is now a matter of going back to find the principles which were briefly taken for granted in public provision, before that led to their demise under a new regime. Compare this with the value system expressed by Matthew Arnold, that 'Culture is right knowing and right doing; a process and not an absolute'. (24) 'Right knowing and right doing' requires a basic understanding of human needs. This places Feelings and Experience at the top of the list, alongside material survival needs.

Culture of 'the inward man' is 'the problem of problems'

Uncle Raymond held that the culture of 'the inward man' is 'the problem of problems', requiring us to 'listen to the true and unerring impulses of our better nature' to find the guiding principles for our common life. (25) Valuing the lives of the people who live with mental illness means providing them with experiences which respect their need to live fully. This does not happen in hospitals and community group homes around Sydney. Their days are a medicated blur and occasional rehabilitation groups do little more than waste away the hours. Which is why most 'clients' do not attend regularly, or only do so because it is a mandatory condition of their community treatment order.

Uncle Raymond stressed that we need to keep culture as an integrated part of all of life, not a separate entity away from the 'main purposes' of society (read politics, economics), or a commodity to be bought and sold. As I understand it, this means offering people, like those who live with intellectual disability, opportunities to participate in the life of their community as full members, not 'special guests' in some freak show. And, for the people who live with mental illness to be able to join in experiences in cultural activities as respected participants.

As uncle Raymond pointed out, the importance of Carlyle's sense of 'reverence' expressing 'the governing seriousness of a living effort' (26), is apposite in this context of seeing the significance of providing ways for individuals and groups to celebrate their culture in community. Carlyle stressed, 'An irreverent knowledge is no knowledge; it may be a development of the logical order or other handicraft faculty inward or outward; but it is no culture of the soul of a man'. (27) On Jurgen's four way test these activities fail all round.

Society's value lies in its conditions for 'wholeness of being'

Quoting John Ruskin, Raymond argued that 'the goodness of a society lies in its creation of the conditions for wholeness of being'. (28) He saw that nineteenth century

English social thinkers stressed interrelation and inter-dependence. (29) It is not impossible to rediscover this aspect of community and to achieve it within the existing system of public provision. Both parties would be enriched by finding ways to interrelate the lives of the intellectually disabled with the wider community.

Currently, there are processes in place which have the intellectually disabled shunted around in buses, herded in and out of sheltered workshops, and organised in groups that have little connection with the wider world. Breaking this cycle of isolation and finding ways to engage them in permanent activities in the community will be part of their emancipation.

Equality among human beings is a given

Williams passionately believed that equality among human beings is a given, part of our natural condition, and therefore should be part of the on-going process of human affairs. Quoting D.H. Lawrence, he emphasised: ' Society means people living together. People must live together...When I stand with another man, who is himself, and when I am truly myself, then I am only aware of a Presence, and of the strange reality of Otherness. There is me, and there is another being...There is no comparing or estimating. There is only this strange recognition of present otherness'. (30)

When understanding of mental illness reaches the point of seeing that many people carry disturbance throughout their day, and that all people have needs for sharing and exposing their 'madness', society will have progressed. As I have observed with my son and his peers, their symptoms are simply suppressed and they, as 'clients', are housed in places where they will cause the least disturbance. Efforts to bring about community integration have been sporadic, and when these fail, it cripples future attempts to find funding. This is not equality in action. The only answer which seems to remain in a democratic society is to move to politically influence the provision of more integrated services. And to persevere with those well-intentioned programs that have occasionally been tried. As well as this, we need to support the many workers struggling under a dispirited system.

Culture is an energy of the soul

Williams explored the work of R.H. Tawney, and 'his argument that contemporary society will move merely from one economic crisis to another, unless it changes both its values and the system which embodies them. Culture is…an energy of the soul. When it feeds on itself, instead of drawing nourishment from the common life of mankind, it ceases to grow, and, when it ceases to grow it ceases to live'. (31)

People who live with mental illness in our society are in the position of being divorced from this concept of belonging to 'the common life of mankind'. Individuals are 'cases' to be managed, more than people with needs reflecting something of 'the energy of soul' that is our whole culture. There is a chance humanity might begin to repair its social fabric when this perspective is brought further into the shared light of community-wide conversation.

Nourishment for all, from all, including the lives of people of difference. As Uncle Jurgen said, 'I know that all learning depends on the formation of inner motives'. (32)

The problem is that management surveillance punishes people who go outside policy limits in their attempts to relate to people's real needs.

To further complicate matters, some of those real needs may be reflecting aspects of shared experience that are actually unconscious, let alone invisible. Uncle Raymond's exploration of T.S. Eliot's work showed how the poet emphasised that 'a large part of life is necessarily unconscious'. (33) Eliot may have been helping people to open themselves to perspectives that could heal many today — those who remain stuck in an attempt to be 'in control', when life is certainly racing beyond any individual's 'control'.

A large part of our common beliefs is our common behaviour, and this is the main point of difference between the two meanings of culture. What we sometimes call culture — a religion, a moral code, a system of law, a body of work in the arts — is to be seen as only a part — the conscious part — of that culture which is the whole way of life. (34)

This common behaviour suggests society would operate better with more sharing of the diversity within our mix. Opportunities for people who live with mental illness to contribute in neighbourhood activities, creative occasions, and times of reverence and ritual, would be a start. Giving priority to such activities in public programs and policies seems a distant goal at present. So, Jurgen's test of rightness seems way above the standards currently being met.

Resist individual, fragmenting 'atomism'

When uncle Raymond investigated the trend towards substituting elites for classes, based on the re-identification of class with 'function', as argued by Mannheim, he was ahead of his time in predicting what has happened to our society's management processes. I have seen that the achievement based, or meritocratic way of classifying people, has largely come to fruition. While Raymond believed it was a mistake not to argue against individual, fragmenting 'atomism', and for continuity of considering culture as a whole way of life (35), the evidence is that modern society has ended up with exactly that. The lesson from this trend is to reapply Raymond's logic and value system in the way alternative community activities and services are proposed, planned and delivered. Piloting examples will assist in illustrating its efficiency, effectiveness and efficacy.

Understanding depends on extending the expression and exchange of experience

In his examination of the literary criticism of I.A. Richards and F.R. Leavis, Raymond Williams showed that art and society did not need to be separated and competitive with one another. He favoured their integration. The lack of creative activities for people who live with intellectual disability and mental illness in the community is a symptom of the disregard with which modern society currently treats them.

The essential values, as I see them, are common to the whole process (of the cultural revolution occurring hand-in-hand with the technological revolution): that (people) should grow in capacity and power to direct their own lives — by creating democratic institutions, by bringing new sources of energy to human work, and by extending the expression and exchange of experience on which understanding depends'. (36)

Art, craft, music, dance, drama and other expressions are more than recreational activities to 'keep people busy'. They are fundamental aspects of community and celebrating humanity. I argue for their introduction on a serious level in rehabilitation. It is not, as Jean Vanier points out, that they desperately want independence and free expression at the cost of friendship and community. But, having their creative needs met, as well as enjoying company and opportunities to engage with society, makes for healing and growth.

Integration for all members of society wherever possible

Uncle Raymond believed that society has a duty to encourage creative energy and give voice to it, to allow cultural expression and development. He saw that 'There is not society on the one hand and these (creative) individuals on the other'. (37)

We can see how much even highly original individuals had in common, in their actual work, and in what is called their Structure of Feeling, with other individual workers of the time, and with the society of that time to which they belonged. (38)

Raymond's view was that all people are included, and that is the priority we need to recapture in public policy making. To remove the current boxes that exclude, and replace them with guarantees of inclusion, where people wish for it, and where it is feasible within community standards of safety. 'The contributors are involved in their society, both in profound ways and in their ordinary human needs, and they usually suffer if they are cut off from it, whether as impractical dreamers or as untouchable spirits'. (39)

Raymond's understanding of the needs of creative artists extends especially to maginalised groups. In the current experience of being 'serviced by the system', those who live with intellectual disability do not experience inclusion in the mainstream. People who live with mental illness find themselves isolated in public places because there is no facility to create a comfortable experience within their own society. Visiting the shopping mall or picture theatre is an outing, but it is not rehabilitation.

Standardisation leads to sloth and vacancy

In the wake of the 'blandification' caused by the mass media, Raymond's resistance to 'mass culture' was for good reason. He believed it reduced the level of possibility for sharing ideas, creativity and feeling among people.

Isn't the real threat of mass culture…that it reduces us to an endlessly mixed, undiscriminating, fundamentally bored re-action? The spirit of everything, art and entertainment, can become so standardised that we have no absorbed interest in anything, but simply an indifferent acceptance, bringing together what Coleridge called indulgence of sloth and hatred of vacancy. (40)

Uncle Raymond was not backward in coming forward to criticise media products. He felt frustrated that standards of cultural expression were becoming shallow. He was not against populism, but defended the need for maintaining a wider scope of provision. This is a choice for consumers, but more poignantly, it is the vacancy of community behind passive cultural consumption which magnifies the disconnection from groups like the intellectually disabled.

When Uncle Raymond said of popular culture, 'You are not exactly enjoying it, or paying any particular attention, but it's passing the time. And in so deadly an atmosphere the great tradition simply cannot live' (41), he was pointing out the kind of passive acceptance that fuels social neglect. While people who live with intellectual disability have active, socially involved lives with their own community, it is a distant prospect that they will be included in mainstream cultural activities as a regular part of the program. This situation can be remedied. In 2000, the Sydney Paralympics was an example of how much general community support there is for sharing such occasions.

Commercialising Dreams

Raymond claimed that the modern media, in order to sell products, has decided to compete on the field of people's dreams by using television and other media to present advertisements which portray invitations to another world of consciousness. He was virulent in his criticism of commercialisation of the media to this end. He believed that the packaging of advertising's consumer media towards its audiences was a negative trend.

While people are being sold ideal images of the ideal life, those who are 'out of the picture', like people who live with mental illness, are more likely to be excluded from acceptance in the 'normal world'. Raymond saw that:

In a sense the product has become irrelevant: the advertiser is working directly on images and dreams. The concentration of such advertisements creates a whole style of life, centred largely

in fantasy, which is in effect a common interest of all adver-
tisers, rather than the recommendation of particular products.
All ordinary values are temporarily overridden by a kind of
bastard art, not clarifying experience but deliberately confusing
it. (42)

According to the image machine, there is no room left in this confused and manipulated world for valuing and engaging with the lives of people who are 'less than'. Looking at what was achieved with the advertisements for the Paralympics, it would be just as possible to use this form of communication to 'sell' messages about the wonderful attributes of character and courage among the intellectually disabled. The fear is that this will not sell products or provide shareholders with profit. But it could lift the standard of understanding and acceptance across society. Campaigns to celebrate disability of any kind are well worth it.

Who are the masses and minorities?

Concepts such as 'the masses', 'mass media' and 'public opinion' were signs to Williams of manipulation of the awareness of ordinary people. His argument is important in underpinning a perspective on where the disadvantaged 'sit' in our society. They are not the masses. Yet they are people, just like the members of the alleged masses. So who are they really? 'It is then a matter for argument whether the masses and the minority are inevitable social facts, or whether they are communication models which in part create and reinforce the situation they apparently describe'. (43) One way to return to active participation in the community is to refuse to accept such implied movements or forces in society. Aggregating to support the concerns of minorities is good grist for the mill of the common good.

Otherwise, people continue to fall foul of presumption and generalisation, ignoring the lifeworld concerns of the disadvantaged because they are minorities. The other side to this story is for these groups to get out and make themselves better seen and better known. This is beginning to happen as more combined support campaigns arise.

Society is a form of communication

Uncle Raymond saw 'new ways of passing ideas, information and attitudes from person to person' as one of the modern age's most powerful improvements and inventions: 'Society is a form of communication, through which experience is described, shared, modified and preserved'. (44) His emphasis here is essential to the gaining of both recognition for the people who live with mental illness, and their further healing and growth through direct involvement in the processes of how society communicates. 'The relationships in describing, learning, persuading and exchanging experiences are seen as equally fundamental. This emphasis is exceptionally important in the long crisis of twentieth-century society'. (45) If we understand that communication is a natural heritage of humanity, then, the process of explaining the concerns of, and promoting understanding of people who live with mental illness, is a high priority for communications. This became a major focus of Uncle Raymond's career. His efforts to demand a more accountable management of communications on behalf of the interests of the common good was possibly his greatest work. Part of reclaiming democracy is to remember that these channels for ideas, feelings and values are just as open to challenge today as they were in his time.

My own view is that we have been wrong in taking communication as secondary. Many people seem to assume as a matter of course that there is, first, reality, and then, second, communication about it. We degrade art and learning by supposing that they are always second-hand activities. That there is life, and then afterwards there are these accounts of it. (46)

With regard to people who live with mental illness, it seems there is a responsibility to share more information about their lives as part of society's acknowledgment of its own reality. Just as the union movement grew out of the efforts of the Tolpuddle Martyrs, and others who struggled for workers' rights under the new industrialism, so it seems there is still a need to take the needs of people to the people.

Our commonest political error is the assumption that power — the capacity to govern other people — is the reality of the whole social process, and so the only context of politics. Our commonest economic error is the assumption that production and trade are our only practical activities, and that they require no other human justification or scrutiny. (47)

What is relevant in this analysis for minorities, such as the people who live with mental illness, is that they and their supporters need to continually remind the political representatives that people's lives are equally as important as production and trade. When it becomes significant in political terms to ignore such disadvantaged groups, the democratic system must respond. So the only way forward, as I see it, lies in engaging in the hard grind of community politics.

Humanity lies in the struggle to describe, to understand

Raymond spent his whole life describing what he saw as the common people's predicament, to seek improvement in their lifeworld:

We need to say what many of us know in experience: that the life of humanity, and business of society, cannot be confined to these ends; that the struggle to learn, to describe, to understand, to educate, is a central and necessary part of our humanity. (48)

He felt for the society he saw crumbling in front of him. What he also probably felt was sad at the prospect that voters were passively succumbing to the new machine of modernism and allowing decisions to be taken that would disadvantage the very people who needed protecting most — 'This struggle is not begun, at second hand, after reality has occurred. It is, in itself, a major way in which reality is continually formed and changed. What we call society is not only a network of political and economic arrangements, but also a process of learning and communication'. (49) For the community of people who live with mental illness and their supporters, the message is: get organised, make yourselves known, argue your case in the corridors of power, and if necessary, go to the streets until you are heard.

Central to Williams' work is engagement with communal custom, where people are able to empower their own ideas and actions within a culture. The strength which the intellectually disabled bring to this notion is that they can add much to the communal custom, and in fact, lead the way back to community. By making their activities public and inviting participation by the general community they show us how to engage in a shared life. The way the people who live with mental illness engage naturally with others is a strength in itself.

Culture is central to common life and distinction of spirit

'The difficulty about the idea of culture is that we are continually forced to extend it, until it becomes almost identical with our whole common life.' (50) Here Raymond thinks more widely about culture than Leavis, but he does not include the contribution and concerns of such marginalised groups as those people who live with mental illness and intellectual disability.

What we now see, is that the concept Leavis had, of seeing literature as the great repository of the consciousness of the race (51), is in fact akin to the role of people like the intellectually disabled. They hold aspects of human consciousness which are otherwise missed in the media, images of society and exchanges between people in the mainstream: 'In their keeping…is the language, the changing idiom, upon which fine living depends, and without which distinction of spirit is thwarted and incoherent. By culture, I mean the use of such language'. (52) Leavis was being something of an elitist here, and uncle Raymond called him on that. But, extending the notion to include people who live with mental illness, for example, it is possible to see the potential in this perspective to inform much more accurate perceptions of the 'distinction of spirit'.

The ways in which we can draw on other experience are more various than literature alone. History, building, painting, music, philosophy, theology, political and social theory, the physical and natural sciences, anthropology, and indeed the whole body of learning. We go also, if we are wise, to the experience that is otherwise recorded: in institutions, manners, customs, family memories. (53)

Here is where Raymond was a believer in the value of general community, and where his views add weight to the argument for more inclusion of the intellectually disabled in mainstream affairs. So, using Uncle Jurgen's four way test, Raymond's views failed on the first two counts, but his intention would have meant fully representative participation.

Culture determines human development

Marxism played a huge part in Williams' life and work. He was seen as a leader of the left in his era, and at the same time engaged in a strong critique of Marxist story telling. A crucial point in his examination of Marxist thought, regarding cultural aspects of life, was to do with 'social existence' and 'consciousness': 'The mode of production in material life determines the general character of the social, political and spiritual processes of life. It is not the consciousness of men that determines their existence, but, on the contrary, the social existence determines their consciousness'. (54) Raymond argued that Marx downgraded cultural activity as a central part of human affairs. Given this perspective, it is not surprising that he wanted to see more done to make cultural activity a central part of social planning. The same sort of central placement that I argue for here, for the people who live with mental illness and intellectual disability.

'I do not see how it can be denied that Marx did in one sense diminish the value of such (cultural) work. He denied that it was this kind of work that decided human development.' (55) Marx was not alone in this. The capitalist system which succeeded in overcoming his ideologies in most countries which had pursued them, also saw little worth in this type of work. It did not represent much more than entertainment value. Now, it can be seen as offering a vehicle for marginalised groups to tell their story.

Inherent patterns of feeling are the substance of community

In examining the work of George Orwell, Williams pointed to another facet of human experience which he felt deserved closer attention as a lesson for further development in human affairs — the ' paradox of the exile', by which he meant that capacity to 'find virtue in a kind of improvised living, and in an assertion of independence. The substance of community is lacking'. (56)

Uncle Raymond's views on Orwell were split. He felt there was a lot of value in Orwell's observations of Western society and its problems. But he could not agree with leaving that society to criticise it from afar: 'The exile, because of his own personal position, cannot finally believe in any social guarantee: to him, association is suspect. He fears it because he does not want to be compromised. To belong to a community is to be part of a whole, and, necessarily, to accept, while helping to define its possibilities'. (57)

Such a perspective is informative. The only way forward for politically weak groups is to stay active within their society until they gain more support from the mainstream. Isolating themselves further can only lead to worse problems.

'His principle failure was inevitable: he observed what was evident, the external factors, and only guessed at what was not evident, the inherent patterns of feeling.' (58) The difference for people who live with intellectual disability, is that they are in fact teachers for general society — their ability to open their hearts and feel is a skill lacking in many members of mainstream society.

Culture is an on-going process

The history of the idea of culture is a record of our reactions in thought and feeling to the changed conditions of our common life. The word, culture, cannot automatically be pressed into service as any kind of social or personal directive...what it indicates is a process, not a conclusion. (59)

Williams began his final chapter of Culture and Society with a call for more engagement with lived experience. It is worth remembering this in the journey to see more integration for marginalised people.

Our engagement with culture always needs effort. Democracy, empowerment, social development, all take effort. Otherwise people end up losing the gains in quality of life that had been previously taken for granted. For the marginalised, who have never even had basic conditions of career prospects, full pay, respectful working conditions or other bottom-line life structures assured, it is essential to maintain solidarity in the process of culture building.

'We have to return to the meanings of experience…The masses are always the others, whom we don't know, and can't know. Masses are other people. There are in fact no masses: there are only ways of seeing people as masses.' (60) This illustrates the implications for reform in rehabilitation services. Political will appears to be lacking in response to calls for more normalising activities for people who live with intellectual disability. But the process of engaging in lobbying for change, and arguing with the system that it is not responding to people's inner needs, is a continuous, on-going challenge. If it is abandoned, it will only worsen the circumstances of these people. If it is continued, it helps to illustrate universal need among all people.

Value the common good above all else

Raymond Williams' gift to future generations was to value the common good above all else in human affairs. In *Culture and Society*, he outlined a view of human affairs that is still relevant today, where sharing our feelings, dreams, ideas and evolving traditions is part of our whole life, as individuals and as a community.

A culture is not only a body of intellectual and imaginative work; it is also and essentially a whole way of life…The crucial distinguishing element in English life since the Industrial Revolution is not language, not dress, not leisure…(it) is between alternative ideas of the nature of social relationship. (61)

It seems to me, that across society, many relationships are deeply empty. In general, in the West, little remains of what used to form community. But what does form it, is the special link between people who get to know one another. And therein lies the reason for getting out and amongst it with as many people who live with intellectual disability as will agree to come. Sharing feelings, news and imaginings builds community. The gift of the weakest among us, is that they build the strong web that binds community. Like spider web, which, pound for pound, is one of the strongest threads on earth. Gossamer fine, but tough and resilient. What uncle Raymond saw residing in the working class, I see in marginalised groups of people who live with intellectual disability and mental illness — if they are given enough support to be able to come together and share their concerns.

The idea that we properly associate with the working class: an idea which…regards society neither as neutral nor as protective, but as the positive means for all kinds of development. Development and advantage are not individually but commonly interpreted…In the general and controlled advance of all. The human fund is regarded as in all respects common, and freedom of access to it is a right constituted by one's humanity; yet such access, in whatever kind, is common or it is nothing. Not the individual, but the whole society, will move. (62)

Here, is the future for reform, opportunities in community for people who live with intellectual disability and mental illness. Standing up for their rights to be regarded as fully participating members of society with certain support needs, but otherwise equal contributions to make to the community. Equal but different. Acceptance that humanity is not just a money earning, product making species. We exist to feel, share, exchange and communicate. At the level of the heart and soul equally as much as the intellect.

Chapter Four

Finding Perspective on Life by
Listening for Echo-logy

Looking through the shadows to the reality

Bernard Smith is a prolific and passionate contributor to world cultural and democratic investigation. He is still writing furiously at the age of eighty six (the second volume of his autobiography), and maintaining great hope for humanity. Uncle Bernard is very like Uncle Raymond, in that both men hold to the notion that humans have choices, and that responsible living means settling on your choice and having the courage to stand by the truth as you see it. They believe that perspectives may differ, but honesty is non-negotiable. Both share Marxist views, believing that the poor deserve to be acknowledged and respected.

In writing about pre World War Two life in Australia, Smith said that 'Banks are pretty rotten things. Still you can't expect an institution to have a soul when most people get along well enough without one…Poverty is a hard teacher but it is one of the few things that can teach us the difference between illusion and truth'. (1)

During a lifetime spent exploring art, culture and ideas, Uncle Bernard has spotted patterns and trends which have helped many people find meaning in the chaos of modern living. He himself was not clear about much of the madness that emerged from humanity during his developing years. His friend, Lindsay Gordon, taught him that art and practical life were two parts of the same thing and that separating them would only lead to self-delusion. 'Truth can only be realised through practical activity', said Gordon in a letter to Smith in September 1939, in the peak of war's unfolding. (2)

This was part of Smith's early learning about integrating life, art, ideas and self-responsibility. As a young man, he had great difficulty balancing life's challenging paradoxes and, thanks to his efforts to work out some of these conundrums, the benefit of his wisdom is now shared through his writings: 'He (Smith) gained no lasting comfort from this image of himself as a sawdust doll pulled by invisible wires of blood and nurture. That was the way of cynicism and self-pity...he began to feel an inner capacity for decision that he had not felt before'. (3)

Smith learned that the value choices people make, colour all their subsequent experiences. People are either victims of their life perceptions or collaborators with the universe in what they choose to see happening 'to' themselves. It is a choice. And Uncle Bernard chose early on to see life as an opportunity to collaborate with his 'fate', and take action according to a positive view of the world as a place where it was always possible to find light.

The great curse of the world today (writing about 1939) has been the indifference and hesitancy of people who see only the shadows of things, who are determined that they shall see only the shadows of things, because the reality is too cruel. (4)

Smith's later work continues to have an influence to this

day. His is a value system that confronts truth and then finds beauty hidden behind the ugliness that must be faced. Similarly, I believe that the 'comparative morphology' of those who live with intellectual disability and mental illness, reveals trends in consciousness that all humans share, and some of these aspects are ugly. Bernard's exploration of art and ideas showed his gift for a wide angle perspective — following history on the big screen; engaging with culture and diversity in a playful, but discerning way.

Such pedigree in thought creates a valuable foundation on which to build a perspective of human consciousness that is complementary to that of Raymond Williams. By examining Uncle Bernard's views, we may find elements that help to give depth to Uncle Raymond's ideas. So, the two uncles combined can help build a framework for the Structure of Feeling and Experience which is relevant across Western society. This framework can then be used to provide background to the Feelings and Experiences of people who live with intellectual disability and mental illness.

Valuing consciousness above biology

While Bernard Smith has written prolifically about art, culture and perspective on an international scale, he also values the basic roots of awareness. In adding a Foreword to Peter Fuller's *The Australian Scapegoat*, he noted the Englishman's shared journeys of ideas, and also their similar, but different paths:

Fuller's determination (is) to work out a fully-fledged aesthetic for himself, and one in which the concerns of society, of morality and of art all have their part to play...He respects intellect but

is aware of the danger of allowing it to override perception…
You may disagree with Fuller but you would have to be a nong
not to know where he stood. (5)

Uncle Bernard could have been talking about himself —
he showed that for many people life and art shine backward and forward between each other with lessons to
share in both directions. It seems his message is that the
main job for humans, as conscious beings, is to keep their
perceptions open to alternative views that come from the
gift of awareness.

Fuller is impressed by the fact (as I am) that we are aware,
simply by looking at the way his face and body are rendered by
his Hellenistic sculptors, that the 'Laocoon' is 'in pain'. But I
cannot agree that this is caused by a biological response on our
part. For as biological organisms we possess no access to art.
Such access requires a state of consciousness and consciousness
is not adequately described as biological, though it can occur
within biological systems…The admiration of a work of art,
aesthetic valuing, requires the operation of memory. (6)

Smith believes that humans are just as much creatures
of spirit as they are products of evolutionary process. He
saw that life unfolded in ways no one could control, and
that history was not facts, but a process of experiences
which humanity flowed through in patterns. These are
good beginnings for creating a framework for thinking
about an alternative consciousness to the mainstream.

   As a cultural critic he has been a leader in grounding
the debate about modernism, post-modernism and how to
construct reality. I will apply analogous and sometimes apparently disconnected perspectives to the deconstruction
(7)of Uncle Bernard's and Uncle Raymond's work – two

different views of human experience can criss-cross with one another to create a more vivid perspective of human consciousness.

My aim is to pursue oppositions where there is potential for opening awareness about shared human traits. Bernard Smith and Raymond Williams both found allegorical and analogous evidence through art, culture and society. It is hoped their efforts can be refreshingly referred to the need for more expansive thought about improving the lives of marginalised people.

Learning that culture and identity are relational

Uncle Bernard's work covers as much territory as Raymond Williams. They were 'soul brothers' in their engagement with the common good. Smith, in his academic work, grappled with the demons that Williams chose to grapple with in his fictional work — spirit, love, decadence, mystery and 'the missing'.

Smith's particular strength is his lateral perspective on human history and the diaspora of the soul that it presents in the modern era. While many agonised over humanity's self destructive behaviour during the last century, Bernard managed to find compassion for his fellows. He saw trends that were part of a long march through history. So, he became an advocate for joining that throng and becoming lighter through the process.

In examining his canon, as a possible framework to complement Raymond Williams' Structure of Feeling, it is possible to see an array of views which allow humanity its lee — to shelter fragile, fickle, vacillating personalities from the hard attack of inquiry through a dialectic artificially seeking some perfect world. This lazy inquiry is what I call 'the drongo dialectic' – it allows for mistakes, for weakness, for habits of repeated faulty decisions and obsessions. It allows for humanity.

This is what we need when looking for parameters with which to frame the consciousness of the intellectually disabled and the mentally ill. They are 'just getting a life', and what we can offer, is the recognition that this is 'normal' and healthy. The key is to link their inner needs to a set of criteria that everyone can understand and value. We are all each other's mirror.

Bernard's message, which is relevant to finding such a framework of the Structure of Feelings and Experience, covers the full scope of human experience — from identity and belonging, to chaos, decadence and perspective. All relevant to determining aspects of self, other, and the common good. This set of criteria can add to how society acknowledges, values and serves the needs of all people through the public estate.

Social is primary in determining identity and being

A view of Identity and Being that sees Social as Primary, not the Dreamworld, dominates Bernard's work. He embraced Australian Aboriginal art and life in his career, but decided that humanity was more rooted in its relatedness than its numinous potential. He believed that 'the relation is all', and concern with human identity should start with 'us', not 'me'. According to his view, people live in a society of human beings more readily than they have a numinous engagement with the Dreaming. Whether one agrees with this or not, it provides a valuable perspective from which to consider the experiences humans share. Most people are born into family, community and social relations. Some are separated by circumstance of environment or biological inheritance from engagement with their group.

Many of the intellectually disabled live in their 'natural state', in a world that juggles being with 'normal' community members and being with peers. This creates both joy and sorrow. Feelings of belonging and separation alternate, but the overall experience is the sense that life exists mainly in the peer group. I believe this is healthy and 'normal'. For those who live with mental illness, consciousness fluctuates between comfort and discomfort with oneself, and with being in the midst of others. Some of those most divorced from group experience, because of their dis-ease with life, are at risk of disconnecting from the world. And there are some similarities in this experience with those who suffer from a disjointed sense of themselves, and about how and where to find meaning. It's a mad, mad world, and in truth there was never such a state as 'normal'.

Peripheral vision connects people and ideas

Possibly no greater reference point comes from Bernard's work, than that he helped the world to see its need for lateral or peripheral vision, as a connecting force in knowledge. By taking the perspective of the Antipodes, and its role in defining and redefining the nature of art, aesthetic, and self-image in Western consciousness, Bernard broke out of a bind.

He determined that 'edge defines centre', and things have not been the same since. If art from the Pacific and the colonies could redefine art and aesthetic in Europe, what does that say about traffic in consciousness? Could it be telling us that people with different experiences of seeing the world, of imagining the world, of Experiencing and Feeling life, have valuable parts to play in the full array of 'reality'?

Bernard said people had to look sideways and back to see what is in front of their face. The arrogance of colonialism had seen us ignore much about the context and perspective of life. So too today, the rational, empirical scientific worldviews can be arrogant and blind to Feelings and Experience in the lifeworld. When Uncle Bernard said that looking inwards towards abstraction only magnifies problems, he could have been describing the nature of both mechanistic science and mental illness.

They both share a kind of compulsive obsessiveness about the 'rightness' of their own inner view which needs a more balanced perspective. Just as one tradition in a rugby playing high school was to have the players in the 'first fifteen' also in the school choir — forced engagement with, and acceptance of, affective experience. Our world can also benefit from embracing the different perspectives offered by the mentally ill, by understanding that some people are given the gift of being in contact with other dimensions, or as Michael Harner calls it, 'non-ordinary reality'. (Harner)

I have seen that a basic mistake in the system is of assuming pathology before exploring shared awareness. If people were to remain open and conversational about consciousness we could create new pathways for engagement. There are as many areas for reverse healing within the rationally schooled psychiatrists and psychologists as there are hidden within the Feelings and Experiences of people who live with mental illness. Smith's work showed that transcultural activities refer outside of themselves in a healthy way. This is exactly the analogy for mentally ill people, to be more integrated into community life, where they can gradually feel more confident about acceptance and hope. Crossing cultures, building bridges of consciousness — there is a lot to be said for singing in the choir with your rugby boots on.

Perspective and experience make for difference

By emphasising common background patterns in human behaviour which criss-cross behind outward cultural differences, Bernard showed there was a shared form of organising life, ideas and images, which brings humans of all different cultures into a shared conversation. While this often breaks down, due to political, ethnic or religious tensions, there are usually ways through to finding some common ground.

The visual rhetoric is appropriate for imagining a meeting of minds, where those who live with intellectual disability, are seen as possessors of consciousness which reflects aspects of humanity that have value and depth. Jean Vanier and Henri Nouwen have both described these aspects of intellectual disability (Vanier, and Nouwen), as being a wellspring of shared humanity in the quiet ability to accept the patience, the stillness, the gentleness and slowness of people who have accepted a different path in life. When Uncle Bernard showed that power does not flow unilaterally, he could have been directing that perspective at this comparison of consciousness. The weak are not less than the strong. They are placed differently. In fact, in yogic terms, you would say they are nicely balanced. Too much energy stuck in one place means imbalance in another.

Moving out of the stuck sense of the powerful and the powerless, Uncle Bernard leads us to see where power best informs the conversation about ideas. In so much as 'knowledge may be that truth may be elsewhere', there is a lot to be said for the vulnerability and receptivity of people who live with intellectual disability. Observing the hectic lives my peers live, I feel that more people need to slow down and find themselves. People living with intellectual disability could effectively act as mentors. But book in early, because they're often out on the town.

Decadence implies renewal

Putting modernity under the microscope, Smith found its practice and offspring showed trends that continue today. When he engaged with the Surrealists who took up the mantle of analysing the 'madness' of 'progress', Bernard saw a healthy embrace of decadence in their work and their cries for change. He took an organic perspective, of the decay and degradation of community, morals and justice, which modernity has as a direct side effect.

Surrealism parodied, and sardonically hung out to dry the damnable results of progress, and the applications of technology and ideology which modernism put on the magnified world stage. Bernard saw all this as a healthy way to understand the cyclic resurgence inherent in humanity's fallible nature. While destruction reigned, the possibility of renewal was being born. This is a bit like Rudolf Steiner's work on creating miraculous fertiliser from treated animal waste, creating bountiful humus. Expressions of decadence in culture can dissolve both past and future. Thereby bringing reality into the moment, where everything actually happens. This is the territory of those who live with intellectual disability — free from too many worldly obsessions, they can often access the moment in an open-hearted way which illustrates something others 'train' for years to be able to capture for a few minutes.

Truth and art, practical living

One of the wonderful links that Bernard brought to light in his exploration of art and cultural process was the concept that truth is realised through practical activity. He has been a pragmatist as well as an idealist, a combination that can loosen perspective, but in his case, sharpened his sense of 'what works'. The Aboriginal notion of 'the business' of life, ie. culture, is that it is alive and requires working, at and in, to remain worthwhile. This is somewhat ironically linked with the Windsor Royal Family's nickname for itself, 'the firm'. Bernard saw that practicality determined how culture panned out. Ideas and dreams were fine, but what actually happened 'in the workings'?

His view is that labour and creation are the context of art and culture — making work a part of the community that is not just slaving away to earn a quid. It is involved in the business of sharing understandings about lifeworld, the numinous, the universe and everything. This seems an appropriate time to invite those living with mental illness to the table. Are they interested in sharing? Yes. How can they get involved? Currently, with great difficulty. But if it is possible to open the doors of legislative, policy-bound rules about where and how people who live with mental illness can join in society's workings, perhaps there will be more opportunity for them to share in it.

Bernard observed that because of the radical restructuring of work since the information and communications revolution, the whole notion of class was being redefined, with the middle classes slipping down to an underclass. In this way, consciousness becomes a much more mobile concept, wandering into the field of real-politik as the groups forming the marginalised come from much further afield than ever before in history. It is my assertion that the time has come to embrace wider concepts of human worth, to involve the mentally ill in looking at how we can restructure lifeworlds and return to valuing everyone's inner life more.

Civilisationally, everything recycles

When examining the schools of primitivism, classicism and medievalism, Bernard saw that certain patterns predominated. Whatever culture was being processed through art, the movement was one of recycling the generic elements of civilisation. The pattern of history showed that humanity often mistakenly followed paths of certainty, only to retreat when that way revealed itself as treacherous and damaging to the whole.

In its pursuit of linear, rationalist thinking, humanity is potentially at its peril — environmentally, sociologically, economically, and organically. Three trends which alone can drastically alter history are: genetically engineered produce and livestock; notions of growth in development and profits; and the separation of large numbers of capable people from being able to contribute to the process of production in Westernised economies. These come at the expense of social cohesion and a basic standard of living.

Yet, so far, authorities seem to be blindly following the ideologues who continue to promote these ideas and practices, in the name of the same 'progress' that has driven modernism. Many believe humanity has entered another watershed, similar to the pre World War Two era. 'Logical solutions' abound, but most people are feeling very ill at ease. In order to respond differently, we need to apply other aspects of the modernist project, rather than logic, measurement, and definitions of growth in terms of profit.

Without sounding like an 'I told you so', for some years now, Bernard has adopted the position that civilisational thinking sees everything as recycling. Understanding follows history, arriving late if at all, and so the message is usually: wait til it hurts then think about changing back. We live in a present that is past, a feeling of déja vu. Which is where the inclusion of people who live with mental illness makes sense, in trying to develop better understanding of what is going on inside a species, which keeps ignoring its best interests and self-destructing.

Signs of certainty are illusions

The Western mythologies of Number and Word have been described by Uncle Bernard as Civilisational Signs. He critiqued the slavish pursuit of mechanistic thinking and rhetoric, as if these two forms of communication and thought would hold all the answers for humankind. In Bernard's view, certainty is an illusion, and yet today it has become the holy grail. Science is no longer to blame for promoting this brand of ideology. Many of its explorations in physics and ecology have led it into mysterious territory, requiring humble pilots. But others have raced into the laboratory to grab hold of the steering wheel and rush towards switching genes and playing with life. This is dangerous territory. They need to recall the lessons from the mythologies of the world. Playing with life is something that ought to be left to the gods.

Into this scenario, those living with mental illness can offer us a perspective of what certainty can look like when it is your sickness. Obsessiveness is not unique to so-called 'schizophrenics'. Leaders and financiers and politicians can fall into the trap just as easily as anyone in a mental hospital. Bernard's message is that art history tells us that images shade into imaginings, and the images represent different orders of seeing. Illusion is a human activity, and modernity has eroded meaning, leaving us with the 'lost shadow of modernity'. Currently this seems to be lost on the powerful elites running the world. But the value in inviting people who live with mental illness to be involved in sharing their perspective, is to provide some counterpoint to the current mad certainty that the world will rush to its future progress on the back of logic and profit.

Culture comes first, always changing

Understanding that culture comes first, is one of Bernard's basic rules for balancing an assessment of ideas and values. If one accepts that, then involving all members of society in the development of new ways to assist each other and serve the marginalised, is a recognition of the importance of embracing all of culture. What is occurring to the least in society is an indicator of what is happening throughout it. Just as the frogs in an ecosystem can be its most telling indicators of potentially deadly pollution, so too the treatment of human beings in society tells its overall state of health or ill health. The experience of those who live with intellectual disability reveals to us that Western society is ignoring its soul.

In most of the circles I have worked, what can potentially be a rich source of quiet energy and shared affection, is often typecast as a management problem in social engineering. One of the deep sources of social capital existing in all communities is seen by the powerful as a daggy, forgettable group of no-hopers. The policy and program rhetoric does not say that, but the reality is their lack of presence and recognition in mainstream environments. It speaks volumes.

But Bernard also reminds us that history is everywhere. It surrounds life, and hollows out arguments for brutal mechanistic treatment of citizens. The answer according to Uncle Bernard? Promoting change and institutionalising restlessness. He sees that part of the role of art and culture is to challenge the popular notions that are running the world; to stimulate the social conscience of humankind; and to build a new sense of what to expect of one another in a civilised world.

Social evolution mixes change and tradition

Bernard has seen some interesting changes through the last couple of centuries. He argues that change and tradition can blend. And the evidence comes from many arenas. Not just art, but music, dance, performance and crafts. Many creative pursuits have proven that the old and new make good partners. He also saw that originality is 'in the mix'. This is one of his great illustrative expressions, showing us that there is great scope for applying this wisdom to 'shaking things up' in the social sciences. Just like what happened in education in the sixties and seventies. Which, under obedience to authority, seems to have been lost over the following three decades by a return to didactic certainty and repetition, driven by fear of missing economic opportunity.

From Bernard we learn that the marginalised have much to share. Their suffering is both old and new. Their experience is both now and then. Their understanding is basic — neglect hurts, and being excluded is harmful to all concerned. People who live with intellectual disability can be leaders in helping many members of society to return to understanding the exercise of communal love. Not a hippy trip through the seventies, but sharing and caring in your street, shopping mall and high rise flats.

Perhaps then, it will be possible to imagine positive outcomes from Uncle Bernard's other perspective: that forms combine. By imagining new forms of social development, and providing inclusion and engagement in mainstream activities with those who live with intellectual disability, there may be great potential for growth and for healing known, as well as unknown, social wounds.

Smith saw society moving from 'form dominating content' to new patterns of human expression. It is to be hoped that such scenarios, towards more loving alternatives than today's mechanistic materialism, can include the marginalised as part of the forefront of social change. Then, the stored memory in the hearts and minds of people who live with intellectual disability will provide a wellspring of positive feeling to fuel some of humanity's renewal.

Cultural traffic is life's essence

Thank God culture flows. Bernard explained this long ago, and showed that whatever 'the centre' may try to do to control, ignore, or reject 'the others', they would infiltrate and change their very masters. This is one of the most hopeful lessons from Uncle Bernard's work, especially for people who live with mental illness, who are increasing in numbers and decreasing in social acceptability.

The very thing that modernism is creating — joblessness, social dislocation, unhappiness, substance abuse and mental illness — is what the image-makers say it is removing. Yet, the information technology explosion, virtual reality impression management, and job removing technology, have all resulted in the above social problems.

Going by Bernard's cyclical culture clock, pretty soon this swell of energy will push cultural flow forward, against the trend of the know-all stock market jockeys and the political spin doctors who proclaim 'everything is going great guns in the modern ship of state.' As people feel the swell rise and the ship begin to float away, breaking its ties, there is likely to be some traffic in the waters ahead.

Mental illness results from the clashing of feelings, thoughts, dreams and imaginings in someone's mind. Similarly for modernism, the traffic's getting busy, clashing around in all the change and profit-boosting progress happening all over. Sooner or later it is going to come across the course of another 'ship of state of mind'. And Bernard is here to tell us that such cultural traffic is life's essence. He said cultures converge and horizons converge, more than they collide: 'There is no need to conceptualise the present in terms of the future…we are more fully creatures of the past than the future'. (8) The image is one of combinations of thought, feeling and imagination, to create new perspectives and understanding.

That is what is needed in looking at the lives, Feelings and Experiences of people who live with mental illness. Not only that they are subjects of pathological investigation of neurotransmitters gone awry. But, that their consciousness has something to tell humanity, about them, and about everyone. The notion that involving these folk in designing, planning and implementing their recovery and rehabilitation programs flies in the face of current scientific expertise. When a psychiatrist has trained for years to 'understand' such conditions, how could the patient be expected to know about their own condition? Yet common sense says that people should be central to their own lifeworld management. Right, Uncle Jurgen? Joining society as predominantly social beings is where patients would be best placed for healthy recovery, once they are out of any critical psychotic risk.

Uncle Bernard found that cultural production happens best, and happens most in cultural traffic. Managers would be wise to take note when they are planning the future policies, programs and services for people with mental illness, that their best chance of healthy recovery will be when they engage with their community, with appropriate support services. I know from experience that this is not happening enough. Some places may be doing this, but the mainstream is not. Patients are certainly not being invited to construct their recovery and rehabilitation programs.

Knowledge is a negotiated conversation

According to Bernard, knowledge is an invitation to a conversation, not extracts from some god-ordained book that holds all humanity needs to know. He examined the way art and ideas reflected Western conceptualisation of knowledge. He compared that with 'the others' in the Antipodes and decided that the exchange of views, opinions and feelings make up the rich mixture of understanding which is knowledge.

When looking at the perspective of people who live with intellectual disability, who are by definition seen to be 'unknowledgeable', it is interesting to consider Bernard's view. Conversation is a sharing and intermixing of both ideas and feelings (Zeldin). The experience of working with people who live with intellectual disability has taught me that they have more than an equal part to play in this conversational exchange.

Often their feelings will predominate. At other times, a quiet observation cuts to the heart of a matter which others have complicated with their own interpretations and competing ideas. The outcome of engaging in many conversations of this type with people who live with intellectual disability, is that they have very valuable, entertaining and enriching things to offer anyone who takes the time to listen. Part of the negotiation of knowledge is to settle on the terms within which it is developed, through this conversation of ideas and feelings. People who live with intellectual disability have much to teach others in their way of approaching the conversations that lead to knowledge. Simplicity in thought is something many people pursue through studying Zen Buddhism. But this simplicity is often innate among these folk.

Life echoes from the edges — it's 'echo-logical'

Listening to the echoes of thought was a process Uncle Bernard spent some time reflecting on. His work explored the waves of Experience and Feeling passing across history, and he came up with the notion that echoes repeated ideas and perspectives through humanity. This is what I call 'echo-logical' thinking. It is a negotiative process, whereby new and old exchange energies in the distillation of knowledge. What is happening now reflects the past, incorporating what has gone before, which is more than just repeating it.

Combined with Uncle Bernard's determination that Culture is not Immanent, the echo-logical concept implies that humanity is in an on-going conversation with itself, about itself. This is not narcissism, but the natural result of mindfulness. Bernard says that by being aware of ourselves and our inner and shared lives, humans have the capacity to grow and change, as individuals and as societies.

People living with mental illness are good examples of how this sort of growth is possible in all people. I have worked in environments in Australia and India, where, given the right conditions of listening, caring, engaging and having imaginative peers and support workers, people living with mental illness can work through many of their deeper problems. It may take a long time, but the echo-logical healing effect of shared understandings and compassionate views, provide as much healing as drug regimes alone.

If we combine appropriate medication, caring conversation and free exchange of Feelings and Experiences, there is great scope for many of these people to recover from deep damage to their psyche. A number of Australians who have gone to live in the schizophrenia therapeutic community of Athma Shakti Vidyalaya, in Bangalore, India, have achieved remarkable recoveries. And just as the answers to healing mental illness do not lie solely in

Western medicine or Eastern thought, there is no immanent answer in any one cultural setting or tradition. What is needed is a response to the eclectic nature of human consciousness. An eclectic regime of allowing healing according to the personality and capabilities of the individual concerned.

Bernard saw that 'Edges and Echoes Think Back and Wander/Wonder Forward'. He is a playful observer of history, culture, ideas and aesthetic. I feel his observations hold great hope for those working with damaged Western consciousness. He has seen the results of modernity ignoring the affective side of humanity. And he has still held a compassionate view of its potential to return to a more holistic way of being.

Watching modernity trying to fill the emptiness arising from its obsession with rational thought, progress and power, Bernard noted there was a process of subordination that occurred among people who could not compete in this game. But he watched them, in the Antipodean experience of the colonised, the other, creating their own meaning. He saw that meaning feeding back to the centre in a way which enriched those who were responsible for sentencing them to relative material poverty.

I believe this is an allegorical story for those people who live with mental illness, in terms of their experience of consciousness in the context of modernity. The very thing that makes them separated from and 'less than' mainstream community, is that they do not handle logical, competitive, compliant thought very well. This puts them on the outer with society. Yet my observations, at Pioneer Clubhouse mental health rehabilitation community in Sydney's Balgowlah, show that this very trait is a strength when compared with the fear behind 'normal' people's struggle to cope in the rapidly changing world of modernity. Hence my assertion, that involving people who live with mental illness in sharing their perspectives, and hearing the echo-logical wisdom going around between people, is a valuable way to encourage healing and build self-valuing.

Place comes from imagination

The exploration of place that forms a central thread in Uncle Bernard's work, has a potentially important perspective to offer those responsible for organising the life circumstances of people living with intellectual disability and mental illness. Bernard's view is: 'We Make Place, Rather than Place Making Us'. The insight that people create the places they experience (which is supported by Simon Schama's, *Landscape and Memory* and John Broomfield's, *Other Ways of Knowing*) emphasises how important it is to allow these two groups to organise the places they inhabit. To decorate them, where possible design them from scratch, and to claim them as their own.

Indigenous people have religious relationships with place. Creation stories are alive and renewing every day. But Westeners seem to have few active equivalents, except their domestic space, where home renovation focuses on the material environment and purchasing products, rather than a more spirit-based sense of place. Individuals have special places they relate to, but generally the experience of valuing place is individual and idiosyncratic. What Bernard found was that an underlying trend of place-making existed within all of us, but was often denied by rationality, circumstance, taste or habit. Understanding that place actually comes from our imagination, promises great scope for the healing that can be created through the way places are developed in collaboration with people living with mental illness and intellectual disability.

Added to this perspective is Bernard's assertion that 'Culture is about traffic, not place'. He saw the significance of places being determined by how people built them up in their imagination, but that even more, the power of cultural development came from exchange of energy between people and their mixed cultures. Place matters, and especially a local focus. But culture, like identity, is transient. Gao Xinjian showed us this in his Nobel Prize-winning novel, *Soul Mountain*. Xinjian's view of the importance of the individual over the concept of identity and culture, reinforces Bernard's point, that mixing, exchanging, growing and sharing make up humanity. Not static understandings of people, traditions or places.

Uncle Bernard has taught that humans need to value a sense of community, but also to remember that Imagination is Primary. This can be compared with Lyotard's view, that 'Modernity carried regret' (Lyotard). Bernard argues it is all a matter of mixing it and matching it, making it up as we go along. Not getting stuck. So, while landscape may have begun as a dream (Broomfield, Smith, Schama), reality is what is imagined right now, mixing past, present and future. So it is, that people living with mental illness and intellectual disability can become the determining agents in their lifeworld, by being given greater opportunities to design and manage their circumstances, places and services.

Nihilistic innerness shadows modernity

Bernard has given modernity a trip to the cleaners. He sees it as sentenced to 'innerness', and 'shadowed by nihilism'. The inner Experience and Feelings that humans undergo, while travelling forward in the machine of modern progress, is one of self obsession and emptiness. The ennui captured in many European films of the post-war era reflects what seems to have spread across modernity. A feeling of 'is that all there is?'.

According to Bernard, the Australian obsession with landscape, while living in the suburbs, is an example of the denial artifice built into modernity. The modern motto of 'development at all costs' has an alter ego of self doubt, like the perpetual stranger in the doorway. When he visited the Antipodes in the 1920s, D.H. Lawrence felt something of this aspect about Australian bourgeois society. In his novel Kangaroo, written while in Australia, Lawrence described the Sydney consciousness as a capacity 'not to care, at its deepest level not to care.' (Lawrence) Uncle Bernard saw Australian art as 'sardonic', not because of the desert it portrayed, but because of the people in the suburbs it was actually commenting on.

People living in suburban cells, either waxing lyrical about the bush, or fearing it deeply, or both, are like miniature portrayals of the modern condition. Nature, society and fate are all 'out there', wild and unpredictable. So it is better to buy a painting of the bush and dream of its connection with one's soul, than to really embrace the experience of being in a land that offers such connection with wildness.

That wildness may also live in the Feelings and Experience of people, such as people living with mental illness. They are actually scary and unknown. Because they are unknown. If more of these people are allowed to express their truth, it creates a healthy route to living the wholeness of their lives. Such approaches are healing, both for those in disturbed states of heart and mind, as well as their 'normal' peers in the suburbs. It is part of the successful holistic healing occurring at the Athma Shakti Vidyalaya therapeutic community.

Life goes out towards culture, not in towards mind

By deconstructing the politics of vision, Uncle Bernard showed that 'seeing' is used as a metaphor for 'understanding'. For example, the use of terms such as 'eye, word, image, blindness and insight,' show that perspectives and views have dominated Western understanding for centuries. According to Bernard, modernism is 'a point of view', and it is time to review that perspective with more 'insight'.

The message in considering the Feelings and Experience of people living with intellectual disability, is that they have particular points of view, but no one takes notice anyway. So when someone is marginalised, their viewpoint matters little, even if it may hold unique visions and possibilities. Uncle Bernard decided the politics of vision needed a shake up. He believes 'what we do and how we live is more important than how we perceive'. Shades of Uncle Raymond's 'lived experience' being the core value foundation for life. The true reception of life is through hearts and souls, as well as the 'mind's eye'.

Bernard saw that suffering was one type of story sharing cultural echoes, stronger than views or perspectives. It represents a universal human attribute, Feelings and Experience. Going beyond perspective into lived experience. This is where he argues that humans 'go out towards culture rather than in towards mind'. Human lives are shared, Feelings and Experiences engage with one another, while views are more illusory and private. People living with intellectual disability have interesting views, and even more interesting engagements when they 'go out towards their culture'. Acknowledging this shared aspect of their humanity is an important step towards providing quality of life, which is everyone's due.

Uncle Jurgen's four way test is currently failing a lot of contenders in this field of rehabilitation.

Context makes life, so celebrate stigmata

According to Uncle Bernard, all things are Connected through Context and Reciprocity. By acknowledging the context within which people live, and the impact of, and need for reciprocal exchanges in life experience, it is possible to plan for better community services. The give and take of life provides for a healthy exchange of ideas, skills, Feelings and Experience. Bernard showed that this exchange process, even between colonised and colonisers, was an inevitable aspect of human society.

The 'wisdom of the centre' has been unravelling for centuries. Bernard interprets this to mean that 'people's stigmata should be worn with pride'. This is a key aspect of the Structure of Feeling and Experience Bernard provides for those living with mental illness. While they may feel isolated, even terrified, the society they inhabit would benefit from their taking a more assertive stance with their unique 'stigmata'. Because the result will be that people benefit from getting a broader perspective on themselves, from what 'the others' show them about themselves. As with Sydney's Gay and Lesbian Mardi Gras parade, the streets fill with people celebrating a shared sense of pride in their sexuality, and, as a result, others begin to reconnect with their own.

Bernard saw the 'absent centre' showing up in universal webbed connections between the colonies of the Antipodes and Europe. Between the Great Tradition and the innovators. Between the rule-breakers and the indigenous. All sorts of webbings showed up in art and ideas, and Bernard used this observation to conclude that varying contexts make for a rich overall combination of life among all of humanity. He claims it is best to celebrate our stigmata. They are all we have, so show them off. This stands as an open invitation for the general community, and the so-called experts managing the life circumstances of 'the others', to be more open to valuing people who live with mental illness. They should be given more opportunity to give voice to and celebrate those aspects of themselves that give colour, depth and individuality to their lives.

Abstraction misses the particular in the general

Watching modernity's unfolding, Uncle Bernard saw its use of abstraction as missing the particular in the general. Sweeping movements in art, culture, education, technology, design, planning and so on, led to everything being taken into a slipstream of progress. The local, the other, the curious, the small, were lost in a morass of certainty and generality.

In the obsessive pursuit of trends and movements, curiosity about 'the other' disappeared. Certainty about notions of 'culture as power' created separation between peoples with compatible lifeworlds. And, according to Bernard, convergence of 'world meaning place', led modernism to its narrow, eroding context.

Because they are 'particular', people living with intellectual disability resist this type of sweeping generalisation. Their needs are not covered universally by modernist, populist experiences. Although many of these things are pleasing and in demand — movies, fast food, clothes etc. In the end, people who live with intellectual disability gravitate, more than anything else, to community. Company. To 'the other guys'. It is simple and inexpensive. And it wipes away notions that providing special services is the priority rather than having appropriate time with peers and integrating with the wider community.

Earth and humanity exist through each other

'Landscape is part of culture' was a strong message in Bernard's reflections on art and its differing traditions across cultures. The overriding perspective he had was that the earth exists through us, given that our awareness of it is how it comes into being for us. Just as we exist through it, because otherwise we would not even be here. This leads to certain responsibilities in both stewardship and numinosity. Because this combination is both contextual and symbolic, humanity is challenged with whether it can 'work the place' and 'dream the place'. In Carlyle's words, highlighted by uncle Raymond, the concept of the 'cultivated' person is really no different to the Aboriginal sense of 'singing it up'.

Both concepts reflect people's double connection with earth's energy and ether, because we 'sit down here', and we 'sing up here'. For people living with mental illness, the acceptance of their experience of the 'other world' of ideas, nightmares, voices, fears, obsessions and traumatic visions, is a key part of healing their wounds of heart, mind and soul. Just as 'losing it', in some Aboriginal communities, is seen as par for the course, 'just going wamba'. There needs to be greater acceptance that madness is part of the condition of humanity, and especially modernity.

Then, humanity can really start talking. About growing closer to one another. Finding common ground for feelings, understandings of how to deal with voices, fears and obsessions. Healing through commonality. Sharing the pain and letting it dissipate. Isolation is the most powerful form of punishment, just as it makes pain and darkness more potent. I believe this is part of what earth is telling humans right now. Listen more, practise dadirri (Stockton) – 'to sit, wait and listen'. Find the voice that includes all voices. The part of each that is part of it all, that is potentially part of the energy of life, providing nurture to those in pain.

Types and styles find authors, and image is secondary

'Not a good look' is a popular late-modernist quip. It speaks volumes. That 'the look' is more important than the substance, the image more valued than the content, the outer form is above the inner scope on humanity's current scale of values. Uncle Bernard has spent his working life arguing that 'image of form is only one level of reality'. It may be valid for creating impressions, but if it is taken as literally the 'way it is' in our world, then it leads to the 'hegemony of the abstract'. Hence the current slavish following of virtual reality as a clever new phenomenon, when many feel it is just a technological game to extend the artificial image-making of commercial promotions.

Accepting 'Form Over Content' illustrated for Bernard how rationality had come to dominate Western thought. He pointed out that earlier on in history, elders had a role in society, to observe from the periphery, and feed back views from the perspective of experience. Now, if the logic works, do it. Bernard questioned this as being a lone dominant value in the same way he questioned 'image above content'. Bernard saw that types and styles moved around through human history and societies, creating echo-logical wisdom. And he saw that they would find authors, rather than authors finding them. Meaning that substance exists before image, and it is necessary to clarify where it lies before making assessments of value.

People living with mental illness are not impression manageable. They will not comply with formulae for image creation, and they are likely to misbehave when required to conform. So I feel they hold out great hope against the passivity that currently besets so much of society, which accepts the rise in image-only experiences, as against real time, real life. From Australia's Wonderland, to the video arcades, to the worlds of fashion and cosmetics, the present modern world has innumerable experiences of images overpowering substance. But, people living with mental illness are so full of images that they do not want to give themselves over to an image-controlled world. It is only another hallucination to go through.

I believe Uncle Bernard's perspective, of involving

people in active planning for their own lives, provides a sound foundation for acknowledging their lived experiences — making the programs, living conditions and services as personal, real-peopled, and individual as possible would help heal the domination of crazy images and deluded senses about the world.

Plurality overcomes duality

Bernard's work showed that modernism lives on throwbacks. It continually redefines, recycles and regurgitates life, style, ideas and images. This is a symbolic and a practical phenomenon which holds both the promise for acceptance of difference and diversity, along with an inability to accept stable states. Intellectual disability represents a relatively stable state. The people whose lives rest in a condition of acceptance of hardship and challenge in difference, and battling indifference among their fellow citizens, provide a particular contrast to the 'rush of the new'. Whether examining promotion and purchase cycles in consumer capitalism, or concepts of adequate activities for people who are 'less than', the energy of plurality should work in favour of better acknowledgment for people of difference. For they are grist to the mill of progress.

Perhaps it is time to engage in the conversation about benefits to the whole, by integrating 'into the mix' of society, those who are 'not perfect'. Selecting out difference, and treating people with disabilities as special cases needing separate treatment, is not a healthy approach to endorse. Embracing difference, providing support to accommodate disability, and then seeking active engagement in 'normal' environments would allow healthy energy flow for the plurality that people living with intellectual disability provide, and we all need for healthy balance in our awareness of what it is to be human.

As Uncle Bernard showed in his examination of the culture of colonialism, progress can harbour many dark aspects, which then fall into decline, followed by a recycling of earlier knowledge and healthy resurgence of humanity. It seems the world is in a particular period of this recycling process right now. Change has occurred in the Eastern block and South Africa. The Internet has globally revolutionised communication and personal networking.

The earth is blowing its global mind with all this change, and old binary forms of knowledge are being replaced by a healthy plurality. The very substance that can feed into new awareness of the value in difference and diversity in human consciousness.

Circling to end the walkabout 'in the mix'

From these elements in Bernard's work, I have condensed five main themes, which will be revisited in the conclusion, as contributors to the suggested framework of a possible Structure of Feelings and Experience. The concept of overlaying, in Mandorla style, the offerings of Bernard's, Raymond's and the four subject groups, fits with Bernard's way of seeking answers 'in the mix'.

Chapter Five

People living with mental illness

What is sane?

The aim of this chapter is to skirt around the broad territory of human consciousness, including mental illness, to see how it connects with the concept of the Structure of Feelings and Experience. I will compare the special boundary posts, the unusual 'geography of mind', and the regular traffic in ideas, fears, notions and noxious weeds of imagination. Mapping the overlapping territory of these two regions, may help in identifying healing places which engage with and value these Feelings and Experiences.

I will examine several areas which act as boundary posts of mental illness, and set that framework against the Structure of Feelings and Experience (developed from the work of Uncles Raymond Williams and Bernard Smith). Two Aunties who are important additional 'elders' are: psychiatrist, Karen Horney, and psychologist, Anne Wilson Schaef.

Madness — mental illness — has varying degrees and images across different societies. For modern Western society it is a complex issue that includes a wide range of states from depression, as a result of stress and burnout, to what is called psychotic 'schizophrenia' from complete mental collapse. So to begin discussing the subject, it may pay to define a common ground that most people can relate to. Hollywood starlet, Lauren Bacall, is quoted as having put into perspective those crazy times most people feel, when she said: 'You can't start worrying about what's going to happen. You get spastic enough worrying about what's happening now'. (1)

That sense of out-of-control and panic, which besets people when they cannot cope with life, is a 'normal' human reaction to extreme stress. But for people suffering from chronic mental illness, life is a continual cycle of worrying about what is happening now, what happened before, and what might happen soon. It all seems to get mixed up in the minds of those living with the challenge of mental illness and it takes over their consciousness completely. I am using that continual cycle of mental stress and delusion as a measurement for madness.

While most people can relate to this as a concept, it is difficult to fully empathise with those whose journey is through much darker territory than most of us usually experience. Because of the extreme and often unique nature of the Feelings and Experiences undergone in mental illness, these people have much to teach society. Their journey through consciousness is full of challenges, of extreme mood swings, of fear, of paranoia, of voices, of obsessions and other delusions which offer analogous perspectives on how the whole of society often seems to behave. Some would say our society is stuck in a delusional obsession with economic rationalism, a value system that hurts many citizens, but is supposed to bring us benefits.

Robert Johnson looked at the dark side of human nature in his book *Owning Your Own Shadow*, and he pointed out that it is unhealthy to try to stay only in the positive side of our personalities: 'To suffer one's confusion is the first step in healing. Then the pain of contradiction is transformed into the mystery of paradox'. (2) Mental illness moves onto another level of confusion than what Johnson described above. Loss of soul, disconnection from the core self, and inability to relate to one's community, are indicators of having moved into deeper and darker mental illness. At times, many healthy, balanced people have travelled through such mental space when they have known they were 'out there and dangerous'. But they most often pass through this moment and come back to regular functioning of Feelings and Experience.

Few people who have been through such territory endeavour to go back in their sane moments and visit the space and place of their nightmares. Madness seems to have been a fluctuating state in the broad assessment of society. For some 'normal' people it is one of the ultimate threats. Many people in the mainstream community find it so confronting to be met by other souls who are completely out of whack with a shared perspective that they shy away and try to avoid contact.

Mental hospitals do not get overrun at visiting times. And as Aunty Anne Wilson Schaef, the pioneer of non-judgemental psychology, based on accepting people's life process, not pathologising their weirdness, says:

Many believe that we try to kill in others what we fear in ourselves. And yet, as we face our fears, we have less need to project them onto others. Going into our fears and processing through them will lead us to places of clarity we have never imagined. And, we will not need the other to project upon. (3)

Some cultures, especially indigenous cultures, have acceptance of madness built into their natural understanding of how people go though different stages in life. When I had to rush off to hospital to be with my son who was experiencing a psychotic episode with 'schizophrenia', an Australian Aboriginal colleague of mine remarked: 'Oh don't worry too much about it. He's probably just gone wamba! Up home we'd just send him up to aunty and let him work it off'.

Mental illness is rife among indigenous communities, especially in post-colonial situations like Australia, where dispossession, stolen generations, incarceration and deaths in custody have unleashed holocaust conditions onto whole communities. As well as this is the destruction of their sacred sites, their land, and their relationship with the earth, all of which have traditionally been part of the normalising influences in their lifeworld.

So it is important to establish that 'sanity, rational or sensible behaviour or judgement' (4), varies from community to community. And the way society decides who is sane and who is not, has as much to say about the state of health of the society as it does about the individuals being certified.

For the purpose of this text, 'sane' is taken to mean: 'able to anticipate and assess the effect of one's actions'. (5) Are the current leaders of most Western socio-political systems, who believe in economic rationalism, then, mad or mean?

Balancing, not judging the shadow

Robert Johnson emphasises that modern society has lost the ability to integrate those qualities which are unpleasant in the make-up of the human psyche: 'It is the task of every human to restore our shadow and redeem our rejected qualities. People are as frightened of their nobility as their darkest side'. (6) He teaches, that if humans ignore the parts of their natures which express the shadow, they are likely to slip into neurotic behaviour.

George Bernard Shaw said, 'The only alternative to torture is art', by which he meant that either we incorporate our shadow consciously and constructively into our lives, to achieve balance, or we will end up doing it anyway through some neurotic behaviour which is likely to be destructive. (7)

There is a possibility of reaching a balance in human nature which is often confused with conflict, or dualism. It is that part of human consciousness which links with the universe's energy — chaos, if you like. So, light and dark, good and bad, yin and yang are not meant to be in conflict, but in balance, by exercising both in cooperation. This is what yoga taps into and turns into a strengthening experience, of body, mind and soul.

For many people, there are regular jolts to consciousness which create disruptions to life, relationships, work, even relaxation. There may not even be a cause. Suddenly a bad mood rises. Its origin is not known. It creates even more frustration, edginess and proneness to irritability.

Aunty Anne Wilson Schaef's *Living In Process*, personal and group life-growth work, concentrates on letting these moments be, giving them room, and allowing the person to work through the feelings, and see if they come to a deeper awareness. Either way, the feelings pass, having generated reaction and negative consequences if suppression has been attempted, or, if they have been allowed to 'pass on by', some unwanted energy may have been cleared from the person's system.

Aunty Anne says it is a mistake to see this sort of event as a good/bad one. That really is dualism – when judgement enters into the equation and we make a decision to mark the experience with a tick in the red column of the ledger of life. She notes that self-blame, blame by others, and a whole series of negative consequences result from this approach.

Robert Johnson adds: 'Every single virtue in the world is made valid by its opposite'. (8) So if people feel themselves suddenly slipping into 'a bad hair day', then, the advice from these experts is that it is often best to 'just sit with it'. It is a challenge to explore paradox. Something unwanted has come upon the person, and they have to deal with it by letting it have space. That is paradoxical, and it seems most people prefer simple logical, apparently 'rational' answers.

Paradox is that artesian well of meaning we need so badly in our modern world... (In refusing to embrace paradox) we only confine ourselves to the useless experience of contradiction,(which) brings the crushing burden of meaninglessness...Paradox is creative, it is a powerful embracing of reality...While contradiction is static and unproductive, paradox makes room for grace and mystery. (9)

Taking Johnson's advice seems to be a positive step, although it involves risk. I have observed the alternative at first hand, in Sydney mental hospitals and suburban homes — where patients, and many citizens, sit in misery and fight the results of human nature — paradoxical Feelings and Experiences. Many cultures have rituals and traditions which engage with the dark side. They vary from vision quests, initiation rites, tests of man and womanhood, opportunities to lead with safe mentoring. And they have other ways of experiencing fear, darkness and the terror of either being alone, or leading with the full weight of social responsibility for the group.

Culture can only function if we live out the unwanted elements symbolically. All healthy societies have a rich ceremonial life. Less healthy ones rely on unconscious expressions: war, violence, psychosomatic illness, neurotic suffering, and accidents — these are low grade ways of living out the shadow. Ceremony and ritual are a far more intelligent and enriching means by which individuals and groups accomplish different outcomes by responding differently to the same inner and outer influences. (10)

An honest public conversation about the universally shared elements of madness, chaos, darkness and shadow within most human beings would help to recontextualise the place we give people who live with mental illness in Western society. If more people processed such aspects of their full humanity in symbolic cultural rituals, from the sporting field, to all night dancing and Mardi Gras marches, to sweat lodges and drumming sessions, there would be a healthier balance in people's lives, and in how mental illness is treated by the majority. Judging another's madness is an invitation to deny the observer's own inner nature. There is a lot to learn, taking a walk on the wild side, with compassion and dadirri (ability to 'sit, wait and listen').

Who is isolated and lonely?

Modern life is increasingly marked by isolation. Success, suburbs full of nuclear families, SOHO (solo operator, home office) work, busyness, workaholism, etc. There appear to be any number of ways that people living in a modern Western society can become isolated from each other. And the corollary of isolation is loneliness. Yet another criterion of modern life, especially in big cities. Separation from relationship is a core problem of modernity. It is caused by the massing of population, removal of time to relate with strangers, and pressure to perform.

What is occurring, here? It appears that people in Western societies are losing the ability to relate to one another. This is seen by some as an endemic problem of modernity. It emphasises the need for sharing, company, story-telling time, and all the other factors Uncles Raymond and Bernard have described as core aspects of the Structure of Feeling and Experience.

Escaping into virtual reality video-computer generated experiences, and finding intimacy through the Internet, are two solutions which have blossomed into popularity. They are available through well established channels of consumption, and have the privacy factor that many people need in order to feel securely in control of their experience of life.

For the diagnosed mentally ill, the above scenario quickly deteriorates into a hell. A place of solo entrapment with all their devils. For millions of people living with mental illness, in a world where finding company and shoulders to lean on is a rarity, isolation is chronic. Hence the increasing evidence of suicide, drug abuse, complete physical collapse and eventual hospitalisation.

Along with this, labelling people with a 'psycho' tag by many in society, reinforces the problem of feeling less than and separate from the norm.

What cures loneliness?

Rudolf Steiner believed that the human experience was one of reincarnation from many lifetimes before, when souls may have gone through a myriad of different experiences. Whether one agrees with this esoteric view or not, the solution he saw for helping the development of people living with mental illness or disability was that these people need carers and teachers who are fully present in their own lives and able to share positive loving energy.

So long as the teacher meets the situation with any kind of bias...so long will he remain incapable of making any real progress with the child. Not until the point has been reached where...a certain calm and composure as an objective picture for which nothing but compassion is felt...is the necessary mood of soul present in the astral body of the teacher. (11)

What Theodore Zeldin (*An Intimate History of Humanity*) and others have called 'welcoming hospitality' is the facility to exercise unconditional acceptance and compassion for others. Herein lies healing potential for those living with mental illness. However, the introduction of budget limitations, efficiencies and pressures to classify and compete between degrees of need among patients, has removed this capability from Western health systems.

Health systems have become so preoccupied with meeting the surveillance requirements of the system, otherwise known as management reporting, that just being with people in need has become almost non-existent in health agencies. The loss of community in society has been matched by the loss of community in places where healing is meant to be available for people living with mental illness.

The evidence from community services for these people, especially where I have worked in Sydney, is that there is an atmosphere of being babysat and watched, while kept on heavy medication regimes. The drugs may suppress any unwanted antisocial symptoms, but they do nothing to redress the inner psychological problems of patients.

Rather than any real engagement in rehabilitation of body, mind or soul, there is a priority for efficient and effective management of people living with mental illness by the use of medication and monitoring alone. In Sydney mental health facilities, nursing staff and former managers have told me that they would personally prefer to engage with patients on a one-to-one basis, seeking to assist self-understanding among patients. But the dominant thinking that 'only doctors know', as well as hierarchical structures, power control measures, the pressure of staffing levels, budget limits, and management priorities, make this not only difficult, but actively resisted.

If mental health nursing, and other staff, were allowed to share with patients in a more natural way, rather than conforming to a legalistic, limited role, they could make themselves available to listen to the lives of those needing hospitality for the soul. They could be themselves in a more personal expression of their role. Their efforts would achieve results.

Once (the necessary mood of soul in the carer/teacher) has come about, the teacher is there by the side of the (person) in a true relation and will do all else that is needful more or less rightly.

For you have no idea how unimportant is all that the teacher says or does not say on the surface, and how important what he himself is, as teacher. (12)

Since my son became psychotic with 'schizophrenia' over six years ago (at the age of 18), and since I worked in the mental health rehabilitation field in northern Sydney, as well as closely liaising with it as a parent – my experience has been that mental illness has a twofold effect on everyone it touches. Firstly, 'normal' people deeply feel their own edge of madness. And secondly, they feel the distance between them and the person suffering, as they either wish to reach them and share a loving connection, or run a mile. Within the present system, the gap is not being closed. The ill remain lonely and isolated.

Political and health administration leaders in Westernised societies need to reflect on the damage being done by continuing to support these isolating ways of living and healing. As Theodore Zeldin has pointed out, the inability of health systems to provide healing environments of care, compassion, individual and group engagement with patients is an indicator of a chronically sick society. This is where we can learn from our indigenous brothers and sisters. As Aunty Anne Wilson Schaef writes: 'The Hawaiian proverb says — *we* overrides *me* — Tribal peoples know how to be a community. In Western culture, we have tried to make the nuclear family the building block of culture…We are afraid of intimacy'. (13)

Isolation and loneliness are spread across the suburbs. It is chronic within the so-called health system. Mental illness remains an unsolved problem because the means are not being made available to overcome the lack of sharing, healing relationships among people living with mental illness and their carers within hospital and community-serviced environments.

How are we meant to be?

German-American psychoanalyst, Karen Horney, decided back in the 1940s that 'individuals cope with the anxiety produced, by the frustration of psychological needs, by disowning their real feelings and developing elaborate strategies of defence'. (14) Horney said this is the beginning of neurosis, and the trail heading towards mental illness. (15)

The sequence of events for people suffering from such a predicament seems to be that they then can no longer 'hold it together'. For whatever reason. Not because they are bad, or wrong, or somehow 'less than' as a person. They are just challenged with other problems than the norm. Horney believed that all people have a 'real self' which we are designed to fulfil, if we are able to exercise responsibility for ourselves and grow through our difficulties. She thought that: 'What is psychologically healthy in human beings is qualitatively different from what is unhealthy. That which is sick in each of us operates by different psychological laws and dynamics and develops in very different ways from that which is healthy.' (16)

I believe that Horney's self-realisation process is our natural inheritance, and regardless of whatever mental illness we may be exposed to, there is always hope for us to re-engage with this process from our deep inner self, if conditions are right. It is not guaranteed, nor is it impossible. Understanding the Structure of Feeling and Experience that is usual for humans to undergo, gives us a set of reference points which indicate why some individuals may go off course. If they are denied these, or unable to give them expression, it is likely they will move into an imbalanced state. Likewise, if these conditions can be restored, they may, with appropriate help, find their balance again.

Knowing how we are meant to be is a lifetime process of learning and growth in self-awareness, towards self-realisation. (17) That is also the ancient teaching of yoga, wherein people seek to balance the energy flowing through them in mind, body, spirit as an exercise in increasing self-awareness, until self is merged with the universe in complete balance.

Aunty Karen saw that when humans became out of balance in their self-awareness they veered towards a distorted view of themselves. She saw this as part of the challenge of growing up, that all people have to face the task of learning to balance their inner selves in order to reveal their true selves:

According to Abraham Maslow, people need physiological satisfaction, security, love and belonging, esteem and self-actualisation. These needs are hierarchical: the physiological needs are the most powerful and the needs belonging to a more highly evolved state are progressively weaker. (18)

Horney saw that all people had the potential to realise their coherent self as the core of their personal identity, while also facing the challenge of having their basic needs met. Maslow developed his theories as complementary to Horney, and the psychologists who followed Maslow's 'Third Force' school (after Freudians and Behaviourists) saw self-actualisation as not only the raison d'etre of individuals, but also of social institutions, 'whose worth can be measured by their success or failure in fostering the psychological growth of individuals'. (19)

This concept, of individuals sitting within a context of society and culture, in an interchange with their consciousness, is the perspective that Raymond Williams and Bernard Smith explored. Healthy individual life depends on people being able to access that interchange between the self and the group throughout their lives, in the same way that the natural condition is in indigenous societies who are undisturbed by Western civilisation. (Cowan, Jackson)

Unfortunately, it can be argued that the 'self' that exists in today's world has a huge challenge finding such conditions. Horney believed 'the self existed within a matrix of concentric fields extending from the intrapsychic, through the interpersonal, to the larger culture in which we are all immersed'. (20) For the majority of citizens today, that set of circles is increasingly impersonal, detached from the individual's lifeworld.

For people trying to heal neurosis, Horney's view was that her work was to be in an on-going oscillation between the outer and the inner regions of the patient's being. For our purposes, this image suffices in portraying the challenge for people experiencing madness. They face the task of trying to straddle that territory and the swinging experience, to and fro in their awareness. Thoughts, ideas, images and voices are continually pushing them into a swaying motion, out of balance with self.

What can we do when torn by conflict?

One of the defining differences between people suffering from mental illness, and those who are not, is the amount of inner conflict occurring in their consciousness. Aunty Karen spent a large part of her career trying to help people out of these inner conflicts by helping them find their own inner guidance and courage, and to persevere with the effort required.

The neurotic person engulfed in a conflict is not free to choose. He is driven by equally compelling forces in opposite directions, neither of which he wants to follow. Hence a decision in the usual sense is impossible. He is stranded, with no way out. The conflict can only be resolved by working at the neurotic trends involved, and by so changing his relations with others and with himself that he can dispense with the trends altogether. (21)

For people suffering from 'schizophrenia', choice about entering or avoiding conflict is not there. In fact, neurosis looks comfortable compared to full blown 'schiz'. This is vividly portrayed in Mark Vonnegut's book about his experience of living with schizophrenia, *The Eden Express*:

Most diseases can be separated from one's self and seen as foreign intruding entities. Schizophrenia is very poorly behaved in this respect. Colds, ulcers, flu, and cancer are things we get. Schizophrenic is something we are. It affects the things we most identify with as making us what we are. (22)

With this much misunderstood and incorrectly 'named' set of conditions, the conflict between 'normal' and 'abnormal' is continuous, with no way of knowing which is which. Sufferers fluctuate in their understanding of what is happening to them, and end up lost in the confusion of what is 'normal' and who they are. The issue arising from such evidence, is that people suffering in this way require caring environments in which to heal their inner conflicts — environments which invite their core Feelings and Experiences to normalise, by being recognised, valued and encouraged to come out and play. Then, when healing has begun, they can be invited to begin taking more responsibility for themselves, their thoughts and feelings. And to open themselves again to caring for, and responding to, the needs of others.

I needed help, but still in the back of my mind was the feeling that I was crying wolf, that there was really nothing wrong. It would be terribly difficult for anyone to understand what was wrong, because what was wrong was such a strange, elusive thing, the sort of thing it would be easy, almost logical to discount…time stopped being continuous; it jumped around with lots of blanks. (23)

While mental illness is isolating, exhausting and debilitating, in terms of how it affects the lives of those who suffer from it, there are aspects to the experience, which shine a light into all human consciousness. Mark Vonnegut is lucid in his memory of what it was like for him to 'be nuts'. And he is able to present the facts in an unromantic, but fascinating way:

There were times I was scared, shaking, convulsing in excruciating pain and bottomless despair. But I was never clumsy. Most people assume it must be very painful for me to remember being crazy. It's not true. The fact is, my memories of being crazy give me an almost sensual glee. The crazier I was, the more fun remembering it is. I don't want to go nuts again. I'd do anything to avoid it. Part of the pleasure I derive from my memories comes from how much I appreciate being sane now, but most of what's so much fun with my memories is that when

I was crazy I found my glass slipper. Everything I did, felt, and said, had an awesome grace, symmetry, and perfection to it. My appreciation of that grace, symmetry and perfection hasn't vanished with the insanity itself. It's regrets that make painful memories. When I was crazy I did everything just right. (24)

What stands out in Mark's account of his 'madness' is how 'normal' it seems. He felt right, and in some perspective seemed OK, but his body and mind were not in sync, and he could not get the whole show to operate in a coordinated way. Confusion and entrapment in the mix of states called schizophrenia are alluring aspects of 'the disease', which can turn on and off like a faulty electric plug. Sufferers are thrown about in a maelstrom of feelings, thoughts, anxieties and obsessions which leave them exhausted and drained. Yet totally involved in the whole shebang, as if it has got a clear purpose: 'Fear and pain would be everything and then nothing. The highs weren't all that different from the lows. Neither was grounded. Both had at best a marginal relationship to anyone's reality'. (25)

It is like getting emotionally electrocuted over and over, and going back for more because some parts of it feel so good. Then the whole energy build-up takes over and causes collapse. For addicts, there is a similar experience, of remembrance being almost a relief because of the freedom of knowing one is no longer stuck in that mad cycle of experiences.

Conflict may not only be like warfare inside ourselves or between ourselves. It can be when something does not fit where it should. And when life gets like that all the time, being in conflict with our desire for peace creates total exhaustion. But something about this sort of experience is akin to what therapists and others call 'world work'. Those at the heart of such experiences are 'carrying the load' for everyone, grabbing that loose high tension wire of life and hanging on like hell. It is scary to watch, frightening to think about, and terrifying to have no choice but to have to go through it over and over. Yet it is exercising aspects of reality that need to be processed, in order for the chaos factor to work itself through. Perhaps being 'normal' is not so different, it just looks more under control. In order to help individuals heal from this sort of combination of imbalanced Feelings and Experiences, they need to be brought into contact with 'normal' human core expressions of Feelings and Experience. These are beyond Maslow's basic survival hierarchy. They go to the aspects Uncles Raymond and Bernard have outlined (covered in the concluding chapter), which reflect shared fundamentals that, unfortunately, are missing in the lives of many modern citizens. If such fundamental aspects of human life can be restored to healing environments, their patients will recover much faster.

How do we get lost and disconnected in the first place?

Karen Horney exposed much about 'normal' modern life that was actually sick. She talked about character types and explored character pathology because she saw these aspects of humanity as indicators of our ultimate potential as conscious beings. Realisation of human potential was her great goal. But, as she unfolded her story of the human psyche, she exposed the down side of 'normal': 'She makes us question the 'search for glory', for many practically a credo of modern life, but for Horney the culture medium of psychic illness. Basic assumptions – about pride, love, the importance of achievement, mastery, the standards we live by, the expectations we have of each other – are all called into question'. (26)

The pressure on many people to conform to these expectations of life, under the burden of mental illness, may be the straw that breaks the camel's back. While not arguing that genetic predisposition, or drug abuse, or behavioural abuse, do not play a large role in creating conditions of mental breakdown, it can be equally argued that the conditions of modernity, and the pressures of life in late capitalism, exacerbate pre-existing tendencies towards mental collapse.

Feeling hounded by the expectations of others, and one's own fears and anxieties over performing badly in whatever life test is being undergone, seems to be able to create the pressure that makes many people snap into madness. Once an occurrence has been experienced, where feelings, thoughts, fears and hopes all crash together under such pressure, susceptibility to more such occasions is created. This begins the cracking open that leaves many people shattered by mental illness.

For Maslow, as for Horney, the real self is not an entity, a homunculus, a thing-in-itself. Its components are 'potentialities, not final actualisations. Therefore they have a life history and must be seen developmentally. They are actualised, shaped or stifled mostly (but not altogether) by extra-psychic determinants (culture, family, environment, learning, etc)'. The real self is actualised only as a self-in-the-world. (27)

Individuals unlucky enough to miss out on developing their real selves in a congruent, transparent and spontaneous way, end up lacking what Carl Rogers identified as openness to oneself. (Horney) The evidence from researchers like Horney, Maslow and Rogers is that such a beginning most often leads to isolation, loneliness and fear. The current dominant value system of modernity operates in a way that puts everyone under pressure to perform according to a narrow set of criteria, for which many feel very unsuited.

Competition, comparison, intellectual regurgitation under pressure, speed of operation in all aspects of performance, efficiency, tightly focused thinking, low concern for heartfelt matters — such parameters make for a narrow shute through which most modern citizens get shot into life. The evidence from Aunty Karen, is that it is no wonder some people just end up flying off into space away from others and find themselves floating alone and feeling like failures.

Karen Horney saw the reason people ended up in a neurotic state was as a result of their life experiences coming primarily from their relations with other people. Then, their problems gradually moved into their being unable to relate to themselves. This combination indicates that our society needs to take more responsibility for how it treats people during their development. Rather than adopting a purely competitive value system, exercising a survival of the fittest, dog-eat-dog approach, it will pay to explore alternative ways of helping people grow up, so they do not only see the 'look after number one' approach to life as their dominant option.

If we want to see how conflicts develop, we must…take a panoramic view of the main directions in which a child can…cope with the environment…a child can move toward people, against them, or away from them…In each of these three attitudes, one of the elements involved in basic anxiety is overemphasised: helplessness in the first, hostility in the second and isolation in the third. (28)

When you are spat out of the high pressure-cooker life that dominates modern societies, you are left out on a limb. Unfortunately, most people see that the way back is by receiving treatment for being ill. When people, who are not labelled 'normal' are rejected by society, it makes me ask the question: who really are the 'sick'? Are they those who may be wholehearted, who do not want to just compete, but who prefer to work in teams and collaborate? Or are they those individuals who fail to comply with ideologically driven approaches to life, who say there is only one way to live?

Only when changes have been made to rehabilitation environments for people living with mental illness, will these people have better prospects of recovery. When the value system applied in those places reflects the Feelings and Experiences that are at the core of humanity (see concluding chapter), then there may be something worth aiming at, for those who are asked to pursue recovery. Otherwise, one could be forgiven for wondering why they should bother.

Seeing the shaman in 'the other'

Uncle Raymond argued in his Structure of Feeling, that humans are not meant to be in charge of everything that comes to us. Similarly, the things that might pass by us, or pass through our awareness, are not always meant to make sense. According to some psychologists and sociologists (Keeney, Jackson), the trap modern people have fallen into is the goal of making sense and finding understanding.

Although many contemporary psychological explanations point to addiction as the basis for our suffering…I believe that the root addiction underneath this fixation on the self involves our desire to understand, the belief that we must make sense of life before we can know how to act in it. (29)

I believe that what might be happening, when 'normal' people experience 'madness', in moments of 'losing it' within themselves, or with their friends, family, or with people in the general community, is that they are being shown something. A sign, an invitation to engage with another form of being, knowing, expressing or seeing life.

Much of modern society's legislation, regulation, mob behaviour and individual prejudicial judgement of others, is based on fear, and the need to protect ourselves from fearful possibilities. When something mad comes our way, it is really offering a different view of the world, which could be quite creative and refreshing.

Human beings are spiritual, not just rational or emotional. They have a dimension that is not always meant to make sense. Madness can be a source of great renewal for individuals and society – it can indicate that conditions need to change, or that there is a shift in the predominant attitudes running the world.

Most of the symptoms described by psychology are experiences that take place because a person feels out of control. The chaos of anxiety, the immobility of depression, and the slipperiness of madness may be seen as panic responses to the realisation that one's life is out of control. Panic may be a wake-up call, not just to a neurotic symptom or repressed memory. Spirituality redefines psychological symptoms as opportunities for growth. (30)

Of course, there are extreme cases where interventionist

help is needed, but in general, by returning to more active expression of the Structure of Feeling and Experience, summarised by Raymond Williams and Bernard Smith, I suggest that humans will allow themselves to 'go back, go way back'. Not in an idyllic return to the native, but a considered, rational decision to revalue those affective qualities of life which are part of our healthy humanity. This is what Bradford Keeney calls discovering our natural abilities to feel in the soul. This is related to madness, and it is where the shamans work: 'I have no doubt that most of what psychiatry addresses are spiritual crises and natural problems in living. The medicalising and scientising of these events in people's lives too often strips away opportunities for spiritual work'. (31)

The two practical implications of this view are, firstly, that the work undertaken in this study argues for use of the Structure of Feelings and Experience as a framework for a healthy return to a more balanced and comprehensive set of human activities; not only among those recovering from mental illness, but also in many mainstream environments which lack an integrated understanding of human needs.

Secondly, while not confusing those cases where genuine madness has beset someone, there are times when all humans enter states where their potential to engage with another dimension of their humanness opens up. If more of these occurrences were accepted as part of 'normal' life, fewer people would find themselves going down the path of madness.

Spiritual experiences occur naturally and effortlessly when one is open as a channel, or, is it when one is as a 'hollow bone' or 'tube' (as Fools Crow an American Indian Elder put it)?

When one becomes a hollow tube and allows spiritual experi-
ence to move through, the idea of wrong notes and right notes,
or more generally good and evil, is dissipated. (32)

Modern society has largely lost the ability for people to get in touch with their souls. The discussion here
has nothing to do with religion, or proclaiming new age
perspectives over empirical logic. It is accepted that humans have a spiritual dimension, as individuals, as well as
shared amongst us in the common human spirit. This is
often referred to in times of adversity, sporting celebrations, and certainly in times of reverence for people who
have died or when disasters beset a whole nation. It is
that sort of spirit I am referring to as a resource for healing mental illness.

Churches and new age activities are not tapping the
common shared consciousness of our human spiritual inheritance. Madness presents society, individuals, families
and institutions with one aspect of the different dimensions which come up when humans engage with other
levels of consciousness. And generally speaking, people
are frightened of it.

To paraphrase Jung, many churches seem to exist to make it impossible for anyone to have a spiritual
experience. One must follow the voice that comes to one,
and only through dialogue and participation in communities of other people and creatures can one's walk be
further tuned to best fit the natural ecology. (33)

Uncle Raymond told us that life carries deliberate
mysteries and unknowns as part of the mix. Uncle Bernard reinforced this message, with reflections on the
value in sharing through relational experience as a natural human attribute. I suggest, that in order to facilitate

healing, part of any effective mental health process should encompass this. Experiences which touch the souls of patients and healers, at levels that human understanding may not be able to reach, will engage with healthy depths of the Structure of Feeling and Experience. This is nothing new. It is where much of the existing healing of madness actually occurs, where human souls get their exercise. Only, the scientific system does not recognise this dimension.

In the Kung bushmen healing dance, some of the healers enter an experiential realm they regard as 'death'. Here 'the fear and pain of that boiling num, the terror of that passage, is faced and overcome as individuals die to themselves. From the death of the individual Kung personality, the rebirth of the Kung healer must come'. (33) Opening and entering spiritual worlds requires experiencing the death of one's previously stabilised identity.

Part of this experience is a microcosm of what society goes into when phases of cultural expression pass through different characteristics. Bernard Smith saw the surrealists as an expression of the decadence of modern society after the wars. In Sydney, Mardi Gras has been used by gay artists to stamp a surreal statement onto public consciousness about where they are at, and how inconsistent human nature can be, in denying difference and diversity.

One core perspective of this book, is that some forms of madness are experiences parallel to the dying that occurs in spiritual quests. Modern medicine has so pathologised these experiences, and the individuals going through them, that it can make no real progress. It refuses to engage with their inner process.

The place of balance in this consideration is understanding that humans need to acknowledge their dual nature. That is, that as well as having a mind and body, we are spirit beings. We need to give expression to our dual nature in the right ways. For example, linked to the Structure of Feeling and Experience parameters, as one balancing framework.

By remaining disconnected from the spirit/soul nexus, humans are denied any real growth, any deeper sharing and celebration with one another, and certainly any real chance of healing from mental illness. Which is why some cultures understand that mental illness is as much a disease of the society, as of the individual. (see Anne Wilson Schaef, *Native Wisdom*)

A combination of good and evil, equally balanced, is essential – for all souls that exist, like all living creatures, must have a perfect balance between life and death. Spiritual work takes place between the poles of light and dark, good and evil are always co-present...the point between...any pair of oppositions is the very locus of transformation where one side crosses into the other. (35)

Reworking western hearts and minds

Experiencing madness is not just a sad and troubling symptom of 'something having gone wrong with people, or their world'. It is also an opportunity and a challenge, for the participants and their communities. If members of Western society are to engage in practical ways to improve quality of life, then political and public health leaders need to embrace a better understanding of the place of madness in society's overall scheme of things.

Madness is both a symptom and a warning that society

is not in balance. Humanity is being neglected, by not 'being worked,' (as Aboriginal people describe steward-ship and practice of their culture and beliefs). The con-sciousness of modern Western citizens needs 'working'. As reflected in SOFE, at the core of our consciousness, we need to engage with one another in sharing, relating and 'singing up' human life.

Local governments, community groups, neighbour-hoods and extended families need to create more hold-ing, more regular social rituals, to bring the shared hu-man spirit into practical expression. We need a working notion of spirit in our daily lives where people are invited to connect automatically with an aspect of their human-ness. This is a basic return to what Raymond and Ber-nard suggest: 'Here we learn that soul is not an abstract psychological or religious concept but a way of feeling the rhythm of life itself. When music has a vital beat, we say that it has soul. Life has soul when we feel a beat that makes us want to move and dance' .(36)

We need to understand that the journey towards chaos is not one of terror, and that nature is meant to express and contain chaos, in the same way that it expresses and contains beauty. Madness has characteristics that are frightening and enlightening. Mental health recovery rates will rise dramatically if Western society can see the balance that is required and move to engage with it in more active healing processes: 'The difference between the real and the unreal is an opposition which hides the greater truth that simultaneously sees both views…when we bring different views in front of us and find a way to see them simultaneously, we are lifted to a higher order of seeing'. (37)

Illness and wellness, balanced against one another, are potential collaborators. We need to agree that wellness means more than behaving safely in society and not being a danger to oneself or others. The notion that human beings are complex, multi-dimensional beings, with hearts, minds and souls, and a connecting spirit between them, needs to be placed on the table in our conversations about mental health.

It is time to get beyond a neurotransmitter based model of consciousness, and its consequent model for healing which is based solely on pharmacological intervention in neural pathways. Until mental health systems apply more holistic versions of what constitutes the whole patient, healing rates will be low, and quality of life will remain marginal. Different views on mental illness need airing and discussion, now, more than ever. Rates of depression, suicide and mental illness in Western societies, are rapidly increasing (*Mental Health in Australia, 2002*). New parameters for holistic intervention in rehabilitation for recovery are urgently needed within the system.

The Structure of Feeling and Experience is one framework for considering affective indicators for informing healing strategies and offers a new approach to rehabilitation. An approach that values the Experiences and Feelings of patients, as guides to their own recovery, not just indicators of required medication levels. By responding to their Feelings and Experiences, it is possible to build rehabilitation processes that encourage reconnection with self, with community activities and with relationships of sharing, caring and celebration. This is the beginning of effective healing.

Rights to be heard, and rites to share

Madness may be 'out there' at times and completely into a fantasy zone. But this is not to say that the experience is wasted. Mark Vonnegut's record of his journey through madness is an exhilarating reminder of the sorts of things that anyone of us may experience at different times. The kind of daydreams or musings which people generally pass over, deny, disregard, and certainly keep to themselves. Some researchers and spiritual teachers claim that human souls are engaging in varied fields of consciousness all the time, moving between different levels of illusion and reality.

As well as being one of the worst things that can happen to a human being, schizophrenia can also be one of the richest learning and humanising experiences life offers...Being crazy and being mistaken are not the same. The things in life that are upsetting... are more than likely things well worth being upset about. It is however, possible to be upset without being crippled, and even to act effectively against those things. (38)

Mark Vonnegut gives invaluable insight into the state of Feelings and Experience which people go through when they suffer from the mixed set of experiences labelled as 'schizophrenia'. His record of consciousness in *The Eden Express* is a travelogue through madness. The reason I believe it is important, is that it illustrates thoughts that are not that different from what we claim as 'normal'. The difference being that they are out of context and out of sync with the rest of the world at the time.

Many observers of society's mad rush to embrace the strategies of economic rationalism claim that this is madness as well.(Raulston, Zeldin, Ellis) If society must be stuck with the madness that currently runs our politico-economic system, then that system could at least respond by acknowledging and recognising the Feelings and Experiences of the allegedly clinically mad.

It's impossible to say whether full insight and understanding would help a schizophrenic or not. We all have vastly greater capacities for experience than for understanding...Schizophrenia multiplies the problem and disability makes the problem more pressing. Since there is always so much to be understood and dealt with, the notion that understanding will clear up the problem can't be tested. (39)

It is healthy for all human beings to share their Feelings and Experiences. Therefore, it is healthy for people living with mental illness to share their Feelings and Experiences too. It is healthy for citizens to become involved in their democratic process, vote, express their needs and aspirations, so that their elected representatives can reflect those expressions in how they make decisions. So too, for citizens who live with mental illness? Or not? This simplistic expression of the democratic process contains a prospect currently far from being realised in mental health. The powerful elites of doctors, bureaucrats and drug-based models of healing, which currently dominate mental health, keep most patients from having any effective say in their healing.

If I were asked to swear on all that's holy that I had no extraordinary powers, I could not do it. As uncomfortable as it made me, I had extraordinary powers. I have no such powers now. I hope I never have them again...The worst thing about the powers was how little control I had over them. They coincided with the blanks. The more rational control I had, the less power I had. So the powers were to me a powerlessness. (40)

Mark Vonnegut moved on from his experience with schizophrenia to become a doctor of medicine. He valued the drugs that helped him stabilise enough to begin to recover. Then he moved on to multi-vitamin regimes and a healthy lifestyle process. And he applied himself to his own healing with a fierce determination.

The example of one person is not enough to warrant changes in government policy and programs. But, there are many, many people living with mental illness, people with brilliance, insight, strong logic, strategic understanding, and compassion for the needs of their peers. It does not make sense to ignore their potential as major designers of their own healing programs. After all, they are not stupid. They are just people living with mental illness who experience occasional bouts of depression, delusions, obsessions, fears, paranoid concerns and so on, none of which should deny anyone the right to participate in managing their own life.

Indicators of the energy of change

There are some aspects of madness which offer unique perspectives on life and can be used to inform how programs are designed and delivered. This will be discussed later and links will be made between aspects of the following attributes, and parallel ones from the other three major subject groups of people living with intellectual disability, the indigenous and the addicted.

Chaos can teach us 'how to be out of control'

Modern members of Western society may well relate to the word chaos, and its accompanying energy in themselves. It has become a household word in Western environments, where life has become so busy, demanding and all-encompassing. In homes and offices, people admit they feel put upon by the constant chaos. Meaning, they cannot handle so much in life at one time, it builds up and becomes chaotic.

For people living with mental illness, chaos is a curse which comes whenever it pleases, and they have to accommodate it in ways that would make others proud. Their feeling of being out of control is exactly what modern 'sane' people need to experience in order to save themselves from becoming uptight, anxious, and detached from their true selves.

Just as the butterfly flapping its wings is said to have the potential to cause a tidal wave on the other side of the globe(Chaos and Gaia Theories), some individual's inner chaos may be waiting to be released in a way that can help others and the common good. The exercise of chaos in one's life is a valuable ground for learning and knowing. Chaos is to be respected.

Mess can free us from restriction

Being a 'neataholic', I am very sensitive to mess. Its chaotic energy disturbs my need to control the environment around me, and to know that things are not 'dirty'. Some part of me became neurotic about this stuff, so now I live with a psychologist who used to be a professional 'flooder' — someone who gets with a neurotic and does the thing they hate the most, over and over, until they just have to give up obsessing about it so much. Needless to say I've given up worrying about my partner's mess. Most of the time. It is actually great to be completely cruddy sometimes and let myself feel how freeing messiness can be.

Mad mess is another deal altogether. You need to be

very present to keep up with it, and it becomes exhausting very quickly. Even mess that means the other person has become absent can be demanding. Because the other person may not know what to do, and it puts everything out of kilter. When the individual in question does not keep up their end of the communications bargain called relating, life can get stressful for both parties.

If you try getting with a messy person and let yourself fall apart a bit, it shows you how to relax in the company of chaos, and how to see that being neat is not that important. It is a more indigenous perspective on life. And perhaps something that people who live with mental illness can share with their health system, in order to provide context and balance, about how healing and rehabilitation programs are planned and delivered. Through acknowledging the messy people living with mental illness, and hearing their Feelings and Experiences, something valuable is put into mental health program and services planning. Because knowing what to expect, and why frustration and blow-outs lead to messy situations, allows us to deal with what is unavoidable.

Wisdom rises from the shadows

People who have undergone some psychotherapy, may become aware of an uncomfortable feeling when they realise they are experiencing their dark selves — an aspect of the expression of personality which represents the shadow or negative side of a person. Mad people very often do not have a choice about entering such a psychic space. But they become used to having to deal with their personality mood swings which seem to come and go according to the temperature, the ether, the energy flow of life, who knows?

This kind of shadow experience, where personality and mood flow in and out of negativity, is an example of what life eventually teaches most people. For some, only on their deathbeds. None of us is in control of our full scope of feelings, experiences, and behaviour, towards ourselves and others.

Sometimes when people get life threatening diseases they suddenly seem to undergo personality changes. It shocks their loved ones and friends to see this person who was nice yesterday, become blunt and demanding today. There should be more of it, until we find our balance in being able to live according to our true selves, and find cooperation and compassion for others. People living with mental illness can show us how to access our true selves.

'Shaman round the mountain'

Mark Vonnegut was sure of it, so is my son William. They claim when you crack up you get some special gifts of vision. So special you can think they should be broadcast on the evening news, so the world can set itself straight! Adults know the truth is that many people have such moments of insight, clarity, and also delusion. It is OK to allow them to come, go, float round and give whatever they have got to give. What is not healthy is to judge people for experiencing feelings like this.

Such experiences, for people living with mental illness, offer openings into consciousness that can uplift the energy of our soul. With a little imagination and patience, I believe it is possible for us all to find special places in our being, the inner knowing which gives us access to unconscious contact with the universe. These places have generous quantities of insight, and exposure to nature with its manifold lessons if only people would stop long enough to 'do-dadirri': that is, 'sit, wait and listen'. The unique experiences of people living with mental illness can not only be entertaining and provide light relief after many painful experiences. They can also give insight to situations for others. This is one of the main reasons why I claim that there is such positive potential in involving people with mental illness in designing and delivering their health and rehabilitation programs. It is not a matter of playing down the dark, but of acknowledging the light.

Insight, energy, vision, imagination and commitment are all attributes employers cry out for. These are available among the people who live with mental illness, and should be tapped for the good of these people themselves, and later, for those who will come after them who also suffer from mental illness, plus everyone else.

Fantasy

Living with and working with the mad energy of fantasy is exciting, crazy, zany and bizarre. Some people tell of almost 'fantasy experiences', meeting a stranger and going on the spur of the moment to a party and entering a completely unknown and unpredicted world. Travellers to other countries sometimes meet someone, get on well and decide to go on a journey together, and have amazing and fresh things open up in their lives.

That is similar energy to what people who live with mental illness go through every day. Sometimes all day. It is possible to imagine that going on such eye-opening, mind-expanding, brand new experiences for breakfast, lunch and tea, would become 'too much'. And it does for these people, subject to delusions, extreme reactions to situations and other people.

But small doses are very healthy. If more people could allow their consciousness to remain in the moment, the immediate experience, and in their deeper knowing, they could exercise awareness on a higher level of fitness for life. The work of many spiritual gurus, therapists, life change workshop presenters and business motivators is based on this exact notion – to stay in the moment and deal with what comes with fresh eyes. It can make life like a fantasy, because preconceived perspectives and prejudices tend to drop away, and some magic arrives.

Designing a lifeworld

It is possible that society can find places for people living with mental illness where they are accepted. But it depends on a more general openness to difference, diversity and eccentricity. They are on a journey in life, just like everyone else, and all people are prone to a degree of madness at sometime or other. These seem fair criteria for integrating people who live with mental illness into more general social settings.

The issue is that Western society is now so rule-bound with regulations about public safety and public liability, that people with life experience on the edge of 'normal' are now labelled as a problem. Rather than moving the rules to allow for more compassionate acceptance, the West seems bent on veering towards excluding anyone of difference, apart from any other reason than because they are too difficult to deal with in the sense of legal responsibility.

Disregarding that hopeless red tape for a moment, it

seems from the examination of humanity's Structure of Feeling and Experience, that most people enjoy engaging with difference and diversity, once it is explained to them. Ignorance is the problem, not difference.

The most hopeful, energetic, and 'in your face' work being done in this arena, is by those advocates of 'Mad Culture'. Letting people be, as they are, valued for being who they are. Sure, go for healing and recovery, but not by suppressing the essence of these folks. Insane Australia is the key lobby group in this field, joining the broader genre of critical disibility studies, which we need to promote into a much wider debate, on inclusion and the essential importance of difference and onto-diversity.

Chapter Six

People who live with intellectual disability

Offering hospitality for the soul

Acknowledging and welcoming others into a family, into relationships and community does not always happen naturally. Fear often rules out welcome and engagement with others, especially when their difference is expressed through disability.

I will examine some aspects of the lives of people living with intellectual disability — how they are different from people in mainstream society; and how their difference enriches everyone. I will show you why these people should be recognised more by the health, rehabilitation and community services systems, and why they should be able to participate in the planning, design and delivery of services for themselves and their peers.

In terms of their integration within mainstream society, these people offer special attributes of personality and social character. Their special attributes add to society's mix in a way that enriches humanity's ability to share Feelings and Experiences. We need to explore how people who live with intellectual disability can be assisted in becoming recognised contributors to society through mainstream social service delivery and greater inclusion in community activities.

When I say that our society has the opportunity to be enriched by these people, I am not trying to present an idyllic spectre of all things being bright and beautiful. Illness and disability are two things we fear. Fear of mental illness and intellectual disability is doubly magnified in Western societies. This is because of the high status modernism allocates to matters of the mind and the intellect. A key component of modernist thought is that progress and change are good, and that the mind is where it begins. Consequently, this value system projects the judgement that if your mind is not right, you are automatically 'less than'.

In the competitive Western world, people born with intellectual disability begin life as 'losers'. It is a world built on achievements of the intellect and fuelled by the ego's ambition. But there are other aspects to the lives of the intellectually disabled which make them richly endowed. In saying this, I do not mean to play down their disadvantage or suffering, but to acknowledge the strengths, endurance and uniqueness they offer us.

One advantage of being unable to perform in the world of intellectual prowess and competitive achievement, is that it gives one time. People living with intellectual disability combine time with an attitude of heart, mind and soul. In other words, they offer 'hospitality of soul' — an answer to one of society's deepest needs in modernity, the need for shared love.

The word intellectual derives from the same root as intelligent (1), and intelligence means 'to choose between'. But it is arguable whether choices made by intellectual processes alone are actually 'choices between'.

Intellectual means 'of the intellect, developed or chiefly guided by the intellect rather than by emotion or experience'. (2) The evidence from uncles Raymond and Bernard is that the Structure of Feelings and Experience needs to be reintroduced into mainstream values and practices. And that its very lack has created an imbalance in the way many decisions, priorities, and evaluations of worth are made in our society.

From my work and personal relationships with people living with intellectual disability, I know that they are very intelligent, highly capable, and deeply caring. They offer to others in terms of sharing, caring, persevering, and creating fun and joy, in a way that is generous and continual. This is not the territory of 'less than'. It is difference and diversity in action.

They can complement the intellectually dominated parts of life. Ideas, ideals, formulae, concepts, structures and processes may have led us through modernity. But it has been at great cost to the state of our hearts, and the commonweal (the general welfare). (3)

With regard to Feelings and Experience, New Zealand ethnographer, Michael Jackson, has highlighted indigenous perspectives, making such aspects of individuality serious parameters of worth (*At Home In The World*) within community. In the field of hospitality for the soul, it is time Western society took similar note of its practitioners who live with intellectual disability. This would benefit not only community services, but society as a whole, through improved integration of difference and diversity.

There is a type of hospitality, to do with the space we share, which comes from the experience of being with people who live with intellectual disability. Henri Nouwen called it 'creating an empty space where the guest (ie. the other) can find his own soul'. (4) This refers to the 'wounds' that all humans carry in their psyches, and which these folk openly display in their being, 'which must be self-understood as signs leading to healing'. (5)

While it is possible to rationalise what is lacking or different among people who live with intellectual disability, I prefer to perceive their strength in this field as one of opening to shared Feelings and Experiences. In regard to this, Theodore Zeldin's concept of hospitality is inviting:

How great a difference to the conduct of daily life, the ability to alter the focus of one's perceptions can make. To be hospitable to the nuances of life, it is no use treating the mind as an automatic camera; only by composing one's picture and playing with light and shadow can one hope to see something interesting. (6)

It is this play of light and shadow that shows up in subtle ways when one spends time with people who live with intellectual disability. You end up dropping all intellectual pretence. In these circumstances, people simply become souls in the playground of consciousness, with no advantage of one over the other. I have experienced this with these folk when they go swimming, play basketball, go to McDonald's, and are out and about on the street.

Zeldin refers to the Ming Dynasty leader and writer Lu K'un (1536-1628), when he raises the topic of hospitality in his *Song of Good People*, which was written as a chant for the illiterate:

What people needed to learn was to put themselves in the place of others, but without illusions, because every individual was different. 'Regarding others like the self, while realising that

others are not necessarily like the self, is comprehension.'…
Recognise first that 'all good people are sick', that there is
something wrong with everyone: it is dangerous to believe one
is right and others wrong. The only cure is to 'share personal
experiences'. (7)

There is an invitation here to engage in one of humanity's great opportunities. The chance to re-engage with
one another in community. People who live with intellectual disability are like catalysts. Their way of being
acts like a can opener of the hearts and minds of 'normal'
people, leading them into the experience of sharing our
unity in diversity, just by making friends and spending
time together.

People in Western societies have lost much of their
ability to relate to one another and get beyond their own
interest in and preoccupation with surviving and thriving.
This has led to a form of selfishness in isolation. For many
people, the muscles in their social heart have not been exercised and have begun to atrophy. People who live with
intellectual disability are open heart specialists.

The age of discovery has barely begun. So far individuals have
spent more time trying to understand themselves than discov-
ering others. But now curiosity is expanding as never before.
Even those who have never set foot outside the land of their
birth are, in their imaginations, perpetual migrants. (8)

Sharing the provenance of absence

Offering others the space in which to reconnect with
their own hearts may be the main gift that people living
with intellectual disability bring to society. They create a
new form of provenance in their effective 'absence' from

the mainstream world of power, image, status and 'intelligence'. They are present and 'absent' at the same time. So, when 'ordinary" people meet them in the shopping malls or on the neighbourhood street, they feel something in themselves reach out and open towards them. They find a new shared place of origin. I believe it stems from the heart.

During personal interchanges around the swimming pool, the basketball court, the video shop and the supermarket, a sort of abandonment to openness occurs. By both parties. Where people give themselves permission to fall into the space of accepting another person's difference and engaging with them, it is a kind of merging of souls, in a moment when all other priorities fall away. Their shared humanity overcomes fear, prejudice or intellectual preoccupation.

That is not to say that people who live with intellectual disability will always be content and available at the moment when others are open towards them. But, they often are. Their frustration and sufferings often shift aside at that moment. This is what Theodore Zeldin has been 'on about' in his work. He refers to Dostoyevsky's claim that 'it does not matter what people say, only how they laugh'. (9)

It is true that you cannot be free or fully human until you laugh, because to laugh means to make your own judgement, to refuse to accept things at their face value, but also not to take yourself too seriously. That means inviting other people to your internal conversations, and discovering that they see you quite differently from the way you see yourself. (10)

This openness is available most of the time with people living with intellectual disability. They are not 'playing a game' with ideas, thoughts, manners or 'jockeying'. Not unless they want to 'try you on', to tackle the resistance in your own mind about sharing in an open exchange, or just having fun.

People are invited to enter the space of hospitality these folk open for them, and experience whatever comes up. Responding like this is a more fruitful way of dealing with dis-ease with life, than the habituated obsessive escape devices many Western people take on by being too busy to spare the time. This is often simply an escape from intimacy.

When people give their consciousness permission to go and play, it is a new Experience of Feeling. They can do this by volunteering to join the support group at their local neighbourhood centre and forming friendships with people who live with intellectual disability. The worldwide movement of Best Buddies International is a great way to make contact. This would give a lot of people what they hope for — a genuine heart connection with another human being.

Such experiences are rare in a modern world driven by stress, timetables, and the pressure to get things done. In these times of mad rationality, most people have not given themselves permission to know their true humanity. I mean this in the pragmatic 'real world' sense that we are all connected through our human consciousness, regardless of intellectual, social, religious, financial, or any other status.

Every individual is connected, to others, loosely or closely, by a unique combination of filaments, which stretch across the frontiers of space and time. Every individual assembles past loyalties, present needs and visions of the future in a web of

different contours, with the help of heterogeneous elements bor-
rowed from other individuals; and this constant give-and-take
has been the main stimulus of humanity's energy. (11)

People living with intellectual disability are a significant group of those 'other' individuals, offering the filaments of openness, vulnerability, childlike wonder, and playfulness, which are part of healthy living. D.H. Lawrence believed that humanity needed to hand over to this way of being, in order to fulfil its full potential. He said, 'It is impulse we have to live by, not the ideals or the idea. But we have to know ourselves pretty thoroughly before we can break the automatism of ideals and conventions'. (12)

Breaking free from compliant ways of being

Helping others to open themselves to greater freedom of expression and sense of self is another surprising contribution from people who live with intellectual disability. The concept of strength in weakness is strongly revealed in the context of their experience with education. Because, there, they are seen as incapable of achieving much in the competitive learning environment of modern education. They are left to undertake activities aimed at a low level of cognitive development. It is possible to experience this concept from another perspective: when people are fully engaged with people who live with intellectual disability, in a respectful and equal sharing, they are given the chance to drop their mask — the forced confines of thought, controlled feeling, behaviour and rules, which have come to stultify our lives, can be removed. Of Western education, Lawrence observed that: 'Our whole aim has been to force each individual to a maximum of mental control, and mental consciousness...But for the vast majority, much mental consciousness is simply a catastrophe, a blight. It just stops their living'. (13) While Lawrence's particular conclusion about categories of potential for mental consciousness veers into a prejudiced corral, his principle of giving priority to the vital and dynamic force within each human being, above training the mentality, is laudable. After people have been educated into oblivion, the task to recover spontaneity and inner creativity, can take decades.

While intellectual disability brings challenges of limitation that are daunting for most people to consider, their ability to 'be' in an unconstrained manner is an invaluable capacity, compared to many people's limited experience of their lives 'from the inside'. Most of us have been educated into monotonous, obedient compliance, and have lost our spontaneity.

Lawrence was arguing for a revaluing of the inner nature of humans, as creatures of natural energy and connection with nature. His view, that life is best lived through this channel, and not primarily the intellect, supports engagement with people who live with intellectual disability as exemplars of unrestrained being: 'The supreme lesson of human consciousness is to learn how not to know. That is, how not to interfere. That is, how to live dynamically, from the great Source, and not statically, like machines driven by ideas and principles from the head'. (14)

It need not be a complex process to involve people who live with intellectual disability in taking more responsibility for designing and effectively managing their own lifeworld. With appropriate care and support they would continue life as it is now, only with greater choice, more self confidence, and a sense of being taken seriously. This simple process will improve their morale, their health, and the quality of community within which they live. Not the Gemeinschaft model, but today's world with an added component of spirit, heart and 'working the culture' in which their whole way of life is taken seriously and given a place among everyone else. We are all one.

Glocalisation — helping people find their way home

Indigenous people in Australia, New Zealand, Indonesia and India, observe that Westernised people seem to have lost a sense of generational continuity and rites of passage. They have reflected that older people seem to have lost a valued role in transferring wisdom and experience, and that the young people have trouble forming an understanding of themselves and how to progress towards wisdom. Compared to those indigenous youth who have remained active within their culture, these youth often seem lost. Two trends seem to be responsible for this. It has arisen from modernism's embracing of rationality, and its denial of the importance of spirit understandings, guided by Feelings, in deciding how life should be. In 1979, Henri Nouwen pointed out in *The Wounded Healer* (15) that he had observed two types of tyranny that had taken over many young people's lives. He said the Tyranny of Fathers led to a sense of disobedience when children chose not to follow their fathers. This created guilt and 'the guilt culture'. Then, when the Tyranny of Peers replaced that of the fathers, it meant that not following one's peers was to become a non-conformist. This created shame, and led to 'the shame culture'.

According to Nouwen, both these phenomena of the last hundred years achieved a loss in the aspiration to adulthood with its replacement by peer conformity among young people. This meant the death of a future-oriented culture, the end of an eschatology — or, in simplistic Christian religious terms, 'no hope of reaching the promised land'. The more indigenous sense of this perspective is that Westernised young people have been robbed of emerging from their youth into an informed adulthood and being observed by their elders as they made their rite of passage. The purpose in our lives seems to come from two main sources: when we feel 'seen', valued and engaged with in our community, with a role to play and contribution to make; and when we feel drawn on a journey towards our higher power, the force in the universe which affects us all, and fulfils us when we are 'in tune' with its energy. People feel whole and integrated with their world whey they are connected with these two sources.

The phenomenon that Nouwen observed happening to many young Westerners, was a loss of that purpose, and a disconnection from those sources. He saw a tendency to stay home, be with your little group, and therefore end up voting for the status quo. That was the end of the seventies, and soon after, the greed of the eighties answered any concerns about the future with its mad rush to have everything right now — ignore the credit card bills. The sequel to this was the neo-conservative push of the nineties, which still impacts on social policy and community lifeworlds. What Robert Theobald called our 'cultural trance'. (16)

Finding new ways of experiencing purpose in community and the shared mystery of a spiritual dimension, comes mostly from sharing in community rituals. Celebrations, local work projects, and ways of caring for each other at the local level, are part of 'glocalisation': the new concept for 'thinking global, acting local' (from Buckminster Fuller), with an emphasis on local community as the locus of action, but in shared movements to aggregate people power.

The relevance of this story for people who live with intellectual disability is that they are a local resource and a local focus for glocalisation. As DJ performer, Fat Boy Slim says, 'Right here, right now', is where the intellectually disabled in our communities are waiting for their friends to get involved in their lives. The result will be a two way benefit: community building, and rejuvenation of spirit. DJ Vinnie Mammolitti from Melbourne's Club Wild dancefloor troupe puts this very thing into action, cerebral palsy and all.

Getting still with the compass of compassion

Henri Nouwen suggested that people who live with intellectual disability teach others that compassion can be the clue to finding a new authority to direct their thoughts (Nouwen). In order to find this, people need time and silence. In the film *Antonia's Line*, there is a beautiful moment in the narration when viewers are told: 'The angels are silence'. Nouwen points out that: 'Deep silence leads us to realise that in the first place prayer is acceptance… Prayer creates openness in which God is given to us'. (17)

This is almost the exact opposite of what is happening in most of the world today. Virtual reality and the information explosion fill people's head space with noise. Information takes over from knowledge and wisdom. The knowledge and wisdom which would otherwise choose to enter silence and contemplate life, to sit and listen for guidance.

Part of the needed contemplation, is to realise that all humans are just 'bit players' in whatever is going on in the world, in the universe, and even in our own minds. As one world famous, but anonymous member of the Twelve Step movement likes to put it: 'My life is none of my business'. In other words, he has handed over his life to a sense of living under the direction of a higher power. Before the 'age of reason' created scepticism about things metaphysical, this was the way people lived. We need a return to valuing these approaches by those in the public sphere who manage our lifeworld.

I am also saying that by engaging with people who live with intellectual disability we will have to face what comes up in this silence. Some of the deep hurt in individuals. It is a silencing moment.

Many people seem to prefer to choose to rush to the nearest shopping mall, to get lost in the muzak, clamour and stupor of consumption. Some would rather do this than engage with the experience of feeling their own hurt through their contact with the life of someone else who has suffered from disability, prejudice and been marginalised.

This is the very moment when humans have the choice of the other option — to allow themselves to feel, and, thereby, feel a sense of connection with people of difference which can be so liberating. As Nouwen says in *The Wounded Healer*, this is the gift we are offered of 'making room for the other' (Nouwen). This echoes the same wisdom from Big Bill Neidjie in *Story About Feeling* (Neidjie), and what Fr Eugene Stockton (Stockton)says about 'Dadirri' in Aboriginal teaching — to sit, wait and listen.

Robert Theobald said in *We DO Have Future Choices*, that humanity is headed towards 'the compassionate era', when such values will be essential to our future development as a species. But he also said people needed tools to be able to return to the practice of this way of being. (Theobald)

Westerners have become outwardly hardened and cynical, unable to make easy contact with their compassionate feelings, except when it is directed towards our loved ones. Inwardly, though, I believe many people are fearful, and often lonely, wondering how to reconnect with 'a feeling of belonging'. It is here that people who live with intellectual disability teach their associates some valuable life lessons, by helping people to experience that space in themselves where they can celebrate life and death — ie. the full gamut of human existence once more. Humanness becomes the common denominator when people stop distracting themselves and realise their shared 'bottom line', their mortality.

In this context, compassion becomes the core and the nature of authority. (Nouwen) Nouwen's view of teaching was that it offered channels through which people discovered themselves, and where people were offered the chance to discover a real, heart-felt, personal connection with people, as they are. We need these folk to be included in mainstream decision-making, exactly so that they can contribute these elements of heart 'in the mix'.

Openness and intimacy

Allowing Feelings to be welcome guests in modern people's consciousness takes a major retraining exercise. Most of us have been programmed to close down our awareness that life is also about death, or that joy often is followed by sorrow.

People who live with intellectual disability do not live this way. They feel. If things occur that are unhappy-making, they will express that. If things are joyful, that is what will be expressed. Henri Nouwen talked about 'naming the space where joy and sorrow meet', as a major part of the intellectually disabled's gift to society. Embracing the truth that painful feelings are often meant for our growth, and are naturally part of life, not something to be avoided.

Many writers have expressed the wisdom that people's misery is also a gift — see particularly Rainer Maria Rilke's *Letters to Mr Koppas*. If people allow sadness its place in their lives, it can bring them into contact with their souls. Just as Rilke said that loneliness can be beautiful in helping us achieve self-understanding (Rilke), and can therefore be a gift. (Nouwen)

This is not some 'new age' truism, but a practical tool for life. Allowing ourselves to be immersed in life's full array of Feelings and Experiences is healthy and balanced. People living with intellectual disability can be friendly guides about how to surrender and fully embrace Feeling. They reveal to us how it comes through trusting that they can 'show themselves' and be open in their expression of what is happening in their lives. It is like the opposite of 'saving face' in the English, Japanese and Chinese shared tradition of controlling manners for the sake of social protocol.

As Jean Vanier points out: 'The journey of each of us is a journey towards the integration of our deep self with our qualities and weakness, our riches and our poverty, our light and our darkness'. (18) The Structure of Feeling and Experience shows us where living with intellectual disability opens areas that have been closed to the mainstream of our society for a long time. Being in circumstances where one's weakness, inadequacy and fear are accepted is an extremely luxurious circumstance in today's world. But for those lucky enough to live in conditions where intellectual disability is accepted, there is then a trust that allows individuals to relax into a natural balance with their feelings and their state of soul.

People cannot accept their own evil if they do not at the same time feel loved, respected and trusted…It is a question of accepting others and loving them with all their egoism and aggression…mutual acceptance…silent, peaceful and tender acceptance. (19)

One facet of L'Arche, (Jean Vanier's worldwide home-based support movement for people who live with intellectual disability), based on Christian philosophy, is to 'work the faith'. To make belief a practical part of daily living, in that life depends on God. And whether one is religious or not, most people can tell the difference in any community educational, social welfare or health service, when it is motivated by a spirit-led purpose, or a religious faith, or is simply a mechanical public service.

Spirit works. It is not a dangerous, irrational concept for the community to embrace. Part of its efficacy is its mystery. Here again, the Structure of Feeling and Experience shows us that we do not need to know why we need to keep engaging with the mystery. Jean Vanier is insistent on this: 'All members of the community have to be vigilant to remain insecure and so dependent on God, and to live in their own way the focal point of fidelity, the essential of the spirit…our faith that Jesus is living in the poor and that we are called to live with them and receive from them'. (20)

To my mind, the purpose and sources of motivation for living are clear. It is a challenge for those who have been brought up principally in a secular consciousness to realise that returning to a practical spirit-based way of living is a possible core component of successfully changing Western society — the world's great secular playground.

(People with responsibility) have to be shown how to find spiritual nourishment. Many people get burned out because this is what they want. Some part of them is rejecting the need to relax and find a harmonious rhythm of life for themselves…they have not discovered the wisdom of the present moment…These people need (to) clarify their own motives and become living with other people, children among other children. (21)

Childlike wonder in communion

People who live with intellectual disability soon learn to 'shut down' and feel wrong or ashamed, or they can push through their pain. It is painful to feel rejected. These people have a deep 'cry for communion', as Jean Vanier put it (22), which comes from loneliness and inner pain: 'To be in communion means to be with someone and to discover that we actually belong together…To love someone is not first of all to do things for them, but to reveal to them their beauty and value'. (23)

Effective examples of community and communion among people who live with intellectual disability, such as the L'Arche households, are creating a model for all people to rediscover their own community. Adding heart and soul as effective management tools. There is work to be done, and they are doing it — working the culture of loving community.

These values are put into practice with effectiveness, efficiency, and above-average rates of recovery and rehabilitation at the Athma Shakti Vidyalaya schizophrenic therapeutic community in Bangalore, India; the Saday Special School for intellectually disabled children and adults in Pondicherry, India; and at the Pioneer Clubhouse, community-based, member-organising, mental health rehabilitation centre, in Balgowlah, Sydney.

Never before has the cry for nuclear disarmament been so loud. But it is even more important that there be disarmament inside human communities and inside each one of our hearts... disarming ourselves in the world of competition and rivalry... People are yearning to rediscover community. We have had enough of loneliness, independence and competition. (24)

Criticism from empowerment advocates, that such sentiments are patronising and controlling, are based on one movement's version of a spiritual priority. They argue that in a secular world of equity and equal opportunity, these matters would be left to the individual, and that those individuals should simply be provided a service, which ensures equal access to all that society has on offer.

Anyone who has worked in, or had relatives receive service from such agencies, knows that they are completely vulnerable to soullessness, which leaves people feeling empty and sad. The force of economic rationalism, tight budgets, staff cuts, managerialism creating overriding surveillance and everyday pressure means these places are almost completely de-spirited. Community services for people who live with intellectual disability and mental illness need to deal in a secular way with the fact that human beings are spirits as well as bodies, and hearts as well as minds. That is, it is more than possible for them to have access to experiences without anyone being brainwashed or evangelised towards one particular version of the numinous.

The work of L'Arche is shining a light for many other human services, by showing that matters of the soul come first. And it does not matter what brand of spiritual faith or lack thereof, which any individual may, or may not have. It is human to be spiritual, and it is therefore common sense to acknowledge that.

Henri Nouwen found that his movement from worldly concerns about justice and rights, to a simple life among people who live with intellectual disability, opened up new fields of learning: 'I am with people who are poor in spirit. They teach me that being is more important than doing, the heart is more important than the mind, and doing things together is more important than doing things alone'. (25)

This echoes Uncle Raymond's and Bernard's Structure of Feeling and Experience categories for humanity's yearning to share in culture, stories, celebration : we want to share; we feel divided; we need to be active in 'working' our culture; telling our stories creates wonder and acceptance; if we surrender to 'not knowing' we can keep engaging in the mystery.

Values and practices are found among those who live with intellectual disability which can point to practical improvements across society. People need to open themselves to re-experience communion with one another and re-value the simple aspects of human life: 'Issues don't save us, people do...My own journey to L'Arche is directly connected with this movement from an issue-oriented life to a person-oriented life...The larger the issues become, the smaller the place where people can return to affirm their love for each other and pray together for God's mercy.' (26)

Joy, play and abandon

The ability to 'be happy' is something many people find inaccessible. Either their worries are too overwhelming, or their lives are so full of escape behaviour that they do not allow a moment when such a feeling could enter their consciousness. It seems that battling away at being independent and capable in the world of power and success can make you very miserable, especially if you cannot remember how to smile.

At L'Arche our basic philosophy is that of learning to be happy together. We believe that the joy of friendship comes before independence. Joy says, 'I am happy that you exist', and thus transforms the broken self-image of the other person. Any form of training which gives primacy to autonomy without this basis of joy in togetherness can be seen as a sort of rejection: 'I want you to be self-sufficient so that I won't have to live with you'. It can force the other person to prove themselves in a way that does not help them to grow interiorly. (27)

There is a deep need in most people to be able to give

in to joy. Many of us have been embarrassed about not being able, 'on cue', to sing or dance in public. We feel inhibited and unable to allow ourselves permission 'to be' in an experience we would most likely enjoy. There is a sense of abandonment to the pursuit of self expression, which many people who live with intellectual disability have given themselves permission to experience.

This has come at a price: the 'normal' world's choice to cast one aside as a 'reject'. Whether it occurs directly, or by avoidance, the experience of rejection for these folk can make them furious, resentful, hurt, and very often bigger people than those rejecting them. Jean Vanier says, 'Men and women with mental handicaps are frequently ignored and cast aside because their existence obliges us to face our own limitations, inner darkness and spiritual poverty'. (28) The ability to climb back up and make life into something worth living is a great achievement among those who live with intellectual disability. But often they go further than that, and make their shared life experiences more effective by expressing their full humanness, more than most 'normal' people.

It is a journey which includes experiences of togetherness, peace, celebration and forgiveness, just as it involves the discovery and acceptance of our own weakness and poverty – everything that we try to conceal behind our capabilities and our capacity to 'get things done'. (29)

The invitation is to 'get down and get dirty' by joining in, hanging out, giving it up and shouting it out. The route to this renewed sense of wonder at being alive, which rejuvenates all those present whose hearts are open, is to increase opportunities for sharing between those people who live with intellectual disability and the wider community.

Being in the moment

People who live with intellectual disability 'have time'. In the apparent back corners of life, with people avoiding them and awkwardness defining many of their encounters with 'normality', they are actually 'taking the time to be'.

Jean Vanier's work with L'Arche has concentrated heavily on this faculty: 'Love is the marriage between time and eternity: it roots us in present experience while opening us to the infinite'. (30) This is something I believe people clamour to find in workshops, therapy sessions, and cries between lovers, family members and friends – 'Have time for me', they all yearn. The key to understanding how this is a special attribute of the people who live with intellectual disability is through their suffering. By recognising that this experience brings with it deep suffering through loss and difference from the norm, people can rise out of preoccupation with their own affairs. Understanding and acceptance of others can then follow. As Jean Vanier puts it: 'We cannot approach the suffering of others unless we have suffered ourselves'. (31)

A lot of life's complications slip away, once we have a shared perspective. This is the challenge Jean Vanier puts to people who get involved in L'Arche and decide to live with people who have an intellectual disability: 'The beauty of (humans) is in our fidelity to the wonder of each day...A community which is just an explosion of heroism is not a true community...True community implies a way of life, a way of living and seeing reality; it implies above all fidelity in the daily round'. (32)

We need the mainstream to engage with these perspectives in their considerations of management and planning for community and health services. Jean Vanier's challenge is an interesting one to consider placing on the agenda of a public service management meeting: 'If we are to live in community, we have to be friends of time…(we don't) fight with time. (We) accept it and cherish it'. (33)

This is vital in rebuilding the commonweal. We are re-valuing the human by using the weakness and need of people who live with intellectual disability as a sign of their strength for the community which cares for them. This is a focus on aspects of life that are not about power, status, privilege or wealth and it balances the perspective shared.

I'm becoming conscious of the limitations and weaknesses of human energy, and the forces of egoism, fear, aggression and self-assertion which govern human life and make up all the barriers which exist between people…(34) All members of the community (of L'Arche) have to be vigilant to remain insecure and so dependent on God, and to live in their own way the focal point of fidelity, the essential of the spirit…and that we are called to live with them and receive from them. (35)

Shared attributes growing from fallow ground

The aim of this last section is to raise some allegorical images which reflect the energy and value that people who live with intellectual disability can offer to social planning. By acknowledging the value that people bring to their community, and celebrating their roles in effective involvement and ceremonial rituals, humans build strong society. These are emotive words, deliberately chosen to come from left field, from where new models of social service and rehabilitation need to emerge.

I see the people who live with intellectual disability as the 'fallow ground' of humanity. With all the limits of their disability, their acceptance of life, nurtures patience and cooperation. They show us how to take time to refresh the human soul in contemplation. This is not true for all of them, of course, but certainly for a large number. The fallow ground of their humanity needs to be returned to active harvest.

Kiss

Gently touching the lips of our lives, this is the energy I get from so many people living with intellectual disability. The light touch of an affectionate consciousness. The gentle pressure to acknowledge the presence of a vulnerable soul, opening themselves to you. Kiss is the energy of intellectual disability – something wounded, open and available for compassion, or abuse. Kiss can be to salute or caress, and this is the energy of soul-connection when someone living with intellectual disability connects with someone living without this life challenge. Affection, caressing and gently pressing are the penetrating effects of people living with intellectual disability coming into your space.

Kissing is not a topic those in the public service readily engage with. But it may be a mood that suggests how to heal the feelings of dried up administrators and field managers. As Theodore Zeldin says, 'A mood is much more powerful than an idea' (Zeldin, *An Intimate History Of Humanity*). I am simply suggesting that we introduce more of this kind of mood into social planning, and get the perpetrators behind 'kiss' into their rightful seats around the table with us. The intellectually disabled might be shy, but they know what this is about.

Child

The child energy of people who live with intellectual disability invites people to enjoy the gift of realising their childlike side at any time. There is plenty of serious business in life, and being playful can lead to freer thoughts. So why not occasionally lash out and be childlike, even childish? This perspective, in management meetings for planning social services, could lead to some fresh ideas about how to develop and sustain nurturing communities.

Feather

I feel the heart energy of intellectually disabled people is like the expression: 'Lighter than a feather'. Compared to the heavy intellectual energy of rational programs and power based decision making, this lighter-than-air energy, can lift people out of life's mundaneness – it lifts their spirits and reminds them to look at the clouds. If we 'lighten up', there are new choices available to us.

Surrender

Our greatest fear is our greatest asset. By holding onto inner terror about decisions, life issues, money, or whatever, people give themselves life crippling stress. The energy of surrender releases unpredictable riches. There are great benefits to be gained from people mixing with the intellectually disabled, because they can feel the sense of freedom that comes from accepting life no matter what challenges it offers. Let life 'get you'. Let the power of the universe show what it wants to show. Let this energy help you 'to cut through the crap'.

Leading from behind

This chapter has explored just some of the indicators that illustrate the energy and capabilities of the people who live with intellectual disability. It is worth a serious investment of political will and effort to create opportunities for such sharing to occur. Progress in material terms has made lifestyles in the West the envy of the world. But this societal model is lacking critical aspects of human consciousness, morals and applied values.

What is missing is our agreement as a society to open our collective consciousness, to begin again to express some of the universal human feelings — awareness, purpose and curious inquiry which people who live with intellectual disability express.

This can be implemented relatively easily by politicians and bureaucrats, parents and community service managers, supporting the movement of 'the others' towards more empowered lives. Allowing them to engage more with mainstream community, and creating decision-making processes that give them more influence over their own lifeworlds. Once such moves are allowed we might see something of what Zeldin has envisaged for a rejuvenated social web across our society:

Once people see themselves as influencing one another, they cannot be merely victims: anyone, however modest, then becomes a person capable of making a difference, minute though it might be, to the shape of reality. New attitudes are not promulgated by law, but spread, almost like an infection, from one person to another. (36)

Chapter Seven

Finding others on suburban walkabout —
indigenous and addicted

Two points on the modernity seesaw

Exploring modern consciousness by going walkabout through the suburbs establishes a perspective on both the light and darker side of late capitalist humanity. The aim in this chapter is to look at two extremities of the Structure of Feelings and Experience: that of indigenous people, and then, addicted people.

Without claiming full representative status for these two groups, as polarities of modern consciousness, there is value in following such an analogy to a point. That a perspective comparing extremities in consciousness from the 'earthed' to the 'spaced out' helps to illustrate important trends in modern life.

Charting the major attributes of Feelings and Experience represented by these two groups, can assist the identification of a framework to be used for healing, rehabilitation and recovery for people living with intellectual disability and mental illness. Once their own attributes are compared with the major points from Raymond Williams and Bernard Smith, a deeper perspective on the lifeworld arises.

The skills of mindfulness, applied by indigenous people can be used to inform the potential rejuvenation of key aspects of the lifeworld process. Those who are actively in touch with their heritage in consciousness, model new applications for today. For Westerners needing more integrated patterns of living, these skills are applicable in rejuvenating their life and in planning services for people who need assistance.

The counterpoint to that is the illustration of dis-ease with life, shown by the Feelings and Experiences of addicted people. Modern life has created and promoted all sorts of addictive habits of life across Western society. They not only debilitate individuals suffering from substance abuse and other dependencies, they actually eat at the heart of our society by undermining Feelings and Experiences which would otherwise be part of healthy individual lives and community.

I am not seeking to show you an ideal way to serve those living with intellectual disability or mental illness, but by using ways of focusing and valuing mindful states, I want to explore how we can improve the policies and programs applied to them.

Indigenous awareness — sustaining echo-logy in action

The major elements of Feelings and Experience that I have observed in the indigenous people in Australia, New Zealand, Indonesia and India, cover aspects of individual consciousness, group consciousness and the numinous. Before entering this subject area, I will state my position on the lifeworld real-politik of the native. No noble savage exists – either in the desert, on the street, in the jungles or on the airwaves. Recognising that indigenous people live in exactly the same conditions as everyone else in modernity should remove any implication of harkening back to an idyllic state of native consciousness.

There are patterns of awareness and ways of dealing with Feelings and Experience, which indigenous people retain from their inherited perspective on life. These aspects of consciousness offer skills we can apply to enable us to see modern life with new eyes. This sort of reapplication of indigenous ways of being is relevant today. The major headings (mainly adapted from Graham Paulson's work, quoted in *Aboriginal Spirituality*, edited by Anne Pattel Gray, 1991, Harper Collins Religious, Melbourne) under which I group these attributes of consciousness are:

- Valuing the group as much as the individual, and seeing oneself as existing in community, not alone.
- Understanding that life is under the control of unseen forces more powerful than the human mind, but which the human mind can access — I call this the higher power.
- That human beings are spirit beings, in touch with the spirit of place, the Dreaming, the earth and stars, and connected with one another in a shared spirit of humanity.
- Sharing is a high-value approach to life, no matter how much wealth one has, because material possessions are of little use unless they contribute to the common good.
- Life is for appreciating from moment to moment, by trusting the higher power and by regularly celebrat-

ing its wonder and mystery through reverence and ritual, everything is under control.

These attributes of consciousness may not be highly regarded in current circles of power, but I believe they are on their way back into mainstream conversation.

In a scientific worldview that believes that the only reality is what we can grasp with our senses, the material world takes on a very exaggerated importance. In fact, it becomes all important because it is the only reality. But since the material world does not feed the spirit, we continue to grab for more and more. As we lose the riches of the unseen, we have less and less. (1)

Uncles Raymond Williams and Bernard Smith and aunty Anne Wilson Schaef express what many Australian Aboriginals, Balinese, South Indian Tamils, and Maoris have said to me: that Western life breeds disconnection with spirit, and that material obsession removes life's balance. Natural, instinctive, intuitive and healthy human values and ways of Feeling and Experiencing life have been deeply erased by modernism. Whether looking at industrialism, capitalism or our own 'individualism and self interest', buying the materialistic dream has come at a price. Former more numinous habits of mind have been replaced by logic, rationality and reason.

Native people living in modern conditions who have chosen to revalue and apply traditional ways of being with their Feelings and Experience, have discovered that these two worlds are not completely incompatible. Early Western thought placed the advances of civilisation ahead of native awareness of living in the moment, in a world still informed by mystery, metaphor, spirits and symbols. The Aboriginal perspective is that Westerners are so stuck on the future, they let the present pass by without notice.

I know of two Balinese restaurants that are run on a spiritual cycle of respect by attending to daily puja ritual celebration and the understanding that their food and work are expressions of respect for the gods. These workers are prospering and happy in their thriving businesses. Customers come to 'be with this spirit'. They respond to the unseen, but deeply felt, aspects of shared numinosity in a commercial environment.

Local Aboriginal Land Councils in south-western New South Wales operate systems of housing management, training and employment creation that includes doing business with the mainstream community in completely Western ways. But the value system informing the operation is the traditional Aboriginal way. They have no trouble collecting rent for all the houses they operate for the community, and their involvement with the local towns is crucial for the survival of those communities.

The main activity of one of these Land Councils is to pursue the return to traditional cultural cycles of large areas of land repurchased from European farmers and to have it zoned as areas for environmental conservation and cultural heritage restoration sites. Interest is growing in the non-Aboriginal community, as to the significance of the restored burial mounds, the carved trees, and the bora bora grounds which are being returned as places of active numinosity.

Uncle Bernard decided that, in his view, history does not repeat, it echoes around again through subsequent generations. This is what I call echo-logy, and the above stories illustrate its relevance to today's world, in modern settings informed by ancient wisdom and mystery. As a result of its pursuit of money and material gain, the Western world has swept away 'beingness', so that understanding what it is to be human has largely been forgotten. We are primarily spiritual beings. Not irrational, mumbo-jumbo merchants, out of touch with life in modern times. We can mix both aspects of our humanity.

In a world of complex, fractal symbols and interconnections that are beyond most people's understanding, it does not seem exaggerated to emphasise our numinous character. There are plenty of things about how the modern world operates that are a mystery to most people – electricity, nuclear power, computers and the Internet, to name a few. The introduction of indigenous approaches to understanding life, relating to our environment and the cycles of nature, are practical skills and benefits for modern life. By looking at how they may fit the Structure of Feelings and Experience of people living with intellectual disability and mental illness, it may be possible to improve programs and services. And at the same time illustrate something worthwhile considering for re-evaluating wider society's values.

Sharing human connectedness

For some time scientists and psychologists, social researchers and spiritual workers have been saying that the energy of love is what makes the world go round (Reanney, Tacey, Jackson, Davies). Indigenous ways of operating, which are able to be transferred to modern conditions, apply 'tough love' as a working process. 'Working the culture' requires elders to remember how the process goes, but once this is applied, it is a natural, logical system.

Such approaches are appropriate for rejuvenating health and community services for people living with intellectual disability and mental illness. The current way we manage human affairs ignores the necessary part of our existence which brings balance. Humans have the need to exercise their full capacities — hearts as well as minds, souls as well as psyches. Indigenous people have ways of factoring this understanding into their daily rhythm of life in the way they relate to each other and their inner lives. Western communities can apply similar ways of being and, as a result, create more effective personal lives and community services.

When I began this book, I spoke of a 'gap at the centre' in Western civilisation due to the breakdown of the old faiths. The clear implication was that this gap needs to be filled. But with what? I repeat, I believe it can only be filled by a renewed sense of the sacred. By this, I do not mean a new set of beliefs, which will inevitably harden into dogma. I mean an experiential sense of trust and caring, a renewed feeling for beauty in whatever form it may be found. (2)

Darryl Reanney died not long after he finished his two books on exploring the numinous with a scientist's consciousness. As a geneticist, he believed passionately in the links between facts and faith, measuring and mystery. It was finally the notion of the music of the spheres that seemed to inspire his view of humanity as part of the hum of the universe.

Most of the atoms in our bodies were made in the heart of a star. We are children of the stars. When we look up at the night sky, when we feel an affinity for the distant lights that burn in the cosmic night, we are not just remembering our origins, we are connecting with our very being…all parts of the cosmos, including ourselves, are deeply interconnected, flawlessly inter-woven, one wholesome unity. (3)

The perspective, which I believe Reanney and other 'hard' and 'soft' scientists have come to see, is that introducing more numinous ways of seeing makes sense. The best teachers about how to 'work the culture' this way are our indigenous brothers and sisters. Those I work with use a combination of traditional awareness and current savvy to 'work' their lives. It is a powerful combination, especially when compared with the divided, dualistic way Western thought limits many modern activities.

'Attempting to move beyond the received opinions which conventionally condemn human beings to isola-tion from one another in the name of essential difference.' (4) This is how Michael Jackson introduced his book *At Home In The World*, written while he and his wife lived with the Warlpiri people in Australia's Northern Terri-tory, and he investigated ways that native people experi-ence being 'at home'.

Indigenous ways of seeing and being in the world add to the dominant ways that inform materialist versions of reality, through logic, reason and rationality. Consider-ing how to plan and provide better services for the dis-advantaged would be much more effective if we took into account these wider perspectives.

Ethnographer, James Clifford, points out that mixing perspectives is a positive way to bring about healthy evo-lution in culture and society.

As Marshall Sahlins (1985) has argued, these (dichotomous) assumptions keep us from seeing how collective structures, tribal or cultural, reproduce themselves historically by risking themselves in novel conditions. Their wholeness is as much a matter of reinvention and encounter as it is of continuity and survival. (5)

People living with mental illness and intellectual disability can be brought into taking more responsibility for structuring their lifeworld by the introduction of indigenous ways of being which may offer them a rich rejuvenation of spirit. One way, is through the tradition of oral story telling — sharing people's life experiences on a daily basis and making that part of the evolving lifeworld mystery tour.

The evidence from the life journalling project is that sharing stories is healing, rejuvenates spirit, and brings fun and warmth into a community. James Cowan found this rich resource when he spent time in the desert with Australian Aboriginal people:

What the elders taught me was simple…People are, in their most profound aspect, creatures of poetry. They like to make up stories out of the deep metaphors of existence. These metaphors are part of our physical environment and resist all our attempts to make them rational. They are bridges to the irrational, that well of supra-sensibility that we go to at times when we experience thirst. (6)

Cowan's work points out the difference between making and perceiving, which I believe has significance for understanding and valuing 'the Dreaming'. It is not passive receiving, it is active creation.

Restoring relationship with place and dreaming

Where we are, has a huge impact on how we are. It seems to me that non-indigenous people have forgotten this, particularly when planning and delivering health and community services. Many environments are de-spirited and depressing. If we find ways to invite spirit back to the places where people gather, their healing improves and their joy rises (metaphyscially). In relationship to place, non-indigenous community is missing the awareness that 'the visible world is grounded in the invisible'. (7)

The visible is set in the invisible; and in the end what is unseen decides what happens in the seen; the tangible rests precariously upon the untouched and ungrasped. The contrast and the potential maladjustment of the immediate, the conspicuous and focal phase of things, with those indirect and hidden factors which determine the origin and career of what is present, are indestructible features of any and every experience. (Michael Jackson quoting John Dewey) (8)

The Structure of Feeling and Experience that people undergo in many Western environments feels either owned and controlled by somebody else, or alien and devoid of warmth. Many public spaces are being developed as more people-friendly, but not, unfortunately, those places designed for rehabilitation. Still, it is people, energy and spirit that create place.

Many of the burial sites, middens and neglected ceremonial sites being restored by Aboriginal groups in New South Wales look degraded and eroded. But once the tribal group has begun re-singing their relationship with place, the lift in spirit is noticeable: 'Mytho-poetry is one of the supreme talents of humankind; we must make sure that its flame never dies out'. (9) Today's Aboriginal communities are re-exploring their own dreaming, and we can join them. The way to find out if there is a shared spirit among us is 'to work it', 'work the culture'. In rehabilitation circles this is a healing strategy. I have seen this working well in Sydney, at Pioneer Clubhouse, as well as at Athma Shakti Vidyalaya in Bangalore, India – people living with mental illness come out of their shell, take risks in trying their skills at new social challenges, and begin learning new jobs. Stuck, obsessive behaviours start to diminish, and are replaced by people openly engaging with others, with a new curiosity about their world. At Te Wananga o Aotearoa in Hamilton New Zealand, I have seen inspiring results in community rejuvenation where the simple exercise of 'tikanga', the Maori way, has led to exponential growth and development in post-school, community-based learning – uppermost is the personal, friendly, fun approach to life and learning.

This is not to say that 'blackfellas have got it all sown up'. There is still conflict of opinion and feeling among native peoples and disputes over 'the truth' of understanding the Dreaming. But the way to explore solutions is available to anyone prepared to listen.

There are so many conflicting interests in a desert community, so many competing points of view, that contentious issues simply cannot be settled to the satisfaction of everyone. Even appeals to the jukurrpa — the Dreaming, the Law – do not necessarily reduce the ambiguity. (11)

The very fact that no one actually knows for sure 'how

the world goes round' is a great relief. Modern people live with ambiguity as a daily milieu. Plus we have only just come out from under centuries of Christianity with its certainty about holding the only truth, and the way it has acted with colonial assertion about its alleged god-given right to bring people into its belief system. Native people are not claiming to have the answer to it all. They just have an awareness which can help others open to their own inner potential for balance.

'I was aware that in telling me his jukurrpa, his Dreaming, Pincher had told me who he was. Without such a narrative, a person was bereft of any connection between his life and the life beyond himself.' (11) If readers feel a sense of familiarity with this notion, it is because we have certainly got homework to do. There are many native people who have to pick up the pieces of lives destroyed by colonialism, dispossession, stolen generations, or even personal choices to 'piss off in anger'. No one is free from trouble or denied help from the universe in connecting with the universal human fraternity of spirit, and relationship to the land of our Dreaming.

Responsible rites of passage

Modern life has lost some essential processes which used to be integral to human societies in placing the individual in the context of the group, the gods and the good. It is not nostalgic 'Gemeinschaft talk' to raise this. Responsible modern rehabilitation can embrace such aspects of knowledge in a contemporary context. One way, is the safe and stewarded rite of passage for young people growing into adulthood. The current rites in drugs, sex, travel and ideologies, may work well for some, but there are many victims of those processes. It appears that Western society no longer has a consistent use of culturally integrated rites of passage. But that is not to say they cannot be rediscovered and reapplied in today's context.

'Jung said that to be in a situation where there is no way out, or to be in a conflict where there is no solution, is the classical beginning of the process of individuation. It is meant to be a situation without solution.' (12) My work with young people and sick people has shown me that modern life does not encourage listening. We are filled up with noise. It takes up every moment. Native ways of being show us realities as important as ideas, ideals and goals, such as feeling, imagining, dream, mystery and metaphor.

In the last few decades Western concerns with reason and rationality have created some fantastic compromises of logic. Citizens continually complain of suffering the madness of economic rationalism which is ruining their quality of community, life, and any shared sense of responsibility for one another. But it seems that the elected leaders and business managers are certain it makes sense. It is the same thinking that brought the world the crash of 1987, the concept of 'killed by friendly fire', and banks which charge extra fees for actually handling our cash.

Indigenous people could be forgiven for thinking Westerners are actually stuck in someone else's imaginary world. Yet, they as native peoples are thought (by the dominant rationalists) to be stuck in superstition with their pagan belief in the Dreaming and the higher power of the spirits of the universe: 'Talking of an imaginary place in the realm of the actual smacks of sorcery and a desire to transcend reality. But, I ask you: is not the security born from the possession of an insurance policy any less an act of sorcery'? (13)

It is not too late for humans to return to practising mindful listening: 'We moderns are killing not only ourselves but all life in our unthinking allegiance to rationality and progress. The rational mind calculates, measures, indeed adores the heady realm of quantifiable relationships…what I am trying to say is, we must give up our belief in the idea that history is centred on 'our' relationship to the world'. (14)

Robert Theobold describes Western civilisation as being in a 'cultural trance'. Yet, the indigenous people I know, claim that the ones in a trance are those who view indigenous people as less worthy because they practise a system of awareness that opens to the numinous in daily consciousness. Western people need a reconciliation to overcome the duality of that situation. There are consequences for having treated the 'others' unfairly and insensitively, as we have treated indigenous peoples. We need to experience more than the rational in our lives.

Claiming identity in belonging

Marginalised groups I have worked with share a common trait. They might be disadvantaged in the wider world, but among themselves, they belong. The uplift in spirit and sense of self worth which they experience from this belonging is precious. I am hoping to encourage this 'group belonging' into rehabilitation circles, and extend it into mainstream environments. 'All human beings share the same evolutionary history. We are social animals before we are anything else. A Common phylogenetic heritage exists for us all. And from this is born the possibility of our humanity.' (15) Yet, Nobel Prize winner Gao Xinjian advocates in his book, *Soul Mountain*, that individuality is the most precious gift of humanity. Much more important than cultural belonging or identity. Where do we find the yogic balance in these apparent opposites?

To speak of any person as a bounded and distinct entity, possessing a unique essence, is as illusory as speaking of a distinct and autonomous society. It is for this reason that it may be wise to abandon our attempts to identify a person as an entity or essence, and give ontological priority to the experience of being a person. Such a shift would accord full recognition to the fact that every human being has life only in relation to others – something the Warlpiri accomplish in their notion of the Dreaming. (16)

I agree with Michael Jackson, that personhood is a more resilient notion than identity or individuality. People living with intellectual disability have great differences compared with people without this disability. But it also gives their personhood a clear frame and marks them for acknowledgment. The fact that sometimes they are acknowledged in a negative way does not negate their personhood, but it might threaten their identity and erode their sense of individuality. Something about indigenous belonging shows the organic way people can be valued in a community and allowed to express their differences. It is in the apparent acceptance of indigenous ways of staying in the moment, that seems to 'handle' this paradox. If people can accept 'others' as they are now, it is not necessary for those 'others' to prove themselves. Identity emerges without a struggle, and individuality is illustrated in the group dynamic.

No human being comes to a knowledge of himself or herself except through others. From the outset our lives are an inter-subjective experience. Ego and alter ego are mutually entailed. Identity is a by-product of modes of interrelationships. The particular person, like the particular event, is an illusion. There are, observes Theodor Adorno, only 'moments of the whole.'… Without the sustaining interplay of self and another, one is as nothing. (17)

Jackson's view may raise the hackles of individualists, but my observation of indigenous communities tells me he is right, and that this understanding is relevant for use in modern rehabilitation processes.

The strength that people living with intellectual disability bring to such concepts is their natural tendency to 'be social'. They form groups and make fun easily, compared with the reserve among their 'normal' peers. While people living with mental illness face a real challenge in this area, I believe the lessons from indigenous and people living with intellectual disability have some clues to help them out: 'Knowledge of others is primarily, not secondarily, a matter of sociality…there is always some shadowy part of myself from which I can begin to reach an understanding of experiences which are foregrounded if the world of the other. As Jadran Mimica puts it, every other is the 'possibility' of oneself'. (18)

Stewarding relationships and places

Where can modern citizens go to find a grounding source for their driven, over-stressed lives? The cycles of Mother Earth, and our inevitability as mortal beings, means we are linked. Indigenous people have employed a rhythmic way of being earthed. This is revealed in the cycles of stories, rituals, totems and other devices which link earth and human continuity.

However, indigenous populations often face a similar challenge to their Western counterparts, in that there is an apparent demise of this way of being among many of their young. Michael Jackson recounted his moment of listening to elders Pincher Jampijinpa and Zachariah (Zack) Jakamarra, alongside the Lajamanu airstrip in the Tanami desert in the Northern Territory:

'Young people got no walya,' (Zack said). He scooped up a handful of earth. 'They don't know this walya. They only got that book, that paper'...I glanced at Pincher. 'We don't use maps,' Zack said. 'We got the country in our heads...'Young people don't know this one, they don't hold it any more...this walya business. Young people don't interest along culture, they don't look back. They only got paper'. (19)

There is something sad about such change, just as there is something hopeful. Bernard Smith's echo-logical understanding of the passage of history, and how the rhythms repeat, shows that chronology misses the point. Change is cyclic and fractal for us all. The message in this story seems to me to be about how people focus their awareness, rather than holding onto particular moments as the only right way. After all, in Aboriginal wisdom, all the moments merge if we enter the Dreaming. Rehabilitation will enhance people's lives if we create processes that link people to their inherent relationship with the earth, and if we create rituals that celebrate earth's natural cycles.

Indigenous attributes for healing through the dreaming

I have chosen five key words to capture something of the quality of the attributes which act as signposts to the territory of contemplative living. These signposts are the felt experience among indigenous people within the practical application of their culture. These are given as indicators of potential areas which should be explored in the creation of healing techniques for those who live with mental illness (who can benefit from 'recovery' work or 'rehabilitation'), and empowerment techniques for those living with intellectual disability (towards 'habilitation'). They are not procedures, tasks or processes. More than this, they are states of being, and ways of opening to the healing energy of the universe.

The dreaming

Generally, people are not resistant to teasing out the Aboriginal notion of the Dreaming. It seems to be an alluring concept. I feel it speaks straight to the soul. In scientific circles, where people are considering how to assist the healing of people with mental illness, there is good evidence to suggest that embracing this perspective can add to the recovery environment. Aboriginal Dreaming is a complex set of lifeworld views which covers creation stories, current responsibilities for place, links between different people and their totems, and the ability to transcend 'normal' consciousness and enter a different state of awareness.

These aspects of mindfulness vary from tribe to tribe, but my experience of modern Aboriginal people is that the Dreaming informs their every moment with the knowledge that they are linked through the universe to higher powers, spirit beings, and mysteries that give their life deep context. This is in accord with the Structure of Feeling and Experience. It indicates there is an innate desire amongst all people to commune with the numinous. Sharing, celebrating, rituals and mystery are part of the human condition. It is healthy to help people enter states where they can transcend the everyday experience of their mind. It is a kind of free association with the natural spirit in each person, linking with the universe, in safe environments, where any fear can be dealt with care.

This task requires effort. Firstly, to gain permission when such activities can be seen as weird. Secondly, to stop the frenetic scheduling of everyday life and allow time for some contemplation. I am advocating the creation of therapeutic environments in which it is a priority to let go of those things that act as distractions from silence and stillness — the space where many people seem unable to face themselves. Some people fear that they might be empty shells inside with nothing to experience and no real inner home of the soul. This certainly sounds true when standing in the middle of today's consumer castles — shopping malls.

For those living with mental illness, creating contemplative space is valuable and nurturing. I have seen this at Athma Shakti Vidyalaya, schizophrenia therapeutic community in Bangalore, India where individuals who normally spend a lot of time talking, doing and avoiding intimacy, enter a completely different mindspace in a contemplative experience. They can then begin 'finding their inner selves', and so follow a path of healing, able to return regularly to this quiet inner space for 'topping up' their equanimity. The indigenous gift to Westerners seeking to find ways of reaching this sort of contemplation, is through their attributes of personal life-flow and community rhythms. There are particular lessons for us in observing and adapting the inherent ways indigenous people have learnt.

Earth

A huge part of my own healing journey has been my coming to an understanding of 'dadirri'. This is the concept that Fr Eugene Stockton writes about, from Miriam Rose Ungunmerr Baumann's spiritual teaching which is shared by Aboriginal people in the Northern Territory of Australia. Dadirri means 'sit, wait and listen'. Easy enough instructions to hear. But, entering that quiet, contemplative zone is another challenge. The particular aspect of dadirri that Fr Stockton's work reveals, is that it is a two-way experience. His understanding of Aboriginal teaching is that the earth is sitting, waiting and listening to us, as much as we are to it.

Waiting. Listening. There. Humming. I believe Earth has so many energies to offer us, and just lying on the ground tells most people they feel 'at home' on the earth. The work of Darryl Reanney (*Song of the Mind*) talks about our shared beginnings, when the universe was totally present in the head of a pin, in the whitefella scientists' story of creation, before the 'Big Bang', and how, ever since, we still all share that reverberating energy.

This is an aspect of Aboriginal relationship to land that is not acknowledged by many non-Aboriginals. It does not mean they are obsessed with ownership (although that is certainly important in restoring their natural heritage), it is more about spiritual relationship, stewardship. The energy of earth is our natural rhythm. Dancing in the dust is an example of getting close to it. I had such an experience at a community Christmas party in India a few years ago where everyone was stomping in the dust, sharing our connection with the earth.

Finding silent ways and places where people can exchange the 'two way Dreamtime' and 'do dadirri' are strategies for healing towards recovery in mental health circles. I have seen this happening in Bangalore at Athma Shakti Vidyalaya. It is ultimately the energy of exchange of love. In the same way as it is our origin in the universe (Reanney), and the same thing people seek in yogic pranayama, chi gong and all other forms of balanced connection with nature's gift of life. Indigenous people reflect this energy, carry it in their being, and can share it if seekers come with listening, with humility.

Blood

Blood is the energy of animal life. It carries haemoglobin, which bears oxygen, which fuels respiration to combust our food and keep us alive. The same chelated molecular bonds that hold this oxygen in blood also work in chlorophyll to capture energy in photosynthesis in plants. And they appear again in humus and dust, holding the energy of life as it returns to earth in the richest organic fertilisers. Blood is life literally, and in its metaphorical links, through genetic inheritance, and the aspect of kinship between species.

Indigenous people in touch with their cultural heritage and its evolving nature, have strong expressions of blood as a continuing energy running their lives. Tapping this understanding could be useful healing territory for people seeking to reground themselves from mental illness. I have heard it works 'in the family' in Aboriginal communities, that is by 'sending him up to aunty' (the person suffering from mental collapse) and letting natural blood relations do the healing that only unspoken, unconscious connection and unconditional love can achieve. I believe there is an aspect in this understanding waiting to be tapped in Western healing environments as well.

When the Neville brothers sing *That's My Blood Down There*, they are sharing the energy of life that circulates in the human family. This heartbeat energy, this unconditional lifeforce, this shared acknowledgment of our equal importance as creatures of the universe, is the source of life, hope and love. By getting down and sharing the blood connection, we become 'blood brothers and sisters', in the metaphorical sense, exchanging renewal and resuscitation of our spirits, which then leads to restoring damaged hearts, minds, bodies and souls.

Echo

Evidence from physics and metaphysics shows that humanity is coming to see the presence of all time in 'the moment'. (Davies, Capra, Cowan). The limitations of linear, chronological thinking are gradually being removed as people begin to imagine themselves living in a timeless universe. Just as Eleanor Dark named her famous trilogy written about Australia, *The Timeless Land*.

Now that people are free to imagine that the universe lives in the tiny as much as the massive, the backwards as much as the forwards, the yin as much as the yang, there is a new perspective available on healing mental illness.

And a new perspective for valuing the more immediate heart presence of people living with intellectual disability who are waiting to be acknowledged and embraced as members of our tribe. One of the aspects of timelessness as a working concept is that people do not have to be ruled by what happened in the past. 'Right here, right now' is a concept which covers all time. So healing can happen to both erase the sense of hurt from the past, and to realise growth and change are available, now.

The understanding that comes, once timelessness is adopted as a practical notion, is that life 'echoes' around between past, present and future. This swinging is a cooperative movement, not a wrestling battle, between 'what happened then' and 'what's happening now'. I have observed that indigenous people can carry this echo energy of life, from past and future 'in the now'. I can hear it in the echoes of Christine Anu's beautiful rendition of Torres Strait rhythms, *Waiting For Me To Dive*, and I believe mentally ill people can access it too, if they are able to find an attitude of surrender, waiting and being with their own presence as nothing but vessels of consciousness. This obviously requires creating subtle and nurturing circumstances for healing. Doing nothing and waiting for the echo can be very therapeutic for people seeking to calm their souls.

Belong

Already noted in the section above, this is the ability to know that one belongs to the group, the family, the neighbourhood, the community. Humans are social beings first, and people who have become mentally ill may need help to find their way back into the shared space of community. Indigenous ways of being illustrate how group processes can nurture self-love and confidence in people who otherwise feel isolated and rejected. While sometimes 'the group above the individual' can be claustrophobic, there is a need in Western society to find balance, to swing back to the group because we have become too individual, too individuated. Hermits like me, and Uncle Raymond, need continuous reminding of the value of staying 'in group', so we do not get out of the habit. It is another example of how the culture 'has to be worked to work'.

If people living with mental illness are able to find a purpose, place and people to share this with, they will begin to gather a sense of belonging. From giving, not taking. From joining and sharing, and building not breaking. My own soul has trouble with this because my addictive side often wants to run. As soon as I remember to surrender, the energy of belonging flows in and fills up that discomfort which used to be an itch I would scratch with alcohol.

Addicted — dis-eased with life

Addicted people have patterns of awareness, and ways of responding to Feelings and Experience that are indicators of some of the deep seated problems of modernity. These problems have not caused addiction, but they certainly exacerbate it and effectively promote it across Westernised societies. These attributes of consciousness are:

- A continual sense of dis-ease with life, and the strong, even desperate, need to relieve that experience by using evasive strategies or habits to distract one's consciousness.

- An on-going sense of inner conflict due to the diseased state and the cycle of relief, because the 'fixes' that are used are the cause of a subsequent sense of failure, entrapment and hopelessness.
- The inability to get out of this cycle of dependence because of no access to the relevant rites of passage that assist people to enter their responsible adulthood, face their weaknesses and receive support in rising above their difficulties.
- Disturbance of heart, mind and soul as a result of the inner conflict, outer habit chasing, and cyclic depression caused by a never-ending sense of 'is that all there is'? This comes from a fundamental lack of balance to do with the numinous and one's place in the universe.
- Feelings and Experience of isolation and loneliness, because it seems that nothing can relieve their problems, and they seem separated from others, who somehow have stability, a sense of worth, purpose, and the ability to say no to habitual fixes.

I will now examine some aspects of addictive consciousness and develop a perspective to inform strategies for healing people who are disturbed in ways similar to those I have outline above.

Society's frontal lobotomy — integrity removal

A favourite quip among serious Australian drinkers is: 'I'd rather have a bottle in front of me, than a frontal lobotomy'. Drinkers consider the potential destruction of their brain cells to be a vocational risk, in the same way that smokers know they are likely to develop lung disease as a result of their addiction. My concern is with the loss of individual integrity that is one of the greatest impacts of addiction, whatever form it takes. Because the disturbance of mind and illness of soul creates the cycle of continually returning to the addictive behaviour, we need to try to ease the pain of dis-ease with oneself that results each time this occurs.

One of the effects of an addictive disease is that it destroys our integrity. We see ourselves doing things at work that compromise our value system, and we say nothing. We are reprimanded for something for which we were not responsible, and we say nothing. We act in ways that are not in keeping with our own personal morality. (20)

On the macro scale, many see that society is stuck in a similar cycle of dependencies, which now envelope the world in a series of compromised arrangements. (Schaef) I believe these are destroying our total environment – natural, social, economic, political and spiritual. Yet the consumer world continues to look for a fix to ease its dis-ease with behaviour which is killing it.

Under economic rationalism, addiction is big business. And big business, is addiction in action. It has the freedom to make profits and expand however it likes, demand that governments comply with its wishes, and it has a total lack of respect for the common good. Business is addicted to growth, shortcuts to profit, and irresponsible behaviour towards the environments it inhabits (personal, social, ecological). It is no wonder the little person with a substance abuse problem, or a co-dependency problem, or a gambling problem, or a bullying problem, stays stuck. The whole world is stuck.

The addiction to doing too much is just like any other addiction, in that it puts us in a position where we are willing to do anything to get our adrenaline 'buzz', to get our 'fix'. We see ourselves participating in decisions that are wrong for us, we neglect ourselves, and we neglect our families. We have lost our integrity. (21)

The cycle that develops under these circumstances is a loss of integrity, behaviour that abuses others, and subsequent further escape behaviour. Individuals turn to the bottle or the bong for relief, companies turn to the profit-and-loss columns and boast of their 'steep rise in rate of growth of profit'. Capitalism has reached a deeply addicted state when profit alone is not enough and it has to have appropriately huge 'rises in the rate of profit'. Understanding this highlights the environment in which people who have 'gone mad' are attempting to 'get sane'. The current climate in late capitalism seems to be insane. There is every reason to have compassion for those who 'lose it' in these circumstances.

In viewing the lives of marginalised people, such as those living with intellectual disability, it is possible to see their very distance from this cycle of mad pursuit of profit and growth, or its corollary, poverty from missing out, as an advantage. There is a pattern of social dislocation which is breeding mental illness and disturbing many people who would otherwise be able to go on with balanced lives: 'For most addicts, the idea of killing ourselves through overwork is something with which we are comfortable. It is the living of our lives at each moment that terrifies us and that we seek to avoid'. (22)

We keep hearing that addictions are spiritual diseases, yet in

Western society we keep looking for mechanical causes and cures...Native people are now seeing the connection between Western culture and addictions: that addictions are not only supported by Western culture, but required so that we can tolerate what we have created. (23)

The universal human needs and aspirations that Uncles Raymond Williams and Bernard Smith have identified as the Structure of Feelings and Experience, are not being achieved. One result is that people like me, who can find life unbearable, become compromised and de-spirited and seek relief in alcohol or other addictions.

My escape into getting drunk was both for pain relief and a rejuvenation of spirit. By taking in the alcoholic spirit I would revive my depressed internal soul spirit — temporarily, and artificially. Alcoholism is huge worldwide and still growing because as people pursue the dollar, their cultures fall away into a superficial materialised unsatisfying blandness or momentary titillation. They become de-spirited. Most of the world is immune to acknowledging alcoholism as an endemic social problem. And use of drugs is its partner.

In developing nations it is rife and spreading like wildfire, aided and abetted by the pressure and social destruction that is wreaked by greedy business practices. As a working member of AA, trying to counteract this force, I know first-hand how endemic the problem is.

I have often said that the addictive system in which we live is an illusory system. It is built on the illusion of control, the illusion of objectivity, and the illusion of perfection. I believe it is also immersed in confusion, dishonesty, and theoretical con-

structs that are built on abstractions and divorced from nature and reality. (24)

Late capitalist societies have all agreed to continue with the frontal lobotomy. Those who 'enjoy' the fruits of living in Western capitalist nations are living a lie. The lie that the world can go on like this and not eventually implode through lopsided, unjust and destructive growth and development. Whether one is Marxist, capitalist, ecologist or spiritualist, this problem needs to be addressed on behalf of the earth and all humanity.

In order to find solutions to these sorts of dis-eased states, what is possible? I believe the Twelve Step, narrative therapy and spiritual program of recovery is a good model. It provides relief from dishonesty, reconciliation for individuals and those they have hurt, and a chance to join a regular process of replacing habitual destructive ways with group support:.

Denial allows us to avoid coming to terms with what is really going on inside us and in front of our eyes...The Addictive system does not like this...We cannot be alive in a system based on denial. It leaves us no real avenue to deal with our reality. (25)

Telling personal stories, disclosing one's addiction and seeking forgiveness and reconciliation, is like receiving a healing balm. Doing so in an environment of freedom, confidentiality and acceptance builds life empowerment, free of dogma, conditions, judgement or blame. Once on the journey of recovery, an addicted person can offer others their story of experience, strength and hope. All can share the wisdom involved in the process. The addictive consciousness, once on the path to healing, has a lot to offer the world as a teacher.

The deceit of addicted minds

The pattern of addictive behaviour is to jump from one evasive behaviour to the next, in order to keep 'scratching the itch' of dis-ease with life. Similarly, we addicts in recovery can see that society has developed endemic 'itches', which it scratches in places that used to be for simple social and wholehearted sharing. Now they have become gatherings of addicts scratching their individual and collective itches, ie. in the pub, the TAB (betting agency), the shopping mall, the stock market, the beauty parlour, the gym, even the church.

No one has just one addiction. Addictions come in clusters. Frequently we use one addiction to support another or to mask another…We can use anything to 'protect our supply' and allow us to stay in our addiction. It is not what I do, it is the way I do it, that will get me in the end. (20)

There are glaring examples of how the individual's experience of this phenomenon is mirrored on a global scale by the forces of capitalism. Witness the MAI (the Multilateral Agreement on Investment) — an attempt by the leading capitalist nations of the West to get the United Nations to agree to a law which makes it illegal for sovereign states to resist the transglobal capital machine from overriding their national interest. If the MAI succeeds, governments that legislate against business being able to do business in whatever way it chooses, will be in breach of international law.

If it is good enough for transglobal capital to legislate, to make it illegal for nations to vote for their own independent decision-making against global greed, then

I believe many nations have been stripped of their integrity. It is little wonder individual citizens have trouble putting down the bottle. Yet, I suggest another way of seeing this is to adopt a homoeopathic view. Like cures like. A tiny suggestion of the 'illness' injected into the situation can bring about the cure. Not like an antidote or anti-venin as much as an energy, a whisper that starts the vortex of change in the chaos.

The more individuals admit to their personal addictions, and begin to heal by surrendering to reconciliation and recovery, the more likely it is that the political and business leaders will examine their own morality again.

The Addictive System is highly dependent upon what we now call left-brain functions. It is founded on the worship of linear, rational, logical thinking. This kind of thinking supports the illusion of control by simplifying the world to such an extent that it seems possible to have control over it...This deceit frequently requires us to ignore or dismiss our own experience. (27)

As we have seen in the work of Raymond Williams and Bernard Smith, humans want to share in a common exploration and celebration of mystery and stories about our common journeys in the universe. This includes admitting our mistakes and learning from them. However, the domination of rational thinking over all other forms of knowledge has taken humanity into a cul-de-sac of denial. This is not to say that rational thinking has no place. But, it has got out of hand and has become the principle tool for denying Feelings and Experience. That is, we are denying the preferred modus operandi of our consciousness.

When looking to heal those living with mental illness, it is advisable to go beyond these territories into more open-hearted spaces and strategies: 'When we lead with our logical, rational minds and try to get our feelings, thoughts, awareness, behaviour, and even spirituality to follow, we almost always get into trouble. When we do this, we almost always find ourselves firmly entrenched in the current mechanistic empirical paradigm'. (28)

The energy of addiction is to flee, to escape. Not to take responsibility and admit error. So rationality is a useful tool because it can serve any master — moral, immoral, lazy, sleazy. Rationality can fit a model to suit the purpose. Conscience can always wait. In Twelve Step programs we talk about people 'doing geographicals'. You can move house, move jobs, move partners, change countries. But the problem is, you keep taking your problem with you — because it is not the place, the other person, the house, the job, the suburb or whatever. It is the dis-ease in you.

Belief in the myth of objectivity and holding that as a value has set up a scientific worldview, that tells us the only valid information comes from being 'objective'. This view so permeates our society that we have systematised cutting ourselves off, from our feelings and our internal information systems. The most effective means of that cutting off are addictions. (29)

The wisdom that comes from understanding healing strategies for addiction, is that once people surrender to their true potential and allow a higher power to take over their lives, there is an invitation to actually participate in their real lives, moment by moment. David Tacey calls this re-enchantment, which has nothing to do with religion, dogma, or 'cults'. It is the same process inherent in indigenous consciousness. Getting in touch with the universe. As Anne Wilson Schaef says, 'Spirituality is nothing but participation, being fully present to the moment and participating in it. The moment is, after all, all we have'. (30)

Minds divided by habits

In describing the Structure of Feeling and Experience, Raymond Williams, and in parallel, Bernard Smith, identified that humans want to be more together and sharing. Addicts are the extreme example of having that desire frustrated and denied. They start life enjoying the bonhomie of the pub, cocaine coffee table, restaurant and 'good times'. Then, when isolation becomes the natural result of an obsessive addiction closing off individuals from society, their real, their deepest longing is furthest away. As they pursue the habit to try to ease the pain of the separation it stays that way.

People stuck in a full blown addictive habit cannot be in the company of 'normal' people for long. Because their habit demands full attention and feeding. If it must be in the company of others, such as for a gambler needing the TAB, the poker machines or the roulette wheel, the addict will shift about regularly to avoid being seen by too many people. Ultimately the serious addict ends up in the company of other serious addicts, so they do not have to worry so much. Generally, there has been a long journey before that occurs, where avoidance, shiftiness and restlessness have become a way of life.

People can feel torn between the persona they are showing in different environments. Chronic adulterers can feel like this — divided between the part of themselves which genuinely loves a partner, and the desperately addicted love junkie who needs a new conquest to feel better about him/herself. It is a split in the soul that eventually cracks people wide open, and they end up in therapy, attempting suicide or becoming ill.

It is the same with drinkers who give up and tell their old drinking buddies they are 'on the wagon'. When a philanderer comes clean to their mates about cleaning up their act, they are often greeted with sarcasm, scepticism and put downs. Their mates cannot imagine how they could face the truth and front their loved ones about their sneaky, slimy manipulative behaviour. These divided behaviours have many parallels with mental illness. The healing strategies used in narrative and group environments, such as the Twelve Step process, offer great hope for shared strategies among those living with mental illness.

Money's too tight to mention

Overcoming the fear which results from this dis-ease with life is the biggest hurdle for individuals and for society in breaking the addictive cycle. Unlike most people, addicts are unable to bear the normal rhythm of life.

All the sequences of our life are regulated by upward and downward rhythm; the undulation that we immediately recognise in nature and as the basic form of so many phenomena also holds sway over the soul. (31)

Addicts panic when they experience the 'swings and roundabouts' of life. Tension builds until they can get release by accessing their drug of choice — something that takes away the fear that life is closing in on them, or leaving them alone, or crashing down all over them, or whatever. All people suffer from dis-ease with life at regular intervals. But addicts suffer from it chronically. They have no barrier to separate their souls from the perception that they are being assaulted by life, which is why they need relief as often as possible.

Considering the analogy with consumer society, a large percentage of the world's population has been bred into habits that make 'buying' one of the commonest 'fixes' sought. 'Shop til you drop' is no joke. Consumption provides daily disguises for many people's dis-ease. Georg Simmel delved into the psychology of this phenomenon in his classic nineteenth-century study *The Philosophy of Money*, which interestingly, did not become available in English until 1978. At the turn of the last century, Simmel already saw that humanity had slipped into a set of habits that objectified experiences in life which used to be more closely integrated into a person's whole being.

Human enjoyment of an object is a completely undivided act. At such moments we have an experience that does not include an awareness of an object confronting us or an awareness of the self as distinct from its present condition...consciousness is exclusively concerned with satisfaction and pays no attention to its bearer on one side or its object on the other. (32)

By being another step away from our internal 'shit detector', those already hooked on finding release from dis-ease could jump into another habit of purchasing. And the advent of 'credit' made it even more accessible to use denial to feed a habit — just 'put it on the plastic'. Similarly, Internet shopping and especially Internet gambling, created instant mainlines into the process of 'feeling that fix' for those addicted to spending on purchasing or punting.

Money represents a process of 'relativity', whereby things are linked to one another through the medium of money as a comparing device, to represent value. In a world where the theory of relativity has begun to release people from a false form of rationality, money is meant to carry some secret relativity that frees it from its effects — 'Money objectifies the external activities of the subject, which are represented in general by economic transactions, and money has therefore developed as its content the most objective practices, the most logical, purely mathematical norms, the absolute freedom from everything personal'. (33)

This objectification is at the heart of what needs healing in Western society today. Heart and soul has been replaced by mind and body. People seem to have 'sold the farm to save the super policy'. Ideas and ideals about how best to manage 'the money economy' have taken over from how best to manage our lives for the good of humanity. Not only do addictions 'cost', they also derive from the process of chasing the almighty dollar.

The philosophical significance of money is that it represents within the practical world the most certain image and the clearest embodiment of the formula of all being, according to which things receive their meaning through each other, and have their being determined by their mutual relations…the projection of mere relations into particular objects is one of the great accomplishments of the mind…The ability to construct such symbolic objects attains its greatest triumph in money…

Thus, money is the adequate expression of the relationship of man to the world. (34)

Anything is possible, once people have bought into the disconnection that objectification achieves. Any activity can be rationalised, so long as it makes sense in the relative value system of a money-rated world — 'To comprehend our separation from our spirituality we need to look at how mechanistic science and technology cannot meet the most basic needs of the creation of which we're a part...We have come to believe that money and material objects are the only true reality as seen and measured 'objectively' through the senses'. (35)

The disconnection from our inner selves, and the continual denial of a true connection between people, keep many people in a dis-eased state. And quite a few moving into madness. It is the reason people seek the comfort of addictions, to release them from discomfort. And increasingly that release is available by 'paying for it', which keeps the money connection nicely tied in.

To break this cycle we need to reconnect with our hearts. To make human life a process of 'feeling first' and 'thinking about it after': 'The real issue is to pay attention to the felt experience, so that each person can own the experience as part of their life process, and to do their healing work'. (36)

We need to provide channels for releasing the confusion and frustration pent up in so many people — people who have been operating out of an artificial mindset, detached from their humanity. Addiction is just a symptom of the need in humans to reconnect with their inner lives, and the link between those lives and the mysteries of the cosmos. Which is where uncles Raymond and Bernard lead us, to our shared Structure of Feeling and Experience.

When the escape 'distraction' becomes necessary to uphold an addict's 'normal' life, they are, in the gambler's rhetoric, 'gone for all money':

When we are fearful, we are usually angry at the same time. When we are angry, it is fear that is most often at the root of our anger — fear of ourselves, and/or fear of others. When we operate out of fear, we are almost always angry because we perceive that world as an unsafe place; when we are angry, we help to make the world an unsafe place because our anger generates retaliatory anger in others. When we let go of our fear, our anger dissipates; when we let go of our anger, we have that much less fear. (37)

Addicts who have faced these steps of 'unpacking their fear and anger' can then be available to aid others who are stuck in the fearful/angry place. And it takes an experienced consciousness to be able to empathise with someone stuck in this place of suffering. Not sympathise, empathise — just the ability to listen, and share one's own story of surrender to a higher power. Such approaches enable recovery in the mystery that Uncles Raymond and Bernard saw at the core of 'normal' human experience. It is that process, which I am advocating should be considered as an integral party of the healing process for people living with mental illness.

Rights of passage

When Raymond Williams wrote *Culture and Society*, he was observing the 'modern' industrial state at its peak. The Second World War had geared everything up for maximum production and workers were in full tilt, focusing on trying to resist the forces of fascism. At this time Williams sensed that people wanted other things in their lives other than slavishly following the 'modern' dream of a job, a home, a secure future and a beer at the pub.

He knew that humanity needed more food for its soul. But something was already afoot that had begun to drain away the traditions and habits of community which had made life both close and rhythmic. What was coming was a rapid swamping of all the old social infrastructure by the shallow blanket of consumer society. As British punk poet, John Cooper Clarke observed in the Thatcher years, life in Britain was to become a round of brain numbing attempts to cope with an empty soul-life and a full television screen. His song, *Ninety Degrees In My Shades*, portrayed the English suburban sitting-room dweller, stuck in front of the television, waiting for someone to fill in the blank where their soul used to be.

Many victims of addiction started their journey in search of some escape from the monotony and emptiness of this media-fed blancmange of life. Whether it was escaping down a back lane to swig illicit alcohol, or smoke illicit cigarettes and dope, the process was one of looking for something larger in life. This results in rebelliousness at school and choosing to stay in dead end jobs, all the while engaging in 'impression making' — hotting up cars, wearing the latest groovy clothes, teenage sex and escaping into early marriages. These were the rites of passage from the sixties. But later they became superseded by 'harder' options, like more serious drugs, and a range of consumer distractions depending on your level of income.

Since the White Male System/Addictive System defines itself as reality, everything else is unreal by definition. Since its referent is the external referent, the internal referent is unreal and nonexistent by definition.(38)

When the industrial state and the post-industrial world agreed to maintain the myths about logical, rational, objective approaches to life, addiction was assured its place as the most likely right of passage replacement available in the 'civilised' world.

Dis-ease — the attributes of addicted consciousness

The words that capture the essence of addictive behaviours are not meant to be scientific labels or precise descriptors. They are indicators of an energy, which may be part of the refocussed healing strategies I am suggesting. Dis-ease reflects the state of not being at ease with oneself, and to be unable to find relief due to an experience than can be compared literally with sickness, or disease. The sense of not being comfortable with ourselves has begun to beset nearly every age group, community, nation and race. This is because the human condition has wandered so far away from its state of natural balance. Dis-ease is chronic. The natural follow-on is to ask what can be done? I believe we need to help each other bring things back into balance, just as I am attempting to develop ways for people who live with mental illness and intellectual disability to be empowered to try out their skills so that they can live more confident, more fulfilled lives.

This is a matter of energy flow. Solving the problem of trying to escape dis-ease in life may help others to realise the only answer lies in surrendering to their greatest fears, and letting the fear engulf us. This is part of the healing strategy used at Athma Shakti Vidyalaya, where people living with schizophrenia and bi-polar disorder can be safely assisted to go inside to those spaces and face their deepest fears and achieve some balance through self-understanding.

Itch

The feeling that things are uncomfortable, itchy, needing action in reply, is a common trait among addicts. When people are frustrated, locked into a situation, made to restrain their natural tendencies, or feeling denied their due, they want to get out of this state. 'Poor me' is the catch cry of addicts. In Twelve Step circles they are famous for it. They cannot bear discomfort in their life. The answer? A drink, a joint, a needle, a poker hand, a sex partner, a huge meal, an abusing relative, a packet of fags. These behaviours can be placed in context when one understands the nature of the dis-ease being suffered by the individual. It does not excuse inappropriate behaviour, but it may be a clue to healing it, and to helping people living with mental illness address some of their inner turmoil.

Scratch

Finding the solution to addictive hunger is half the story of life for addicts. So much energy and strategy goes into maintaining supply that this becomes an obsession in itself. Since the whole world is made up of 'relief stations' — pubs, bars, TABs, poker machines, sex shops, fast food outlets, shopping malls, and relatives who can be hassled

— they have no trouble finding access to feeding their habits. Until the money runs out. Then stealing comes onto the scene. As they say in the Twelve Step program: you will only be able to fully participate in your own life when you have dealt with this escape behaviour.

Trick

The energy of lying rests inside every addict. They need to lie regularly because their desperate need to feed the habit becomes so dominant it soon removes morality and constraint. The driven, desperate addict, inveterately lies to 'get the fix'. People who are co-dependent can even invite the lying in order to feel content in their superiority. They do this to escape their insecurity and dis-ease with themselves. It is paradoxical, cunning, baffling and powerful (as the AA *Big Book* puts it). But, the trick can be played on itself, and ended forever, by learning to sit with the discomfort long enough, until eventually, it passes. Then you need to make a habit of facing such difficult moments over and over, until you no longer need a trick. Life is hard. So, build a bridge, and get over it.

Escape

Ultimately every addict yearns for 'the total trip'. Release into oblivion, probably best imagined in the heroin addict's collapse into momentary ecstasy, when they have finally got their hit. The energy here is of desperation for release and escape into a state of consciousness that cannot be touched by 'reality'. It only lasts a moment, like orgasm, or like being stuffed with too much Christmas lunch, but addicts keep seeking that quality of experience. The natural outcome of such desperate searching is that each time the quality of the original 'hit' is harder to find. Addicts need more and more of their fix, to keep feeding the habit for the same degree of 'hit effect'. It is little wonder addicts experience the energy of fear. Their uneasy friendliness in order to get something, and a certain 'shifty' distracted attention, is really always focused on finding the fix, not on whoever else is present. Such preoccupations are shared with people trying to cope with living with mental illness. Healing strategies that arise from the Structure of Feelings and Experience, address these problems by responding to the inner areas of loss. They enter the same space as the indigenous Dreaming, where access to the Higher Power provides motivation to resist the temptation to escape and gives them the energy to persevere with their lives until the darker moments pass and move into the light.

Chapter Eight

Suburbs

Personal space — biological privacy

'Ingenious man has developed ingenious methods to ensure his biological privacy', wrote dedicated evolutionary biologist Robert Ardrey in his 1970 book, *'The Social Contract'*. Ardrey saw humanity's love affair with the city from an evolutionary perspective, and he saw something 'in the mix', which pointed to why we ended up developing our parallel love affair with the suburbs.

We face in the urban concentration something new under the sun, something unanticipated except by the biologically, genetically directed termitary: but we lack the insect's genetic directives as we lack an evolutionary common ground. While we may live in our cities like ants in an ant-hill, as vertebrates we are genetically unprepared for such contingency. (1)

While humans gathered together in great numbers, finding their space being encroached upon by one another, something needed to be balanced in this 'trade off' of advantage, something which needed to be practised over centuries. Ardrey tried to understand this balancing act in evolutionary terms:

In that grand tradition of the modern human being, we oppose nature, master our environment, and, victims of nature's tricks, we are threatened by the urban environment which we in our hubris have created...Let us write down one more extension of the social contract: The group must present to all its unequal members equal opportunity to develop their genetic potential; in return the individual must, by coercion or consent, sacrifice any right to produce young in greater number than society can tolerate, or the fulfillment of the individual must be suffocated by indiscriminable numbers. (2)

This notion worked pretty well in the West, where populations are ageing and falling. In developing nations, overcrowding and increasing birth rates have led to government attempts to limit population by decree — almost as impossible as prohibition of alcohol. So what happens to the social contract, when the numbers begin to explode?

Glen McBride (Queensland animal behaviourist) was struck by the way people pose themselves in a crowded room. Almost never do two people in conversation face each other directly at close distance. Yet if we sit side by side on a bench or couch, no matter how uncomfortably we may be jammed together, we speak freely and without feeling self-conscious. McBride developed a concept of personal space from these observations:

Surrounding each individual is a portable territory with its deepest dimension in front. As the robin will threaten and fight an intruder on his fixed bit of exclusive space, so we resent intrusion into our personal space. (3)

On a continent where the first peoples lived in relationship with the land without fences for tens of thousands of years, Australians have made an art-form of boxing in space, of erecting fences. We enclose our dwellings, our belongings, ourselves and our souls. Yet we find little to value in the horded goods we are protecting behind these fragile ramparts.

While Uncles Raymond and Bernard are telling us that humans want company, stories to share, mysteries to explore in wonder, and to 'belong', we are in the living room with the blinds pulled down, the television on, and our consciousness closed to our engagement with a world we find threatening and alienating. No wonder some people go nuts, commit suicide, commit incest and other atrocities in their suburban 'castles'.

Somewhere in our 'evolution' some of us turned down a dead-end path, ending in the cul-de-sac of suburban blandness, now developed into miniature form in the apartments which have sprung up in our cities and surrounding feeder suburbs. Others experience this suburban precinct as a rich source of nurture, for the self, the soul and the social. What happened to create these different range of responses? Another animal behaviourist had some clues three decades ago:

By studying the behaviour of infants and lovers, it becomes clear that the degree of physical intimacy that exists between two human animals relates to the degree of trust between them. The crowded conditions of modern life surround us with strangers whom we do not trust, at least not fully, and we go to great pains to keep our distance from them. (4)

The so-called advance of civilisation obviously omitted a few essential ingredients that were needed for healthy living. Humanity was not meant to end up stressed to the limit by huge populations, nor locked in ticky-tacky cells hiding from 'the others', while trying try to cope with the accumulated stress from each excursion 'into the world'.

When we examine the Feelings and Experiences of people living with challenges like mental illness or intellectual disability, it does not seem much different from the 'normal' life of the suburbanite, yet these people are marginalised because of their very difference from suburban 'normality'.

The human animal is a social species...hemmed in on all sides, he defensively turns in on himself. In his emotional retreat, he starts to shut off even those who are nearest and dearest to him, until he finds himself alone in a dense crowd. Unable to reach out for emotional support, he becomes tense and strained and possibly, in the end violent. (5)

Thirty years ago in Britain, Desmond Morris saw that simple solutions lay in admitting we were on the wrong track, and that we could change. But nothing has changed, because the marketing of the suburban dream home, and its miniature apartment clone, along with the lifestyle accoutrements that go with them, have overpowered any contrary messages about scaling down our pursuit of suburban Arcadia:

In a way, our ingenious adaptability can be our social undoing. We are capable of living and surviving in such appallingly unnatural conditions that, instead of calling a halt and returning to a saner system, we adjust and struggle on. (6)

While so-called civilised humanity has battled with the emotional results of material success, those with 'less than', the 'others', have carried riches in their backpacks of personal 'heart connections' and intimate friendships that work to support their lives. Uncles Raymond Williams and Bernard Smith, along with Aunties Anne Wilson Schaef and Karen Horney, would smile at the comparisons.

Some commentators have seen the light side of the suburbs as indicating human potential for growth in the use of communal and personal space. Notably Australian planner and social intellectual Hugh Stretton:

What the clichés about suburbs call for is really a rejoinder about life. Plenty of dreary lives are indeed lived in suburbs. But most of them might well be worse in other surroundings: duller in country towns, more desperate in high-rise apartments. Intelligent critics don't blame the suburbs for the empty aspirations: the aspirations are what corrupt the suburbs. (7)

This points to the problem that the 'others' illustrate. In their difference, they create fear among those seeking 'normality' and 'belonging'. In their difference, they also declare that it is possible to live with a diverse range of 'beingness', and they provide an invitation to 'normal' people to open themselves to their own diversity of being.

What has happened that makes the suburbs so tragic is that their support mechanisms and feeder processes — schools, health services, churches, shopping centres — have moved more and more towards banality, and, in most circumstances, have excluded engaging with people of difference. In areas with public housing, where the less fortunate are more likely to congregate, most often including the 'others', people choose to 'move away' rather than see the strength in living in diverse social groups.

Hugh Stretton saw the positive in the suburban house and garden and believed that the solution to human community, lay not in the physical creation of space, but in the attitudes that predominate.

Stretton's defence of suburban structures and use of space is illustrative of the potential for change in places which are often seized by attitudes of conformity. When it comes to having people living next door who are indigenous, or who live with mental illness, are you going to be comfortable with difference and diversity, or fearful of it?

What we hope to move towards is a way of being that sees communities accepting each other's weaknesses with more compassion and engaging with the local support networks of those with particular needs.

Happy or helpful or creative human relations are not confined to any type. Good and bad relations appear within the closest families, and equally in the busiest open markets. Everyone has an individual pattern of need and response, in relations of both kinds. It is not hard for good cities — especially urban-suburban cities — to offer their members wide and compatible opportunities for relationships of every kind. (8)

This is OK as far as 'normal' people go, but it is very unlikely in the case of seeking equitable access to living space, activities and services for the 'others'. An increase in integration for groups of 'others' would generate greater diversity and character in the bland suburbs. As A.S. Neill says in his introduction to his famous 1962 book on *Summerhill* (the British student-governed, free school that began a focus on child-centred, person-centred learning):

Maybe there is original sin after all…the sin of opting out. If Summerhill has any message at all it is: Thou shalt not opt out.

Fight world sickness, not with drugs like moral teachings and punishments but with natural means — approval, tenderness, tolerance...I hesitate to use the word love, for it has become almost a dirty word like so many honest and clean Anglo-Saxon four letter words. (9)

Neill's fury was with the 'poisoned emotions' that dominated modern life because of judgements and demands for obedience from independent, self-responsible young people.

In a similar way, we can argue that the presence and absence of the 'others' in our society provides examples of where the human condition has a chance to revive itself by exercising love — to explore difference; engage with mystery and archetype; and to see oneself in the life of another.

Suburban consciousness — the path of social memory

Once we had decided that the suburb was a good idea for dealing with urban crowds and class distinctions, people began to find reasons why they worked so well. As modernism began its sprawling growth, all sorts of logic was applied to the suburban raison d'etre to reinforce its efficacy.

Nineteenth-century advocates of the American suburban idyll, like Frank Jesup Scott, prescribed carpets of front yard lawns, undivided by fences, as an expression of social solidarity and community — the imagined antidote to metropolitan alienation. The designation of the suburban yard as a cure for the afflictions of city life marks the greensward as a remnant of an old pastoral dream, even though its goatherds and threshers have been replaced by tanks of pesticide and industrial-strength mowing machines. (10)

Human nature tends to follow us wherever we go, and something began to gather in the suburbs that continued a dark tradition. If we had delved deeper into the places that were being buried beneath bowling green lawns and hydrangea hedges, we could have unearthed some pretty scary old shibboleths.

It is just because ancient places are constantly being given the top dressings of modernity (the forest primeval, for example, turning into the 'wilderness park') that the antiquity of the myths at their core is sometimes hard to make out. It is there, all the same...'Landscape And Memory' has been built around such moments of recognition as this, when a place suddenly exposes its connections to an ancient and peculiar vision of the forest, the mountain, the river...it is our shaping perception that makes the difference between raw matter and landscape. (11)

While the Structure of Feeling and Experience for modern humanity was showing the need for a return to shared stories, surrender to mystery, and engagement with the way our lives reverberate around us, the modern suburban project tried to give nature a new paint job. Rather than embracing the ghosts and ancestor stories surrounding every local neighbourhood, there was a pastiche process undertaken, to fill the holes with spackle and paper over the cracks.

Writing about Western society, Aby Warburg believed that 'beneath its pretensions to have built a culture grounded in reason, lay a powerful residue of mythic unreason'. (12)

In the context of how the 'others' are 'seen' by much of 'civilised' society, it is ironic to begin to see the degree of myth-making and self-delusion that goes into a suburban life, while at the same time, judging those of difference as 'something strange and other'.

Perhaps some of the illness, that has welled up from 'normal' humanity over the past century would not have held so much sway if we had been in the habit of engaging more with our people of difference as a natural part of sharing life's diversity.

Just as Clio, the Muse of history, owed her beginnings to her mother, Mnemosyne, a more instinctual and primal persona, so the reasoned culture of the West, with its graceful designs of nature, was somehow vulnerable to the dark demiurges of irrational myths of death, sacrifice and fertility. None of this means that when we, too, set off on the trail of 'social memory' we will inevitably end up in places where, in a century of horror, we would rather not go, places that represent a reinforcement of, rather than an escape from, public tragedy...landscapes will not always be simple 'places of delight'...memories are not all of pastoral picnics. (13)

The 'burbs' can be pretty psychedelic when it comes to both behaviour behind closed doors and communal outbursts of zany personal expression. Witness suburban Christmas lights competitions all over the Yuletide panoply. I have to ask, just who are the real nuts, when neighbours are competing over having bigger transformers to generate electric necklaces around their homes?

What can be learnt from this small piece of suburban communal madness, is that more such instances could open hearts, minds and souls to a much more eclectic life, if only we allowed ourselves to imagine it. What Simon Schama sees in landscape and memory, I see in the people who have been squeezed out of view by the veneer of suburban sameness, or by the patronising effect of health and welfare corrals.

For notwithstanding the assumption commonly asserted in these texts, that Western culture has evolved by sloughing off its nature myths, they have, in fact, never gone away. For if, as we have seen, our entire landscape tradition is the product of shared culture, it is by the same token a tradition built from a rich deposit of myths, memories, and obsessions…Instead of assuming the mutually exclusive character of Western culture and nature, I want to suggest the strength of the links that have bound them together. That strength is often hidden beneath layers of the commonplace. So landscape and memory is constructed as an excavation below our conventional sight level to recover the veins of myth and memory that lie beneath the surface. (14)

The 'others' have great potential to reinvigorate suburban localities with their presence in the mainstream. People need more people of difference. And people of difference need more opportunities to be 'normal' — in the sense of engaging in worthwhile work, social roles, community support functions, and general sharing of the joy and wonder of life. Just as Uncles Raymond and Bernard have said.

'This is how we see the world', Rene Magritte argued in a 1938 lecture explaining his version of 'La Condition humaine'… 'We see it as being outside ourselves even though it is only a mental representation of what we experience on the inside.' What lies beyond the windowpane of our apprehension…needs a design

before we can properly discern its form, let alone derive pleasure from its perception. And it is culture, convention, and cognition that makes that design; that invests a retinal impression with the quality we experience as beauty. (15)

Touché, say the 'others'. Our exploration here is to see whether the consciousness of these four groups can be embraced again as part of the rich web of life in its full metaphoric complexity. The scary, the angry, the shy and the anxious are all parts of ourselves. But, in a world where impression management and virtual reality have merged with public life, we have made it unpalatable to expose these realities to public view.

Leave me alone with my dreams

Theodore Zeldin is a troublemaking thinker. He will not comply and he will not restrain his curiosity about the inner workings of human consciousness. He even invaded Paradise to find out what suburban life was like there:

Each century, each generation, each person finds in Paradise what they are looking for. That is the best reason for visiting Paradise, to discover what it is that one is looking for. Most people unfortunately arrive too late in life, when they have stopped looking...They forgot what they had left behind, they had no room for regret about the debts they had not paid or collected, or for worrying about what would happen to their possessions, who would feed the cat...They were shaken by becoming aware they were totally independent souls unable to lean on others, on family or friends. They did not know how to be souls. (16)

Just like us, here on earth, which is no different a place to be a soul. And the 'others' are evidence that souls do not always behave in predictable ways. They can be varied in their expressions of difference, and in their engagement with our differences. They can even be curious about us, which can feel threatening.

If curiosity was a necessary condition for happiness, happiness was also a necessary condition for curiosity…that was the trouble with the happiness…on earth: it was made up of vicious circles. (17)

On the surface, suburban life seems safe. But, scratch this surface and you will find it is a mix of chaos, energy, surprise and fate. We have insurance, superannuation, even unemployment and sickness insurance to stave off life's exigencies. But sometime, and certainly inevitably at the end of life, we have to face the music, that life is unpredictable in its ultimate nature.

The 'others' are neighbours who remind us of this. And they tend to do it in ways that do not always feel comfortable, even if they are strangely attractive — like meeting people who live with mental illness in the shopping mall. They have a disarming habit of just fronting up and talking to you, with frankness and a direct heart connection that does not take no for an answer. What do you do?

(In Paradise) There was no…tasting of the different vintages of bliss…The ability to imagine one's body to be what one pleases can be exhilarating for those who have the courage to let go their fantasy…how souls see themselves can be very different from how they are seen by others.(18)

Suburban life can be either a place where one will be seen, or a place where one can hide. The 'others' have the gift of already being different and learning to cope with being themselves. They may not always have an easy ride on this journey of self-coping, but they cannot avoid it. 'Normal' people have every inducement to avoid facing themselves for as long as they can find distractions.

Life without props can be a terrifying prospect. If you are left without the certainty of acceptance and support from your surroundings, life becomes unbearable. It is often this way for the 'others', who find themselves in circumstances where 'normal' people assume everyone feels comfortable.

Suburban living provides many places and spaces for engagement with difference. Trying it out is another matter. And often the 'others' themselves are traumatised into not reaching out to find those who want to share some true heart connection, to get beyond the props.

Stagnating consciousness

To understand the darker side of suburban life, we need only wander down *Beasley Street*. John Cooper Clarke, Britain's 'Poet Sir Lancelaureate' of the Thatcher years, chronicled the dead end that many suburbs become.

Again, as Zeldin says, it is lack of curiosity, otherwise known as boredom, that kills in the suburbs. Michael Bracewell tracked Cooper Clarke's journey through this territory, and linked him to a generation of modern jesters, pointing the urban bone:

'Beasley Street' begins with a vivid description of the street as both a real location and as a metaphor for stagnating consciousness; like the Thames for Eliot and Conrad, Beasley Street is a river to the heart of darkness:

Far from crazy pavements,
The taste of silver spoons,
A clinical arrangement
On a dirty afternoon;
Where the fecal germs of Mr Freud
Are rendered obsolete –
The legal term is Null and Void
In the case of Beasley Street.

Cooper Clarke's Waste Land is a place where love and procreation have not only worn out but become their reverse; Beasley Street is a state of living death, as removed from drama as it is from hope. It is a place for the discarded, the lost and the forgotten, where nothing ever happens save further decay... The horror of the poem lies in its subject's mute acceptance of boredom as the lobby of death. (19)

Australia has plenty of equivalent places spread around its coastal fringe of dwellings snuggled up to the cities. But the sun shines on them, drying out the depression so that it maintains a suntan and regularly complains of itching.

With empathy for the circumstances of the 'others' who are judged and compared by 'normal' folk living in the suburbs, we can also breathe a sigh of relief for them, that they escape the drudgery of hopelessness that besets so many people – like those who have 'made it' with their brick home and above-ground pool with outdoor barbecue.

This is a place where the living have become ghosts, haunting the ruins of home and hope; their situation is described through images of domestic decay, playing on humour in a way that twists the comic punchline into tragedy:

Vince the ageing savage'
Betrays no sign of life,
But the smell of yesterday's cabbage
And the ghost of last year's wife.

As Beasley Street reverses life and confounds hope, so there is no chance of redemption; the dream – if it can be called a dream – is simply to be a different person in a different life.

The boys are on the wagon,
The girls are on the shelf;
Their common problem is
That they're not someone else...

There is a final, glancing blow in this description of an urban oubliette* for society's lost souls, and that is a sarcastic reference to the sociological solution:

It's a sociologist's paradise –
Each day repeats...

Thus Beasley Street's only value to modern society would be as a model for some social theory; life itself, as a gift turned into a burden, must simply be endured. (20)(*oubliette is a dungeon with an opening only at the top; from oublier – to forget; from the Latin 'oblivisa'.)

Who needs freaks when you have suburban decrepitude? The 'others' live under the stares and glances of the same folk who go home to *Beasley Street*. What everyone could do with is a good jitterbug around the shopping mall to mix up their zest for life, and create more imaginative spaces for communal living. Raymond and Bernard can double on sax.

We all need these things that the Structure of Feeling

and Experience has chronicled. But the life that surrounds the suburbs in most Westernised communities is being rapidly mesmerised by new forms of virtual reality — fast-food chains 'just up our street'; and movie houses that provide weekly updates of the Hollywood version of our lives. These elements add to the shopping mall muzak to ensure that more consumption replaces any chance of rejuvenating self-generated community interaction and integration of difference and diversity.

Cooper Clarke's scenarios are telling in both hemispheres, and the 'others' are part and parcel of the consumer queues.

Cooper Clarke bears witness to all of the banal suffering that is rendered invisible by its very familiarity… (his) subject is the fate of vulnerable humanity at the hands of advanced consumerism in a depressed or archaic region; his particular balance of comedy and protest is drawn from the increased vulgarity of cut-price glamour in a local culture weighed down by economic collapse and a redundant industrial heritage. (21)

American films such as: *Requiem for a Dream, American Dream, Mulholland Drive, Safe,* and the earlier, *Drugstore Cowboy,* chronicled the hopelessness of young and old in urban and suburban consumer life, depending on escape through substance abuse, obsessively expanding consumption, or fear-laden 'environment illness'. Pop music went on to finish the job.

Bowie, Roxy Music and Kraftwerk were British versions of the trend to create a decadent way of sending up the whole modernist show, while at the same time, mimicking its best images. Difference became an industry and people like the 'others' would have to wait.

Pallid as opposed to tanned, skinny as opposed to muscular, Bowie was Beaton with a bouffant and reversed the idea of what a pop idol and sex symbol might look like…(He) became the Pied Piper of handbag…it could be seen as a liberation from mere fandom into a cult of mass individualism…the army of impersonators represented a triumph for suburbia and the provinces as the home of revolt through style. (22)

While in America and Australia there was also the popular World Wrestling Federation attracting huge 'projectile audiences' on television and at live events, their suburbs were also ringing to the cabaret, lounge lizard rhythms of Roxy Music. These guys were part of a trend to mesmerise ourselves into a painless way of enduring the consumerist weather front that had swept over the modern world.

Luxurious and melodramatic, Roxy Music, like Bowie, were essentially time travellers…And in inner space…the mind loses its bearings. What's the date again (it's so dark in here) 1962? Or twenty years on?…the real mission of their cool theatricality was a kind of fin-de-siecle swoon into the arms of technology…This was playing with history as a cosmetic version of itself. (23)

The story went on, through many forms of cultural packaging, which expressed a sort of passive acceptance of the overruling techno-classes and vested interest groups, which had assumed the political powerhouses of democratic Westernised consumer societies. But their success lay on top of a hollowing out of the suburbs, and the 'others' became a series of groups scattered through these curbed and guttered streets, who were signals of some other form of humanity than those identified in the sixties graffiti slogan: 'consume, be silent, die'. Thank goodness for those who cannot help being stuck with 'Less Than' as a designer label. They hold up hope against the tide of lifestyle television, reality television, like *Big Brother*, and the home renovation programs that are more like sitcoms of self-obsession.

Die a little everyday

People and nature have to get on together. In figuring out how to do that, we have mapped out three territories (according to Evan Eisenberg, author of *The Ecology of Eden*): the Mountain (Eden), the wild place; the Tower, the city; and Arcadia, the suburbs. Eisenberg's point about these concepts that humans have invented, is that they have created artificial ways of being in our world.

Responsibility is what the Arcadian most wants to be free of… Arcadia is not a place, it is a phase…The suburb is meant to be a mean between city and country…(it) tries to solve the problem of our relation to nature by finding a place where it is already solved. (24)

What is revealed about the suburbs, from Eisenberg's ecological viewpoint, is that humanity has closed off its options by securing a 'safe' place in the myth of Arcadia. He sees our natural place on earth being 'on the edge', not ensconced in one place or another, and he points out that we are paying a price for this compromised solution to our desire to achieve safety and security 'in the middle'.

Humans…are fond of edges. Many of us feel safest – physically, psychically – on the edge between civilisation and wilderness. Either one in its pure state can turn demonic. We want to be able to run and take shelter from one in the other. If the edge spreads endlessly,...it eats up countryside and drinks up the sap of the city. (25)

In the Feelings and Experience of humanity, as recorded in culture and society, literature and art, we know that Raymond Williams and Bernard Smith have found the patterns of desire for sharedness, mystery, stories, and celebration of the mystery. Maybe we thought all of that could be found in the safe confines of the suburb. But in fact, it could not and what we found there instead were the empty shells of stale memories.

Given that we are not going to dispense with these massive blocks of life in a short period, the positive option for seeking solutions to their chimeric nature would seem to be to create occasions of validity and true-heart between people. The physical structures may be one level of ecological challenge, but they are nothing compared to the soul and psychic barriers now constructed around and between souls. Save us from the shopping mall sameness, freeways and parking lots. Who will lead the break out?

Here the 'others' are ghostbusters worthy of a call. Their tendency to live openly and in pursuit of some heart and soul connection offers energy and hopefulness to a shallow grave-like indentation on the earth's playing field.

We can break down monotony by opening more bland suburbs to diverse populations, where people of difference receive support to live independent, integrated lives in the community. The idea that an exclusive lifestyle belongs to 'the right people' is setting itself up for a death sentence from within:

The one question the resident of a deluxe suburb…must never ask himself is: What if everyone lived this way?…But though (this question) has not been asked, the question is now being answered (in energy wastage, pollution etc)…And since both the wildness of nature and the wildness of the city are far away, the main form of adventure is consumption…beneath the glossy surface, reality decays. (26)

Eisenberg's point is that we need to regain the ability to listen to rhythms other than our own. Hence the 'others' rise up as inherent teachers in the midst of this society of self-seekers. By creating more diversity in our communities, and decreasing our walled-in mentality towards human development, we may be able to return to a more healthy balance in our relationship to Earth and Gaia.

To be workable, a model for human life on earth must leave room for humans to move around. Somehow, it must find a way to make us feel responsible for the places we leave and the places we arrive in, as well as for distant places touched by our actions. (27)

These implications require balanced engagement with praxis, not 'logical solutions' alone. People's feelings, circumstances and their implications for whole ecologies, all require intuition in finding new approaches. The 'others' are part of suburban life now, but not as acknowledged contributors to its wholeness. When they are, we will all be 'weller'. Just as biodiveristy is necessary for ecological sustainability, I claim 'onto-diversity' is essential for 'suss-tainability' of humankind.

Your private sky — Buckminster Fuller

In 1962 when A.S. Neill wrote his book, *Summerhill*, he was in despair — about the state of humanity's pursuit of 'infantile idiocies'. But he was also calling for action, to change the trend towards a nihilistic future for humankind. One reference on his mind at that time was Selby's book, *Last Exit to Brooklyn*, which had been recently banned in Britain:

It is most difficult to keep thinking of schools and teachers. Think of the book 'Last Exit to Brooklyn', by Selby. It was banned by law in Britain. The banning was another instance of official Bumbledom, of ignorant puritans. The book is full of four letter words, of sexual perversions, of humanity at its lowest, but as a picture of one aspect of our boasted culture I think it should be read by millions. It really terrifies.

It shows the other side of American Cadillac-status-seeking-anti-life-commercial-life, shows what slums and a bad education and commercial exploitation can do to human beings. And in one degree or other these conditions obtain in every city in the world. They are the corollary of our welfare state, our 'never had it so good'. A culture that is not there. (28)

At the same time, across the Atlantic, was Neill's soul brother, Buckminster Fuller, a genius inventor, 'anticipatory design scientist', artist and imagineer. He worked towards the betterment of mankind and felt, like Neill, that life was not meant to pursue the shallow options. He saw truth and the reform of people's environment, not reform of people, as the answer to the earth's ills under human occupation.

Fuller's aim was about 'doing more with less', 'without

one individual interfering with or being advantaged at the expense of another'. He spent a long life assisting others to create new ways of serving the human condition, and tried to express his beliefs in his daily life. Trusting that 'nature would provide', he regularly gave away his money and started again from scratch. He saw life as an adventure and he went to the edge on every possible occasion. Not a likely candidate for suburban living.

But Fuller's message is crucial to the conversion potential of today's suburban, urban, and all other configurations of human ways of being together. He saw that life is energy, and he knew that it was part of a complete mystery in the universe, but offered us clues to its energy connections in all sorts of unusual places:

Your Private Sky: the self-confidence with which Fuller said the sky under which he stood was his sky, and encouraged us to do the same, is also the attitude of an artist who produces something, not that of a scientist who recognises only what already exists. (29)

Fuller's views were informed by a deep sense of the metaphysical. He believed that humans should replicate the wisdom of nature's designs. His belief that 'the flow of energy through a system acts to organise that system' (30), gives a clue about how the 'others', as sources of alternative consciousness in human society, can add to the mix in our suburban blandscapes.

The 'tensegrity' principles that Fuller applied to energy in physical structures, to minimise use of materials and construction resources, were also relevant for people's connections: 'Nothing in the universe touches anything else. The Greeks misassumed that there was something called a solid…both micro-cosmically and macro-cosmi-cally nothing touches…(so) tension and tensegrity have no limit of clear spanning'. (31)

What we have yet to apply in human social 'mixes' is the understanding that 'don't fight forces, use them' (32), is a philosophy for bringing diverse people together, and not having to separate them for fear of their difference. The key is to provide appropriate environments in which to do that, and some suburban precincts achieve this mix well.

The 'others' are seen as 'health and welfare cases' by the system which applies the compromised values Fuller abhorred in the real-politik. But suburbs as places for lightening the links between people of difference, and allowing transfer of energy to enhance human occupation and interaction, are a whole different ball game. Fuller would applaud such a process unfolding.

In the updated version of Goldilocks and the Three Bears, that Fuller wrote and produced in twenty lithographs called *Tetrascroll*, when he was eighty years old, he had Goldilocks explain the laws of geometry in nature and the development of human civilisation from sea travel:

Goldy and the bears agree that the Austronesian water people constitute the prime on-going organism of human evolution, designed and conditioned by multimillion years of experience to withstand the mania of rationalised selfishness, and eventually capable through ever-more-with-ever-less artifacts of rendering altogether obsolete opportunistic myopia in general…selfishness can no longer be rationalised as inherently valid. (33)

The prospect of finding suburban circumstances where

the 'others' can be housed, integrated into education and work, and engaged in full social and celebratory spirit occasions, offers a scenario that is Fulleresque in dimensions. It is only when we see humanity take the risk of mixing difference and diversity, and supporting group mutual assistance as a way of community life, that we will reinvigorate the human spirit.

Imaginary homelands — what's your excuse?

Australian rock group, Midnight Oil, challenged suburban audiences for two decades, 'to get up and get on' with changing the world. These performers were serious about the way society had been eroded from the inside by selfishness and apathy, leeching away any active participation by its citizens.

Lead singer, Peter Garrett, often wore a T-shirt emblazoned with 'What's Your Excuse?'. It is bold stuff, and the 'others' would all agree, although they may feel threatened by the idea of having to 'extract the digit' themselves – as so many of us would.

But that is the life for future citizens who choose not to accept passive consumption of mediated images of democracy, while decisions affecting our world are made half a globe away. 'Think Global: Act Local' is a good way to start a rejuvenated civil life.

If you have trouble remembering why to bother, try Salman Rushdie's 1984 thoughts on the matter, (at the time he was reflecting on George Orwell's work, whose novel gave that date particular fame):

Returning to Henry Miller, Orwell takes up and extends Miller's comparison of Anais Nin to Jonah in the whale's belly.

'The whale's belly is simply a womb big enough for an adult... a storm that would sink all the battleships in the world would hardly reach you as an echo...Miller himself is inside the whale,...a willing Jonah...He feels no impulse to alter or control the process that he is undergoing. He has performed the essential Jonah act of allowing himself to be swallowed, remaining passive, 'accepting'. It will be seen what this amounts to. It is a species of quietism...

The truth is that there is no whale. We live in a world without hiding places; the missiles have made sure of that. However much we may wish to return to the womb, we cannot be unborn. So we are left with a fairly straightforward choice. Either we agree to delude ourselves, to lose ourselves in the fantasy of the great fish,...or we can do what all human beings do instinctively when they realise that the womb has been lost forever – that is, we can make the very devil of a racket. (34)

We have created this world the way it is. The 'others' are screaming already, and they can always do with some partners in the suburbs. And Rushdie provides reminders as to why those who experience difference are valuable cases for engagement for those in mainstream life:

It may be that when the Indian writer who writes from outside India tries to reflect that world, he is obliged to deal in broken mirrors, some of whose fragments have been irretrievably lost. But there is a paradox here. The broken mirror may actually be as valuable as the one which is supposedly unflawed...it (is) precisely the partial nature of these memories, their fragmentation, that made them so evocative for me. The shards of memory acquired greater status, greater resonance, because they were remains; fragmentation made trivial things seem like symbols, and the mundane acquired numinous qualities. (35)

The 'others' are symbols of aspects of all our lives that are worthy of reflection, protection and sharing. If more of us engaged with people of difference who show their inner natures, personal challenges, psychic and soulful paradoxes, we would all be able to grow richer in our shared understanding of life in the suburbs.

As Richard Wright found long ago in America, black and white descriptions of society are no longer compatible. Fantasy, or the mingling of fantasy and naturalism, is one way of dealing with these problems. It offers a way of echoing in the form of our work the issues faced by all of us: how to build a new, 'modern' world out of an old, legend-haunted civilisation, an old culture which we have brought into the heart of a newer one...we are at one and the same time insiders and outsiders in this society. This stereoscopic vision is perhaps what we can offer in place of 'whole sight'. (36)

While Rushdie was talking about expatriate writers, we can form an analogy with the 'others' in our suburban world. They experience life in the stereoscopic (or sometimes kaleidoscopic) perspective, which Bernard Smith has so valued in his review of Western art meeting antipodean expressions. What we can explore, in engaging with one another and finding our points of mutuality, is that territory for all humanity that rises up and out of the suburban morass. That hope for human potential which is helped by the experience of the 'others'.

Streets lit with cathode rays
in our global village suburb

For over thirty years, the closing of the urban-rural gap has been a topic of concern. At the same time, people have been using 'the village' as a salvationist descriptor, for what human beings need for their peace of mind and community, as an appropriately scaled living environment.

As we consider the place of the 'others' in 'normal' society, and the way 'normal' society could benefit from embracing the perspective the 'others' can give us about healthier ways of understanding the human condition, the village-suburb nexus is a place of strong focus. Former United States Vietnam War correspondent, Richard Critchfield, studied the notion of 'cultural loss' in village life, after deciding 'that it was knowledge of culture and character, not just battles, which often changed nothing, that would decide the issue of the (Vietnam) war'. (37)

What Critchfield discovered about origins of culture, change in cultural patterns, human nature and trends affecting Western consciousness, is directly relevant to our concerns with the 'others':

Overcrowding on the land, all kinds of scientific advances and the nearly universal spread of television have quite abruptly ended the old, autonomous, isolated and culturally self-contained village... (yet) No substitute for the rural basis of urban culture has yet been invented. In other words, rural life is the source, and the only source, of such aspects of our culture as religious beliefs, the agricultural moral code, the institutions of family and property, and the work ethic...All culture...has a rural origin. (38)

Something about this notion, which Hilary Clinton's work on *It Takes A Village* briefly brought to world notice, engages with the energy that the 'others' offer suburban life. Those people who are able and content to 'sit, wait and listen', provide a healthy heartbeat of soul in the midst of a society gone mad with 'busyness' and virtual reality. So do the 'fruit loops', drunks and suburban natives.

We have lost contact with just watching the folks go by on the street, chatting casually with neighbours, and allowing our shared energies to slow down. Jean Vanier invests in this as his total healing method in the L'Arche movement. And many urban and suburban people would love to find the ability to stop and reconnect with this style of being.

But back in the villages themselves, in developing nations, things are changing at a cracking pace. The arrival of television, phones, access to consumer goods and marketing are all creating pressures to change the family dynamic. Richard Critchfield tried to understand what forces were at play in influencing the evolution of village life, and he sought help from Arnold Toynbee's colleague and biographer, historian William H. McNeill:

McNeill sees human life and society resting on physiological (molecules), ecological (organisms) and semiological (symbols) balances. How we act from day to day, he says, depends on symbolic messages in and out that define our consciousness. Experience of what happens when we interact with the natural world feeds back into our vocabularies and concepts in such a way as to alter and correct, refine and redefine the symbols we use to guide our further behaviour. Science guides human actions today, just as theological and magical ideas did in the past. One wonders just how powerfully television will alter this process in the villagers' minds. (39)

The 'symbolic messages in and out' have become pretty distorted as a result of two things about television: its ubiquitous penetration into homes across the world; and its apparent 'no brainer' morals and manners. Despite censors being employed by television networks, the standard of presentation of news, entertainment and 'lifestyle' programs seems to keep degenerating. Fellow American journalist Michael J. Arlen (another person deeply engaged with the Vietnam War's effect on the world, and its televised presentation) looked into some outcomes of television's role and presence in 'civilised' lives.

The universal takeover of popular culture by American television is not complete yet. But it is the main modelling house for such products and presentation styles. And it pumps out the images, moods, styles and dreams, so that there is little room left for an individual to have dreams of their own. Consciousness has been colonised through the living rooms and tea shops of the world. Or one could think so.

What the 'others' are offering society is a reminder that life comes in varied experiences, rich in colour and movement, Feelings and Experiences. Something like what Raymond Williams and Bernard Smith were saying society needed and wanted. Can we hope that television will also package that and make it a program?

We have a strange way of fetishising suffering and making it a commodity that can be detached from our real lives. Ignored in the streets, cried over in the living rooms. But there is something missing in that assumption, because we are all connected through our consciousness, and so our shared experiences do count.

What comes as a natural follow-on to the admission that relationship is central to human life, is that the grounds for relationship need to be nurturing. People need to be able to meet in comfort – psychic, physical and social. Acceptance of difference needs to be part of the fabric, of the human waft and weave, not a principle adhered to by ideologically sound devotees of 'do-gooding', therefore resisted by folk who do not want to comply.

Chapter Nine

MANDORLA — the Overlap of Opposites

Mapping consciousness using allegory to make connections with each other and the world

Going Walkabout has explored some of the territory of the 'others'. They have perspectives of consciousness, and Structures of Feeling and Experience that are part of us all, and all of our parts. And they keep changing, just as we do.

By engaging with the 'others', we have access to a rich source of learning. Sometimes this Experience might scare us; sometimes it might unlock memories, causing shattering and emotional explosions we did not expect; at other times the experience might be numbing, silencing; or the source of passionate angry outbursts; or bursts of quiet joy and compassion for the whole world. We cannot predict and we cannot control. It is life in the raw.

In exploring the 'ontology of the unthought', Michel Foucault speaks of the unconscious as an 'obscure space', an 'element of darkness', which lies both inside and outside thought.

The unthought (whatever name we give it) is not lodged in man like a shrivelled-up nature or a stratified history; it is, in relation to man, the Other; the Other that is not only a brother but a twin, born, not of man, nor in man, but beside him and at the same time, in an identical newness, in an unavoidable duality. (1)

I am not suggesting that you go out to meet the 'others' in order to meet yourself, though that is certainly a likely result. The only way healing will happen is by adopting a position of respectful acceptance of our shared humanity. And waiting. Who knows what will happen when you listen to the boomerangs?

Of course, Zack was in a sense 'growing me up' too, as well as imparting to me something of the spirit of initiatory praxis. But in enacting this episode from his Dreaming, Zack was also revealing that knowledge is both mimetic and eidetic. He could not have actually embodied his Dreaming without possessing a keen first-hand knowledge of the behaviour of these marsupials in the wild. I was reminded of what Pincher Jampijinpa once said to me about myth. 'You learned them from the boomerangs.' In other words, one grasped the meaning of a myth not with the mind alone but through sitting on the ground, close to other initiates, the impact of the singing felt bodily along with the rhythmic clapping of the boomerangs. (2)

The 'others' extend this invitation: your own life, your family, your neighbours and your community are full of souls waiting to re-engage in this sharing. Just as Uncles Raymond and Bernard discovered — that what our culture and society were actually telling us all this time is that we have been preoccupied with the movement of modernism, rationalism, and egoism.

Being in 'this' moment offers the chance to engage with more than your own narrow view of life, the world and everything. The 'others' are everywhere, waiting for your arrival as friends.

For many people who have lost contact with the human community, engaging with one of the 'others' could open up their lives again – to mystery, to wholeheartedness, to surprise and wildness. We are not meant to be disinfected from our inherited amount of chaos. It is part of being human and alive. Likewise, we become unhealthy if our egos, wills and power driven intellects are allowed to continuously 'run the show'. It literally becomes 'a show'. Which is why politicians have made impression management into an art-form that passes for democratic representation of the people.

We need to activate that aspect of our lives in order to stay healthy. Staying in our natural, human, social milieu is good for us, just as too much of it (as Gao Xinjian says) can be stultifying and claustrophobically bad for us. Staying in our intellects alone, where ideas can run amok and ideals can magnify into dogma, is dangerous:

One thing that made a deep impression on me when I lived among the Kuranko was that knowledge was neither reduced to practical skills nor formulated as abstract principles. Knowledge was grounded in social being. It was a 'vita activa', a form of 'savoir faire', of knowing how to comport oneself socially with gumption, nous and common sense… The measure of understanding was thus unequivocally social. The same principle holds true in Maori New Zealand. Knowledge ('maatau-ranga') draws upon notions of 'oranga' (necessity for life) and 'taonga' (cultural wealth), suggesting that it is like the land through which one's identity is affirmed… knowing has no other value apart from sustaining the life of the community whose 'taonga' it is. (3)

My tendency to slip away from social being and drift into solo being is not ultimately healthy, either for society or me. If I had grown up with different 'elders', I would have been given the feedback not to allow such a trend to close me off to my people. The 'others' have this experience from both sides — sometimes too much togetherness, sometimes too little. We can learn from both ends of the spectrum, and celebrate our common humanity.

Ultimately, our social practices, formal policies and programs, will have to be better informed by the incorporation of this life knowledge into activities that are now managed for groups by 'the system'. This is especially true for marginalised and disempowered people, who cannot access independent activities and services.

In our global village, where irony has become fashionable, hyper-reality is celebrated without a hint of irony. Surrounded by self-referential signs, sound bites, and fetishised things, we have a long way to go if we are ever to regain a sense of that world of birth, death, initiation, pain, separation, and struggle, which precedes knowledge. (4)

Tell me the old story — allegory plots our path

The 'others' are allegorical presences, 'other narratives' in our world. In the same way that we are allegories for our families, friends, neighbours and workmates. People who know us learn from 'the stories of our lives'. The trick is to actively re-engage with difference and diversity. In the same way people do when they travel. They take time to talk with the milk bar staff, the bus conductor, and the seller of tea and coffee in the street. They make a decision to reach out to others and make a connection.

Robert Johnson, who revealed this notion of the

Mandorla connecting the overlapping aspects of life's mysteries, life's opposites, talks about what Carl Jung said on a related part of this story:

When the unstoppable bullet hits the impenetrable wall, we find the religious experience. It is precisely here that one will grow. Jung once said: 'Find out what a person fears most and that is where he will develop next.' The ego is fashioned like the metal between the hammer and the anvil. This is for the brave, and one does not easily find a moral or ethical nature strong enough for the process. Heroism could be redefined for our time as the ability to stand paradox. (5)

The 'others' shove that paradox right in our face, or even closer, right up our nose: whether you have a person who is living with mental illness in the family; or a neighbour who is living with intellectual disability who disarms you; or you are an alcoholic, controlaholic, workaholic, co-dependent-aholic (and still denying it); or your camping holiday is on the traditional land of an indigenous group and their ancestor spirits are stirring your soul for fun every night around the campfire – you are in it. Face it. Embrace it.

We all have lives that, every moment, are being invited into some form of closure: closing off from learning any more; shutting out the love we need and crave; or stopping ourselves from giving that love, in case we fail to do it right, or get hurt by rejection.

The 'others' face this every moment and they have to deal with it whether they like it or not. But, we can choose to hide:

The way to cowardice is to embed ourselves in a cocoon, in which we perpetuate our habitual patterns. When we are constantly recreating our basic patterns of behaviour and thoughts, we never have to leap into fresh air or onto fresh ground. (6)

The 'others' are our guides out of this stuck place. Like the one I enthusiastically get into when I am writing. Why shouldn't I stay in this world that I am creating? If we go on fooling ourselves that what our minds think is all there is, then we are limiting ourselves to a small number of options. When we engage with their Feelings and Experience, the 'others' remind of us just how stuck we are.

When we are faced with our fears, we can take note of the Twelve Step wisdom that tells us we have to do it for ourselves, but, we do not have to do it alone. There are guides around, some of them right in our backyards — the allegorical stories of our own and others' lives, including the 'others' who are shining the torch and showing the way.

Truth has no form. A change therefore is required. You must make a change within yourself, an internal change. You question the content of what you have put into your mind. You question that. In this questioning is the strength of integrity that helps you to undo. We all need to undo a great many concepts, fears, and doubts – the many, little knowings that have become our bondage and by which we live. We are always so 'sure', and yet we are divided, separated. A miracle, then, is that which ends the separation for that moment. (7)

What do we mean by healing through narrative?

The poet, Rainer Maria Rilke, had a gift for understanding life's rhythms and mysteries like few other Westerners. But his intuition and instinct were really only reflecting the quality predominant in most indigenous peoples. He saw that life was a story lived from us and through us, as much as it is visited upon us:

Because we are alone with the alien thing that has entered into our self; because everything intimate and accustomed is for an instant taken away; because we stand in the middle of a transition where we cannot remain standing…We could easily be made to believe that nothing has happened, and yet we have changed, as a house changes into which a guest has entered. (8)

So-called civilised life has robbed us of the element of mystery and surprise that gives life its ultimate purpose and motivation. Without surprise, who could be bothered? This is one of the secrets known by indigenous people, and practised in their daily lives.

It is also an aspect of the lived experience of the 'others', who, I believe, are born, or enter into, a life on the margins of civilisation, with a consciousness linked to the Dreaming, and who have access to levels of truth that 'normal' people no longer hear. Hawaiian healer and kupuna (teacher) Angeline Locey explains:

Hawaiians speak on three different levels. There's the mundane (physical), the symbolic, and then there's the spiritual level. There are meanings on all these levels. That's the way it is with the body too. Feeling happens on a cellular level. While we are loving the body, we are healing on a cellular level. (9))

The stories we tell, the stories we participate in, and

the stories we inherit, are all part of our larger human story. Rilke provides encouragement for us to see life in a more indigenous way:

The future enters into us in this way in order to transform itself in us long before it happens. And this is why it is so important to be lonely and attentive when one is sad: because the apparently uneventful and stark moment at which our future sets foot in us, is so much closer to life than that other noisy and fortuitous point of time, at which it happens to us as if from outside. (10)

This is one of the functions of 'going walkabout', to recommune with the story that is telling us. Rilke somehow knew that humans are meant to surrender to the unfolding of a narrative, over which we have 'control' by submitting to its natural process.

We will also gradually learn to realise that, that which we call destiny, goes forth from/within people, not from without into them! Only because so many have not absorbed their destinies and transmuted them within themselves while they were living in them, have they not recognised what had gone forth out of them; it was so strange to them , that, in their bewildered fright, they thought it must only just then have entered into them, for they swear never before to have found anything like it in themselves. As people have long mistaken about the motion of the sun, so they are even yet mistaken about the motion of that which is to come. (11).

Going Walkabout through the Suburbs follows a process that respects mystery and seeking to remain open to the messages provided in the lives of the 'others'. They are marginalised and require justice, but they also own

Experiences and Feelings that are significant healers for our community. We should all take our life stories much more seriously, and forget our egotistical self-deluding concerns at the same time. Just watch and listen to what the universe has to tell us. As James Cowan saw among the desert people:

Exoteric story telling had an important role to play in the continuing process of cultural renewal, particularly since the myth-making process had ceased at the end of the Dreaming...The role of the storyteller for each Dreaming site around the Rock (Uluru in the Northern Territory of Australia) was always left in the hands of the man who had been 'possessed by' his respective Dreaming, usually at birth. (12)

Living life as story

Humans are meant to be in touch with our stories, to be conscious of them. When Aboriginal people ask: where are you from? They mean who are you? Or, what is your country? Whitefellas are increasingly learning that their country is the life experience they have come through in returning to an awareness that they need to re-connect with place, spirit, metaphor and blood. And the experience of the 'others' offers a pathway back to reconnecting with our original poetic natures:

What the elders taught me was simple, even if it was difficult at first to understand. People are, in their most profound aspect, creatures of poetry. They like to make up stories out of the deep metaphors of existence. These metaphors are a part of our physical environment and resist all our attempts to make them rational. They are bridges to the irrational, that well of supra-sensibility that we go to at times when we experience thirst. (13)

Stewarding our stories

Narrative is a healing and a re-birth of meaning. So, in telling the stories of the 'others', it is not about judgement, being patronising or placing people in categories, it is an acknowledgment of the human experience, that brokenness is part of the norm:

Likan and bundurr (connected respectively with common words for elbow and knee) are words which label and enable the linkages within Yolgnu reality. They are what keep the Yolgnu cultural body moving. They can be understood as naming the connecting and articulating points within the complex web of relatedness in which stands every individual, group, totem, song, plant, animal and piece of land, and into which everyone and everything is born. (14)

Perhaps now, you can see how this is an indication of the human tradition — stewarding our stories, taking responsibility for our real human affairs in relation to country, family and our roles within that web:

So far as Yolgnu are concerned, there is no single universal structure suspended over the whole of Yolgnu life, it is the absence of this structure which allows individual groups to articulate their separate identity, and ties them into their particular histories and geographies. In fact throughout Yolgnu philosophy, identity can be seen to derive as much from ruptures within the overall system as from the system itself. (15)

Reading the symbols and signifiers of the universe

David Mowaljarlai, of the Ngarinyin people of the northeast Kimberley region in Western Australia, has a gift (to rejuvenate human culture) — spirit power or 'wungud': 'Your culture is based on economics, my culture is based on art'. (16)

'Mowaljarlai sees black and white coming together to work towards a new law. A new 'wurnan' (relationship between people and land) is needed to rebalance our being here on earth. Mowaljarlai's people have been marginalised through colonisation, dispossession and despair since the arrival of Europeans on their land:

Relocated to the townsite of Derby in a camp called Mowanjum... people have taken to the trappings of socio-economic subjugation, sex and alcohol, indulging in escapisms during the limitless separation from culture and identity. (17)

But Mowaljarlai, and Paddy Neowarra (his kinship son), and their fellow custodians of the Wandjina paintings — world famous as evidence of the world's oldest culture — are applying traditional wisdom to rejuvenating the culture of their people. Through their Bush University, the Kamali Lands Council and Ngarinyin Aboriginal Corporation, they are advocating a communion between black and white cultures.

The key perspective Ngarinyin people apply to their daily life, the rhythm of their awareness, is that the primal energy of the universe (the 'wungud') spreads across the country in a pattern for which they are responsible'. As Mowaljarlai explains:

'Wungud is the beginning, it's where we come from, our life, Wandjina (the paintings and their magic) is wunguna, it gives us sweet waters. Without sweet waters, we die.' Wungud is the primal energy source. The land is the body of which the (Wandjina) paintings are merely points. The Ngarinyin are lawmen of wurnan. Wurnan is the system of responsibility for protecting the symbols that protect the transmission of energy patterns through the country. (18)

This knowledge is echoed by Raymond Williams in *Culture*, in which he concludes that modern civilisation has resulted in culture becoming predominantly a 'signifying system', compared with his earlier thoughts about culture being a 'whole way of life'. He assessed that society had become so multi-layered and influenced that 'no aspect of cultural production is itself wholly specialised, for it is always…an element of a quite general social and cultural production and reproduction. This is why the strictly "intellectual" functions can not be isolated'. (19)

Williams saw that human affairs were organised in a system of 'signifying relations'. This is the same as David Mowaljarlai's relationship with his country, its stories and art, and the stewarding responsibilities held by his people. Something has become divorced from the indigenous way of running this set of responsibilities and their organic link with the rhythm of daily life.

It is not only that intelligence, in the most general sense, is involved in all social and productive activities. It is also that 'ideas' and 'concepts'…are both produced and reproduced in the whole social and cultural fabric: at times directly as ideas and concepts, but also more widely in the form of shaping institutions, signified social relations, religious and cultural occasions, modes of work and performance: indeed in the whole signifying system and in the system which it signifies. (20)

Here we have the connection between a cultural analyst's understanding, and that of the people of the first nation. The connection between signifying systems is direct and relevant to how we rebuild communion in our community — by finding ways to regain responsibility for the patterns of meaning and continuity of spirit which inspire our lives as a group of social beings.

So far we have succeeded in making so much of this 'abstract', in terms of ideas, notions and concepts, that most people have lost touch with their communion with the universe. The result of this is fragmented, dis-eased lives.

We may rejuvenate our numen and heal our disaffected souls with a return to the process of ritually connecting life with its symbols and signals of meaning. This would mean returning to their rightful place the responsibilities we should all be allowed to carry, for our shared communion with the mystery and wonder of God, the universe, our higher selves.

As Raymond Williams saw in 1981: 'Indeed the social system and the signifying system can only ever be abstractly separated, since they are in practice, over a variable range, mutually constitutive'. (21) It is time we rejoined them.

The voice of the infinite in the small

From Joanne Lauck's writing on *Revisioning the Insect-Human Connection* (after which the title of this section is named), we can pick up some final clues about symbolism

in our totemic journey back to noeisis, poesies, numinosity, enchantment, call it what you may:

*In establishing our basic attitude toward the world around us
we might simply reflect on the awakening of consciousness in
our earliest years. As soon as we awaken to consciousness, the
universe comes to us, while we go out to the universe. This intimate presence of the universe to itself in each being is the deep
excitement of existence. (22)*

The story goes round and comes round again. The 'others' are just another form of the allegorical way in which
the higher power gives us the clues to the mystery in this
universe we share:

*After differentiating, all things turn back to that primordial
unity where each is fulfilled in the others. To go far is to come
near. Such is the basic law of existence. We are at the moment
of turning. (23)*

Beetles, weevils, cockroaches, flies, caterpillars, butter-
flies, bees, spiders, ants, you name it, Joanne Lauck has
had a close look at and made friends with these creatures.
It is the same process we are undertaking — to see beyond the surface impression, and find the Feeling that
resides in symbol, metaphor, and universal life energy
shared between creatures, plants, rocks and all God's
creations in the universal energy of space.

Some of that territory is not so comfortable. Joanne's
deep engagement with the insect 'queendom' shows us
patterns and maps to consciousness that are directly illustrative of our journey with the 'others':

*When an archetype is activated it releases a power comparable
to the power released by splitting the atom. The resulting energy*

restructures external events and aligns our inner, subjective worlds with them... The psychological and symbolic aspects of our fascination with the dangerous creatures are complex but have a common denominator. They are all connected with a push toward psychological maturity and the cultivation of certain qualities – process of inner growth, a turning toward our soul of true nature, that Carl Jung called individuation. (24)

There are direct parallels with the 'others' here. Each group of 'others' sparks fear in some 'normal' people. Although no one has done anything wrong, there is an energy of negativity in the air between them. Something archetypal is occurring, just as it does when we travel into 'dangerous country' inhabited by 'wild beasts' or 'dangerous creatures':

We sense in the potentially dangerous creature real power, and, unless we panic, we are likely to quiet our own noisy thoughts and restlessness and try to match its depth of silence. Sometimes our well being depends upon how well we match it. Silence in the presence of such power is the only appropriate response, because it anchors us to our own centre, where the power can be matched and used to transform and initiate us. (25)

If you bear with this allegorical story a little longer you may see, feel, hear, and sense what is similar in our engagement with the 'others'. We are really talking about ourselves, not the scorpion, or the person who lives with mental illness.

What is often humbled in painful encounter with another creature, especially a small creature like a scorpion, is the self-important, inflated parts of ourselves.

Those parts mask our general fear of the unknown and our

resistance to the pain of being overcome and changed. 'Forget about transformation and renewal,' protests our personality who fights for order and predictability. I suspect our task, and a monumental one at that, is not to withhold ourselves or defend ourselves from that which would help us grow strong and help us move close to our true natures. 'What we choose to fight is so tiny, what fights with us is so great,' Rilke reminds us in 'The Man Watching'. (26)

What is emerging in this tale is the way other creatures, people, and the results of our engagement with them, can be our greatest teachers and profoundly enrich our lives — if we manage to find the humility to let it happen.

In shamanic traditions it was understood that other species are way-showers to the mysteries and messengers for the divine powers operating within us and within the universe. We can neither appease nor bargain with them. Their task in dreaming and waking is to arouse us out of our complacency and push us past the edge of what is familiar and comfortable.

Life 'in your face' is like the drunk who scams you for a fiver to buy his last drink, or like the junkie looking to score who is desperate for your assistance and annoyed when you are not forthcoming. Or, when you engage with an Aboriginal person in close circumstances and their natural earthedness and belonging disturbs your equanimity for days. Likewise, a person who lives with intellectual disability can invade your complacent space and leave you wondering about who they are, who you are and what is going on?

Our gift for each other, of soul, wanders the streets, sits in the homes of those who are worse off, and waits for us to find it in a mutual search for soul. It is a process we are invited to everyday, but most of us try to avoid the pain of 'fronting up'.

Australian novelist, Tim Winton, made this observation about the time our 'exploring European discoverers came' (to a land inhabited by our Aboriginal people for thousands of years):

He feels himself within himself. There's nothing left of him now but shimmering presence. This pressing in of things. He knows he lives and that the world lives in him. And for him and beside him. Because and despite and regardless of him. A breeze shivers the fig. The rock swallows the quoll. He sings. He's sung. (27)

What we need is a commitment to make more shared space available in our world, so that more of us can join in the experience that helps us all 'sing and be sung', as equal souls in our inheritance, in our Feelings and Experience.

Chapter Ten

Diamonds and dust

The value in difference

Exploration into the lives of the 'others' has shown us that we need to value difference and discover ways to accept it in our everyday lives. Accepting difference is about the balance that comes from embracing the collaborative energy of life which pulses within apparent dualities.

I believe progress can be achieved by borrowing the yoga challenge 'to address your resistance'. In this way we can embrace new perspectives about how to make better use of the positives and negatives in individual lives and within society.

People who live with mental illness

Chaos freeing up 'control'

Chaos is part of the natural mystery and wonder of the universe. Perhaps that is why other people feel deeply disturbed when chaos is apparent in the behaviour of people who live with mental illness. This energy touches something deep and universal among humans. So if it is possible to 'sit with' fear long enough to let the chaos ride itself out, a natural process will be allowed to work, like with a bushfire, flood, tornado or earthquake. Society can benefit from accepting the chaos in mental illness, by not viewing it so much as a pathology, but simply as a different state. Freud said the First World War was a symptom of the repression of the strongest and deepest feelings of ordinary people. That humanity had ended up living 'psychologically beyond their means'. (1)

This understanding is applicable to the way mental health, rehabilitation and recovery programs are designed and delivered — to allow natural energy to move through people, and as Anne Wilson Schaef (*Living In Process*) says, we should let people go through their process. We can learn a great deal by allowing fearful feelings to be expressed.

Mess can help remove obsession

'Mess' originated from the Latin 'missus', a course at a meal, from 'mittere', to send (2). It signified sharing food. In Pondicherry, India, people's eating houses are called a 'mess' (as it is in the military tradition). We all need to relax more with mess. Me included. It feeds something in the soul which has been starved by the ordered efficiency of modernism. Some great insights occur out of messy thinking. If people are allowed to stretch their mess just enough to know how it feels, some positive results can come from such 'disorganised situations'.

We need to allow diversity in consciousness to inform our thinking and planning about change and development. As well as this, we need to understand that keeping policies and programs neat and ordered may be the exact opposite of what a well informed doctor would order for effective rehabilitation among people who live with mental illness.

Wisdom rising from the shadows

Another aspect of mystery in human life is the shadow or dark side. All people have it, and when someone goes 'mad', they reflect the worst fears of those who know that their own dark side lurks not far from the surface. It is healthy to accept mystery as part of reality. Some spiritual teachings say that your life is just 'maya', an illusion. Mental health recovery happens when both mystery and shadow are faced.

To generate healthier conversation in 'healing circles' about the shadow side of all humans is to allow the energy to flow safely. American Indian teaching says that the dreaming occurs in the shadow — the way some people, such as Australian Aboriginal people, with advanced awareness and initiation, can use a transcendent state to 'dream someone', or influence them without their knowing it.

Some serious shamanising around

Magic is one thing modernism set out to challenge. Yet many inventions of modernism seem exactly that — aeroplanes, electricity, computers, satellites, the Internet. Mental illness can give rise to shaman-like states, where individuals are given powers of prophecy and apparent understanding of mystery. This is unplanned, and certainly uninvited by health authorities. But, we should explore whether we can be more respectfully attentive to the passing awareness states that people experience (this was R.D. Laing's approach). It does not mean pretending to earn a shaman's wisdom, but to respect different states of consciousness as valid.

This aspect of mystery traverses into wonder, where awe and humility are inspired. Not great features of modernism's project which wants results, now, under control of logic and will power. While not claiming that delusional states are shamanistic, I believe we need more respectful listening to what people are experiencing to help them process their energy into a more balanced place. Shaman energy is 'out in left field'. It provides a perspective on life that is not the norm. Having seen people experiencing altered states of consciousness, I believe they were processing healthy mind stretching, and afterwards, they were able to place their experience within a framework of self-understanding.

Fantasy invites the unknown

Creating images and ideas from an unrestricted imagination is one definition of fantasy. It is ironic that a world producing megabytes of virtual reality, would be frightened of the fantasies that people who live with mental illness might undergo from time to time. Freud's reflections on the way the nation state 'forbids wrongdoing and violence, not, however, in order to abolish it, but in order to monopolise it', (3) is telling. Reminiscent of the array of new laws emerging against all sorts of human misbehaviour, and the subsequent growth in privatised prisons. We seem to be so afraid of breaking out and experiencing fantasy states, that we legislate and regulate to protect ourselves from our own darker sides. We need to trust the human condition more and listen for what lessons might be coming from these different states of human consciousness, from experiences of 'non-ordinary reality'.

Perhaps the prospect of people experiencing fantasies could be seen as a permissible part of the journey of healing, rather than something to be repressed with drugs. The root word for fantasy is the Greek 'phantos' (4), meaning visible. Bringing people's inner views to light, in safe environments, could be a healthy safety valve for society.

People who live with intellectual disability

Refreshment from fallow ground

'Idle, unsown, dormant or inactive' (5) are all definitions of fallow, which seems applicable to what most people in modern life need — time out. Too much time out can be wasteful. This is often the experience of people who live with intellectual disability, especially in regard to their being contributors to their own development. But the concept of tapping their fallowness and sharing this energy with others, is what Jean Vanier has been celebrating in the L'Arche houses for decades.

If more people can be invited into sharing time with people who live with intellectual disability, there will be an automatic benefit for both parties. People who cannot stop suddenly have no other choice. And they say it is heavenly, once they learn to stop feeling guilty. As Jean Vanier said, when inviting Henri Nouwen to join a L'Arche community: 'Why don't you come and waste some time with us?' (Nouwen) There are benefits in remembering to learn the lesson of stopping, and then quiet listening. As Stockton urges us, 'do dadirri' — sit, wait and listen.

The kiss from an open heart

'To touch with the lips as a mark of affection or greeting'. (6) In Maori culture it is touching foreheads at the 'third eye' spot, in order to share the energy of soul and 'catch up with each other'. But, in Western culture, the kiss is vulnerable to being colonised by romantic imagery, where it certainly has a place, but not exclusively. 'Affection and greeting' are exactly what people who live with intellectual disability teach others to remember, as an ordinary exchange of unconditional love. We need more of this kind of exchange in our everyday connections between people who seem starved of affection in their frantic chase for success or survival in modern life.

In a world full of competition, open-heartedness has been turned into a naive weakness. But, just as Jean Vanier points out, people are worn out with being alone, many people yearn for open-hearted connections with one another. This is not Gemeinschaft nostalgia. It is responsible humanness.

Childlike wonder restores hope

'Marked with the innocence and trust associated with children.' (7) 'Innocence' almost feels like a dirty word in today's version of modernity. When corruption is rife across the political and corporate sectors, people become numb to notions of softness and vulnerability. But, if humanity is to reclaim its fullness, such values and behaviours need to be advocated and practiced among all people. People who live with intellectual disability are powerhouses of innocence and trust, ready to top up those who have forgotten how to do it, be it, give it and receive it.

The sharing of ordinary 'life time' can renew harrowed business people, administrators, and young people looking for a way out of the veneer of cynicism they picked up in response to the adults they observed while growing up. My risk taking, by advocating such concepts, reflects the strength of what I know from sharing life's journey with these folk, and learning more from them every day.

Freed by the incredible lightness of being like a feather

An Australian friend of mine, Peter Tumminello, who is a world leading innovative homoeopath, is currently 'proving' the energy of 'feather' as a possible homoeopathic remedy. This may seem weird to those unfamiliar with homoeopathy, but then new awareness makes for interesting Feelings and Experience. There is, within 'the light horny outgrowths that form the external covering of a bird's body' (8) some real magic. Not the stuff modernism set out to remove. The stuff it has yet to engage with. The miracle of flight rests between the fronds of a feather, the energy of uplift and freedom.

There is a message for us in the fractal nature of life, in which all things are connected and 'the whole is in the part, and the part in the whole'. People who live with intellectual disability carry a potential. They have a way of inviting others to open their hearts. It is enlightening to see a harried shopkeeper or bureaucrat meet a person who lives with intellectual disability and release their pressing worry. Somehow they are allowed to do unconsciously, what they would not do for 'normal' folk. This feather energy of soul is a valuable commodity. Not to be exploited, to be shared.

Surrendering to the mystery

The mystery of life's lottery is what baffles many people during their struggling years, of 'making it', and then bemuses them during their redundant (modernism's latest version of forced retirement) years. A more universally 'indigenous' sense of life, would have us all able to accept mystery, and surrender to it as part of life's gift. Not experience it as threat. People who live with intellectual disability invite that learning. They do not even charge to teach it. Many successful, over-stressed, harried people need to learn the value in surrendering more to life's unknowns. Learning and accepting that we are not in control could be the ultimate salvation of Western society.

Addicted

Curing modernism's infectious dis-ease

If 'ease' means 'freedom from pain, discomfort or anxiety' (9), then, 'dis-ease' is the exact opposite. Like the old blues song, *Easy Street*, life would be so easy if we could just get to live on easy street. Under the influence of profit making, advertising feeds modern citizens the notion that life will be like that, if they just consume enough of the right stuff. In pursuit of good business, the media has performed its task excellently, and now modern citizens are stuck with habits of consumption they find hard to give up. Addiction is the magnified version of what happens when the dis-ease cannot be fixed.

Acknowledging this aspect of consciousness is not only important in healing mental illness, it sits at the heart of modernism's current discomfort with itself. The cure lies in letting out the Feelings and Experiences that drive the addictive desire. That comes through honest sharing, telling stories that help heal oneself and others, in our community of souls.

Finding a way to watch the itch

Understanding how to watch discomfort, bear pain, and enter into delayed gratification with a feeling of gratitude, may sound crazy. Yet, in order to balance their lives, that is what people pursue to great lengths. Vipassana meditation training, which has come down from Buddha, is experiencing great interest in the West. People know they need to learn to watch the itch, not scratch it. Addicts are here to help teach us that. Shunning their experience, is like scratching itself. It refuses to hear the message, that things need to be, in cricketing parlance, 'let go through to the keeper' of the soul.

Healing the scabs by not scratching

Finding alternative sources of supply does not just come from meditation. Moderns need reminding that life is for other purposes than earning, consuming, doing and fretting. Sharing, conversing, imagining and seeing in perspective, are ways of deepening what can make a life. Seeking expansion of life through risk taking will ultimately help stop the scratching and help us lift something off us, rather than continue to indulge in self-destructive habits.

Seeing through card tricks

The trickster is a major figure in the archetypal canon. This teaching says that part of each of us is unconsciously trying to trick ourselves into mistakes, crazy blow outs, things we would normally not venture to do. (O'Connor, von Franz) Addicts are the prime examples of giving in and following the trickster. I should know, I have been there many times myself. Self-delusion is part of the modern condition. It leads to existential angst and further addictive behaviours.

Openly sharing this part of ourselves would do us the world of good. This can be achieved by incorporating such sessions into rehabilitation and recovery work for people who live with mental illness, where they can 'let it rip' with the full gamut of stories about the trickster's inner tales of grandeur and self-deception. Something like this happens in Twelve Step meetings that are working to their full potential.

Renewing the escape hatches

It has been said that addiction is modernity's rite of passage. The corollary to that is how to replace such a destructive habit with something life-building. What has been missing for the past few generations, especially since the Second World War, is the role of taking responsibility for something in our society. We need to relate to the community in a way that defines a role for ourselves. That is the indigenous passage. It will fill the void previously taken up by the escape habit. Finding such roles in the relational world is the challenge in forming rehabilitation and recovery programs for people who live with mental illness and intellectual disability. The need is to get beyond nominalism into something actual.

Indigenous

White people getting a dreaming

Indigenous people have many troubles in modern times. Forming relationships with them allows a perspective on what is still possible in human awareness. The Dreaming is a reality beyond modernism, although one could suggest that ostensibly, its 'front' has been to 'sell the modern Dreaming'. Transcendent consciousness, exercised by indigenous people remaining in touch with their heritage of spirit, has much to teach the rest of humanity. And a lot to offer healing programs for those living with mental illness. By learning to listen to the elders and learn the respect for spirit and place, people who live with mental illness can be encouraged to open themselves towards healing. This is not a form of neo-colonial, 'cultural tourism', it is serious cross-cultural relational exchange. A matter of discernment and honesty. Uncle Jurgen's territory.

Getting down and getting earthy

Earthing ourselves is a powerful metaphor for modernity. Full of the electricity of change and movement, we need a release into mother earth to get some relaxation of spirit. People who live with mental illness are full of this 'electric eels' feeling. But, so are half the executives running our world, and many people are buzzing inside their homes with frenetically paced lives. By designing programs to 'get down', I believe it will be possible to assist people living with mental illness to take hold of some of their unhealthy over-charged energy. Not just by taking Outward Bound courses and bashing cushions. But by developing a listening relationship with the earth, forming reverent relationships with place. They need to celebrate those in some ritualistic ways, which develop meaning and significance specific to them.

Critics will no doubt see 'the Jungle Jim of Gemeinschaft', donning the loincloth and reaching for the tree vine. I am not suggesting 'going native'. This is a simple matter of small domestic rituals, and personal development of gestures towards meaning and connection. In Uncle Jurgen's words, the intention counts, and the four-way test works as well with truly meant symbols as with the real thing. This is another process to be designed for healing people's illness, but suggested for anyone seeking a new opening of awareness and refreshment of spirit. It could also come to life through public sector agencies.

'That's my blood down there'

Forget genetics, I am interested in seeing a reconnection with the energy of blood. Only, these transfusions are not 'in the arm', but in the spirit. This miraculous energy carrying substance sustains all humanity and links us with nature. Through the shared chelated molecular structure, from humus, to photosynthesis, chlorophyll to haemoglobin. In symbolic terms, this is a connection with the iron of life, the electrochemical essence of humanity's link with the sun, where all earth's energy originates.

Forming groups that talk about, act out, celebrate, ritualise and share the 'stuff of life', puts us 'in the bloodline'. This way of meeting with all types of different ethnic groups and indigenous peers is a path to healing for people who have lost connection with their fellow humans. We build perspective by remembering our one-ness in diversity, through the blood of humanity.

Whispering echo

Songlines in the two-way Dreamtime. A concept that covers so much territory that it is only necessary to refer to its link with healing. People who have lost connection with their core self, and their peers, can somehow make connection with the notions of an informed universe working through songlines. There may be pathways across the country which trace the stories of the gods, the ancestors, the creation spirits. And they are accessible today, if we open our minds and use our imagination.

For people who live with mental illness, whose imaginations have been having a field day, this is territory where you need to wait until they are feeling balanced and grounded. Then, on the way out into their re-enchanted life, I believe it is possible to explore ways of connecting with this part of universal humanness. One way, is through the simple choice of a totem: animal, plant or place. This may not work for some people, but it is possible with other rituals, to engage with each individual's way of imagining their link with the higher power, and through its values, to the higher good. It is part of the echo of humankind, in the spirits going round in the timeless zone.

'You don't belong here!'

Individualism is one of the attractions of Western life: 'I', before 'we'. But it comes at the cost of belonging. All of us yearn to belong. That is why we buy designer label clothes, to be seen as the same among our peers.

The downside of individualism is loneliness. Cities are jammed full with lonely individuals.

Indigenous people can manage to be both individual **and** belong to a supportive community, where 'family' means 'my people'. That is how I, and many of my peers, are choosing to live these days. It is one way in which those who live with mental illness can be encouraged to form new relationships in community. People who live with intellectual disability already seem to have this. They somehow have an innate way of automatically forming extended family groups. But some individuals need help with this, diversity is across all aspects of the disability community.

Diamonds – a model for feelings and experience

Picturing the process of mind

Models and formulae have been part of modernism's fascination with 'understanding' and 'capturing' information. Whilst I am sceptical of models, I believe this work suggests one. Borrowing from Buckminster Fuller, one of the great futurists, I have created a diamond shaped model, to combine the five pointed contributions from Uncles Raymond and Bernard. Last century, Fuller made a major discovery when he developed his 'Jitterbug Transformation'. (10) By combining two geometric conceptions and realising their combined energy capturing and strength bearing potential, he opened up new dimensions in architecture and industrial design.

Thus were born a multitude of modern devices, processes and ways of thinking. I use the analogy of Uncle

Buckminster's process (named after the American dance craze of the time) when partners would jive and swing each other to and fro. This visual concept of energy exchange provides an image I like to use when I imagine the energy of consciousness going around in our awareness. Fuller said that 'how nature builds' is the way that humans should replicate the wisdom in its designs. He believed that the 'flow of energy through a system acts to organise that system'. (11) This is a simple illustrative concept, which can be used to create new parameters for meeting human needs. And of understanding where differences in consciousness sit, on the 'jiving' cycle of 'normal' movement in human Feelings and Experience.

Fuller emphasised 'emphemeralisation', 'doing the most with the least'. This harnessing of energy, has an equivalent in the points of engagement with the Structure of Feelings and Experience.

Fuller's philosophy was 'don't fight forces, use them' (12), similar to the principles in Eastern martial arts, such as judo and karate. The message here, for understanding human consciousness, is that it is better to 'go with' than 'go against'. So, finding points of engagement and cooperation, sharing and exchange, are more natural and healing, than suppressing with drugs or isolating.

Just as Fuller believed 'there was a regularity function at the deepest levels', I believe there is a shared energy of life, and a 'circumference of consciousness expansion' by combining the two five-pointed models drawn from the perspectives of Uncles Raymond and Bernard. With the merging of these shared aspects, I see these two five-pointed summary focus points, joined dot-to-dot, forming a diamond shaped model. It creates an eight-sided, six-pointed reflection of human consciousness. This is a serious metaphorical way of considering the subject at hand. Engaging and contextualising the Feelings and Experience of two marginalised groups, to create more empowered lifeworlds, but working 'with them' to address their inner needs.

So while being metaphorical, this is also a practical exercise in helping to see the dimensions of opportunity for regenerating human Feeling and Experience, expression and fulfilment. The 'swinging crystal model of consciousness', from the model Fuller used to conjure up his energy and tension synergies with integrity of form – tensegrity. I envisage the energy flows and swings, which apply here, as two poles of a diamond's furthest points interchanging, within the integrity of consciousness.

The four-pointed belt of the 'waist' of the diamond is circulating. The two apex points are oscillating, constantly shifting the energy with life's changes. The four energies of noetic awareness move from highs to lows, intense to fallow, dark to light, front to back, side to side and so on. Multi-perspective and multi-relational. The two peak poetic energies express the transcendent aspects of consciousness.

Sharing the energy of awareness

First, we can consider the shared four-pointed 'waist' of the diamond shape, formed by bringing the bases of the two Raymond and Bernard pyramid shapes together. There are four points of agreed focus on human Feelings and Experience between these uncles. And they are essential for healthy, balanced lives. They are presented here with a balancing set of collaborating yin and yang, light and dark 'opposing energies', with mention of examples of attributes of consciousness from the four subject groups, seen merging with these points of shared awareness (none of this is claimed to be comprehensively representative — it is only a catalyst, a starting point for thought and further conversation).

1. **Relational** — Sharing for the Common Good, in a Working Culture with Practical Activity, Belonging, Co-operating, Responsible for one another.

- Aspects from the four subject groups that fit here may be: Belonging (indigenous); Sharing Dreaming (indigenous); Kiss energy (people who live with intellectual disability); finding new Roles and Responsibilities, ie. Passages (for addicts); and Lack of relationships (people who live with mental illness).
- Some balancing 'opposites' in this area, to be given room for healthy 'processing' are: Rejection, Anger, Aggression and Hate.

2. **Perspective** — Where Experience allows Difference and Truth to Combine in Plurality — Leading to Truth, Acceptance and Oneness in Diversity.

I believe establishing processes, which respectfully encourage difference in life perspectives, is another area of priority. This could mean creating services that mix people of different disabilities or illnesses, with enough support services to be able to interrelate and interact safely and effectively within their limitations. Living circumstances that allow different levels of disability, illness and support service need to be met, in order that communities of varied perspective can be valued. This is creating wealth in plural social capital, and potential for stronger, healthier lives.

- Aspects from the four subject groups here are: Mess, 'out-of-orderness' (people who live with mental illness); Fallow (people who live with intellectual disability); Blood connection with earth and each other (indigenous); Watching the itch, observing (a lesson from addicts).
- Some balancing energies are: Obsession, Prejudice, Separation, Judgement and Blame.

3. **Conversation** — Shared in the 'Cultural Traffic' of Life, it is how Knowledge is Negotiated, Leading to Exchange of Empathy and Understanding.

Creating circumstances, where interaction and communication are the reasons for coming together, requires deliberate decision-making. Group decision-making, problem-solving, and working the concept of community into action. These values need to be acknowledged and allowed to emerge into daily practice, in a way determined by the participants, not some outside 'authority'. Thus valuing the lives and views of the participants, and creating a stronger community among them. Such is life's cultural traffic and its way of sharing and evolving knowledge and wisdom.

- The four subject groups provide perspectives here, such as: The Trickster (addicts); Sharing Stories, joyful and sad (people who live with intellectual disability); Dis-ease in communicating (addicts); Echo-logical awareness shared between people and the earth (indigenous); and No one listening (people who live with mental illness).

- Balancing energies here could be: Isolation, Paranoia, Loneliness, and Ignoring others.

4. **Imagination** — The Primary human activity, expressed and exchanged through Communal Celebratory Signification, which includes Creativity, Inspiration and Intuition.

Combining for group story-telling, music-making, song, dance, celebration of good spirit. This is a universal human need, too often ignored and replaced by passive consumption of media productions. People who live with intellectual disability and mental illness can really 'get down', and the healing, restorative effects of such gatherings, provides evidence to the wider society of its need to reclaim a full experience of community. The issue is that time, money and intention have to be devoted to valuing these sorts of activities, and honouring their symbolic and affective role in nurturing communities. Such priorities have to be consciously reset in order for society to recognise them again.

- Some aspects from the four subject groups revealed here are: Shaman energy (people who live with mental illness); Earthed feeling (indigenous); Risk growing (addicts); Fantasy tripping (people who live with mental illness); Childlike wonder (people who live with intellectual disability)); and Building one's own life by valuing what is (people who live with intellectual disability).
- Balancing energies could be: Self-delusion; Psychosis; Nightmares; and Groups creating 'mirage' experiences.

Balancing on life's swings and roundabouts

The above four aspects of human life, the 'compass points' of Feelings and Experience, or consciousness, are only illustrative. But I believe they point the way for helping people who live with mental illness and intellectual disability to claim their rights to improve their lifeworlds. The way society responds to their need for these engagements with life, and the resulting Feelings and Experiences, can be a strength for humanity or a weakness. Too often decisions are made, allegedly in the interests of 'efficiency and effectiveness', which are denying these core aspects of people's life needs.

The task now is to find ways to reintroduce such experiences into the lives of these two groups, and for many 'normal' people to explore whether they have the courage to follow the same examples and give vent to their true inner natures. This would be a valuable acknowledgment of how much more can be experienced by everyone — if the marginalised in our society, and those aspects inside ourselves, are served with proper respect, safe from ridicule, judgement and artificial 'protection' in the name of 'official due process'.

Finding this ability to 'swing free' in our consciousness, can come much more easily if we follow the two other points on the tips of the pyramids, creating a 'soul tensegrity' diamond. At the apex and base of the diamond are the two main energies. They are identified as the peak points for concentrating the rejuvenation of consciousness in all humans: mystery and wonder. Not Gemeinschaft nostalgic idylls. But, working aspects of human awareness, reintroduced as recognised attributes

**One way of looking at consciousness:
Using affective indicators from the structure
of feelings and experience as points in a model.**

<u>1. From Raymond Williams</u>   <u>2. From Bernard Smith</u>

<u>3. Model of consciousness</u>

Combining the above,
plus perspectives of
'the others' to form
the structure of feelings
and experience.

that need education and practice to be properly under-stood and 'worked'.

These aspects of human consciousness show up in all four subject groups. The indigenous have clear engage-ment with these aspects of daily life, and addicts suffer under the shadow side of both, finding chaos and terror where healthy mystery and wonder can reside. I believe what arises from the walkabout journey through con-sciousness, is that these attributes of human Feeling and Experience need to be officially acknowledged, and fac-tored into programs, to ensure holistic provision of life services.

James Cowan's work shows that noesis and poesis re-quire 'working'. As Darryl Reanney said, 'we are chil-dren of the stars, literally'. So, if we came from the same 'stuff' that was there at the first Big Bang, I believe he was right in suggesting that we all need to regularly commune with our source. Allowing mystery and won-der to oscillate through our consciousness, is like keeping the pathways of consciousness clean and healthy, flushed with the original energy of life. Otherwise, the 'others', become jammed in magnified versions of their balanc-ing opposites, which can create delusion and terror in a worst case scenario.

5. **Mystery** — Where we keep Engaging, Allowing Echo-logical Recycling to Renew, Giving our Lives Con-text and Reciprocity.

Stories from traditional culture, and ones emerging from today's experiences, are gateways into mystery. So is visiting nature, experiencing its beauty, and seeing that there is so much we do not understand. Mystery is a natural part of life. The certainty and determination to be right and understand everything, which modernity has thrust upon us, can be placed further behind, where it belongs in a more respectful place, exercising humility in the vastness of the universe, not 'planning to invade Mars'.

Hearing about human history, engaging with elders, and sitting still long enough to hear our own feelings and imaginations at work, can restore humanity. This is particularly needed among those who live with intellectual disability and mental illness. Gaining official approval for this serious 'work' is the issue. It is time the system began to practice the understanding that work is a life issue, not only a matter of vocation. Cultural work builds the soul of society, and when it is not done, the society lacks soul. And just as individuals can end up with exaggerated versions of the 'opposite' of whichever life energy of consciousness they ignore and fail to exercise regularly, so does society risk 'archetypal blow outs' when these matters are ignored.

6. **Wonder** — Having a Sense of Wonder in a Meditation on Life, Wandering Back to go Forward — 'Applied Dreaming', Replacing Narcissism.

We need to acknowledge that humanity is a tiny part of the universe. By creating more exposure to the wonder of life, in simple and reverent occasions, we can help people to rebalance and heal. Rituals designed to acknowledge the numinous and wonderful aspects of life refuel the human soul.

Not any particular 'brand' of belief or explanation of the universe is needed. Just simple processes to celebrate our oneness with life, and our part of the natural cycle of birth, life and death. More natural, more indigenous ways of being in our lives. These phenomena may lead to more spiritual occasions, attendance at funerals, births, community occasions and other ways people celebrate things bigger than themselves.

To ignore this aspect of humanness, is to negate a fundamental part of life. Daily life, ordinary life. Not life limited to 'the church'. Systemic incorporation of activities that connect with the numinous is part of healthy 'work'. Especially in the healing professions, but basically in all human fields of activity. The equivalent of an old Australian advertising campaign for milk, which used the catchline, 'Drink your milk Freddy ', as a message of daily protein, vitamin and mineral intake. In the same way, society needs to 'drink its milk' of numinosity on a daily basis. Or, as Hindus in India might put it, 'there's a point to the puja' (daily offering to the gods).

What it all means for policy, programs and service delivery

What does it mean in practice?

Put simply, I believe the above six parameters create a working framework for suggesting areas of development; for exploring aspects of healing and rehabilitation; and re-valuing processes currently missing from the health and community services provided for those who live with intellectual disability and mental illness. The aim of the follow-on project from this work, now underway, is to test these areas of lifeworld, in the daily context of involvement in community programs for these groups. It is developing a process for engaging with the two target groups and their support workers by using life journalling of their Experiences and Feelings over twelve months. By recruiting 'buddies' who can assist in the recording and experiencing of day-to-day sharing, interacting and individual activities, it is possible to create support for this process to occur. Recording times are fortnightly, and peer support groups meet to share their perspectives.

The six parameters above are factored into the program, designed to test the efficacy of bringing these aspects of life into full engagement. Imagination, Conversation, Perspective and Relational activities are shared, discussed and reviewed and recorded. Wonder and Mystery are built into the activities and a cyclic pattern of reverence for the mystery and celebration of the wonder. And the impact of these elements on the lives of participants is recorded, as part of the evidence of the 'health' of the individuals participating. The Feelings and Experiences of participants, facilitators and volunteer buddies are recorded during the exercise to provide tracking evidence of the lessons which are emerging from the project. The results will be fed into policy and program design and community service delivery for those living with intellectual disability and mental illness. Aiming for improvement in quality of life seems a simple target. But so many programs have promised that sort of goal before, so many are sceptical of its 'outcome potential'. This work promises to add the dimensions that have previously been ignored, because of slavish worship of rationality above holistic human understanding. And I believe the outcomes will be cost effective, recidivism decreasing, and beneficial to the community as a whole.

What will make it work?

The point I am making, without pre-empting the results of this current action research project, is that work-a-day ways of respecting and engaging people's potential for these activities, makes good pragmatic sense. The numinous can be any form of opening to a higher awareness. As Irish comedian Dave Allen used to end his weekly TV show, 'May your God go with you'. No specific identification need be made in these rituals with any sectarian point of view. In fact, the spirit of place is probably more likely to relate to 'generic' Australian circumstances. It will be up to the participants to plan, design and deliver. The 'driving energy' for all this, and the exchange of the six attributes of healthy human consciousness, is sharing them. People want to share, so we should let them. Uncle Raymond will be smiling, as it is his first point on the Structure of Feeling.

Equally important are the four circulating aspects of consciousness which engage people in the full range of human sharing of life skills. 'Working the culture', relating with each other, developing a perspective on life and its healthy plurality. Conversing in the cultural traffic, mixing imaginations, negotiating knowledge, and being encouraged to do what Aboriginal people in the 'native' cycle of life do, in the suburbs as much as the outback: 'When they're not *in* celebration (of the wonder of life) they're preparing for the next — that's life', (paraphrased from Fr Eugene Stockton's work, *The Aboriginal Gift: Spirituality for a Nation*).

What does Uncle Jurgen think?

Going by Uncle Jurgen's four-way test, I believe introducing these aspects of awareness into policy, program planning and service delivery will result in the following:

Reflecting the Truth of Human Nature in Healing — Creating activities and experiences relevant to people's lifeworld brings them into context. Nurturing Feelings and Experiences which help people rebalance their lives will achieve healing. As well as this, it will reflect the fullness of human nature and 'working'.

Truthfully and Responsibly acting for the Common Good — By admitting that previous activities have ignored large slabs of shared human reality, these approaches have greater potential than existing programs to add to the common good. They aim to reflect the fullness of humanity, and heal people holistically, not in segmented symptom suppressing impression managing ways.

Adding the Right amount of Wisdom and Compassion for Healing — Refusing the existing mechanistic value system and procedures which are applied in the system, this model engages with real needs in ways that address the full nature of individuals, and therefore of society. It requires risk-taking, and professional management.

Making Comprehensive Sense for Society's Evolution – Engaging with the inner aspects of humanity as a 'working' part of normal individual and societal functioning is long overdue. Modernism's true supporters will embrace a move into the territory too often ignored in the project over the past century. It makes sense to me, and only the results can show if it makes sense to humanity.

And the limitations?

The down side of all affective, person-centred approaches, requiring trust and sharing of ideas and skills, is 'the human element'. So much legislation now exists to try to negate this factor, that policy restrictions and regulations have created as many barriers as budget squeezes. But, mistakes will happen, and the only defence is to advocate taking the risk because the overall gain will outweigh any losses.

While risks lie in the approaches I am advocating, there is also an appeal to reintroduce true professionalism. In this way, nurses, teachers, social workers, support workers, families and community members, along with doctors, can all be part of 'the mix' that creates healing and rehabilitation.

Where to next on walkabout?

Returning to Uncle Raymond, where this story began, he ventured a view on 'the truth about a society', which I hope can be addressed in work to follow this. He believed a set of guideposts could be picked out from the actual daily life experiences of ordinary people. His Structure of Feeling led to the suggested guidelines above, but, his insight went deeper than there being a set formula to save the world. I risk repeating his words, to invite imagining whether these parameters cover Raymond's broad sweep of life:

The truth about a society, it would seem, is to be found in the actual relations, always exceptionally complicated, between the system of communication and learning, the system of mainte-nance and the system of generation and nurture... Our con-temporary experience of work, love, thought, art, learning, de-cision and play is more fragmented than in any other recorded kind of society, yet still necessarily, we try to make connections, to achieve integrity, and to gain control, and in part we suc-ceed. (13)

My hope is that the above work begins to 'make connec-tions, achieve integrity and to gain control' (in the sense of greater understanding, not 'power over'). Model-makers might have a go at overlaying Raymond's seven points of life experience mentioned there, with the consciousness points on the diamond model. It is all a way of seeing and feeling, towards more informed ways of being.

I am grateful for the journey to this stage. It has taught me a lot about myself, and the potential in sharing more with others as the substance of life; and it has taught me that giving is getting. 'You've got to give it away to have it' is the maxim of Alcholics Anonymous. I feel the world would be a better place if more people tried exchanging Feelings and Experiences.

I see Marshall Berman's point — about the future of the modernist project. For me, this work has been a 'way back to the future' after many years of being critical of modernism, because of its negative, mechanistic side. It can inspire feelings of freedom and new growth as well.

Nietzsche's... aim was not to promote any particular escape route. Rather it was to convince his readers that they didn't have to let themselves be absorbed by gigantic institutions: to strengthen these readers to the point where they could believe in their own inner strength. If powers of social control grew strong, men and women could grow even stronger. If people found themselves devalued, they had the capacity to create new values. Thus Nietzsche affirmed and deepened the modernist faith. (14)

The final word on the walkabout journey is about sharing from all of Uncle Raymond's and Uncle Bernard's writings, and my own work with the four groups covered here. I believe sharing is the principal missing factor in modernism's current 'mix'. A return to sharing more between human beings will answer the needs of the two marginalised groups we have focused on. It will be an expression of the love, which I see in indigenous terms, needs to be 'a working part of this culture', 'the business of life'. To Uncle Buckminster, it was purely logical: 'Selfishness can no longer be rationalised as inherently valid'. (15)

Glossary

awareness
the phenomenon of human thought either, when you are engaged with the world or when you are detached from worldly activities and sensing your existence in the universe

belief
a trust and confidence in a particular set of ideas, morals and values that are reflected by, and pertain to, how the world operates when it is working according to its ultimate plan

common
humanity
what we all share in our experience as social creatures, needing relationship with one another

common good
the shared set of experiences, values, equal rights to life, and the understanding of truth and fairness that exists among all human beings; and the process of ensuring that this comes about for all people

community
a regional group of people sharing place, socio-economic processes and broad values that determine rights and responsibilities among them

consciousness   daily human awareness of a persons thoughts and feelings as a whole

culture   a whole way of life among human beings, including traditions, beliefs, rites, rights, responsibilities and signifiers of meaning shared across a particular society

citizen   people who share a responsibility to participate in community life in order to preserve the common good

dadirri   to sit, wait and listen

deconstruction   two opposing terms help each receive its meaning from the contrasting perspective thrown up by its difference from the other — exactly what happens when concepts about culture and society, art, ideas and consciousness, are compared and contrasted with the Structure of Feeling and Experience of the 'others'

democratic   the process of free choice in deciding how people are to be governed and for what ultimate purpose, whether solely to administer logistics, or to represent the citizens regarding their morals, rights and responsibilities

Dreaming, the   that other reality of consciousness that links to the numinous as part of our natural inherited awareness

drongo   Australian colloquial expression for 'a slow coach'

drongo

dialectic — a phrase the author has coined to distinguish the slow, meandering way of examining things and waiting for knowledge

earthedness — connected to our roots in the earth: through our cells, our blood, our minerals, and spirit as part of being 'children of the stars'

echo-logical — the way the author sees history entering the timeless zone and echoing throughout human experience, providing perspective on past, present and future as aspects of the now(as against the idea of history repeating itself)

ego — that part of human consciousness which represents the personal will, reflection and personality of an individual

eidetic — reproducing a copy of any scale; taking the shape of

elders — those who hold the memory of a society and reflect back to the young how they can grow through rites of passage

elites — select groups of people, organisations or institutions which receive favoured treatment in particular circumstances between people, within society, or within an organisation

energy — the source of life for everything in the universe that provides the fuel for life, movement, power and force, in organic, inorganic matter and in human affairs

esoteric	belonging to the inner circle
exoteric	belonging to the whole circle; public story-telling
experience	the process of engaging with an activity, understanding, feeling or set of circumstances in life
feather energy	the uplifting 'unbearable lightness of being' captured and harnessed in the wings of birds
Feelings and Experience	representations of consciousness, lived out in people's daily lives, which are affective indicators of the basic human needs of heart, mind and soul
feeling	the experience of emotion that is linked to experience which leads to a positive or negative assessment of a circumstance
glocalisation	the ability of humans all over the world to act locally while remembering our global responsibility to protect and preserve Mother Earth
group	people who share a common experience such as: belief system, ethnic background, illness, disability, suffering or prejudice
higher power	the force that empowers and guides the universe and all of us

higher self	that part of each of us that connects with what is true, just, loving and good
identity	the image and associated implications of a person's nature, behaviour and position in society
impression management	the way politicians, business people, media and others can appear to do the right thing, but are not doing it in truth or practice
'in the mix'	what eventually shows up in the outcome, or turns out in practice
individual	the wholeness and distinctness of a person
knowledge	the capacity for individuals and society to both hold information and understand its meaning, in the context of time, culture and history
lifeworld	the daily lived experience of people
love	the quality of unconditional affection for another person, place, thing or idea
mandorla	the almond-shaped segment formed when two circles overlap (as in a Venn diagram) which is the overlay of opposites, such as heaven and earth
marginalised	individuals or groups in human society who, due to poverty, disability, illness, or some other difference that separates them from the mainstream, are unable to receive normal services or access to life conditions enjoyed and expected by the majority

mainstream	what the majority of 'normal' people in a society deem to be the accepted way to live, work and aspire in life
metaphor	when a description serves to illustrate another truth relevant to different circumstances
mimetic	imitating other creatures or people in mimicry of pose or action
mind	the place of consciousness, thought and feeling of/between individuals
mystical	those occurrences which are beyond the normal daily experience of life, through connection with higher powers in the universe, unable to be explained by rational thought alone
noesis	to perceive through metaphor, making stories of life
non-ordinary reality	where one can experience a state of consciousness where the 'rules' of ordinary reality are suspended
normal	the mainstream set of behaviours, habits and mores which determine how society operates 'in the centre'
numinous	feeling of attraction, awe and communion with the higher power in the universe
onto-diversity	the natural range of difference and diversity in human consciousness, necessary for our survival
other	the concept of someone or something that is not the subject in question, but a

	separate person or thing, identified by difference
poesis	to create harmonious compositions, making life a story
power	the ability to influence other people, things and events, and to make a difference in the way worldly activities unfold, in individual and group lives
reality	what people experience in their day-to-day engagement with life in nature and society
schizophrenia	a term coined by Emil Kraepelin and Eugen Bleuler between 1911-13 for a set of unrelated symptons of mental disturbance, which have since been falsely seen as 'an illness', when they are actually random assortments of 'non-normal' behaviours varying with every individual, and not scientifically proved to be mental illness.
sharedness	the ability to give and take between creatures; our common experiences of life
shaman	one who travels between the worlds of ordinary and non-ordinary reality
ship of state	the real-politik expression for a society and its ruling structures
ship of state of mind	a play on words to expand the above concept to include a society's (Western) or nation's state of consciousness
society	the whole population of people within a nation — their customs, conventions,

	traditions, and understandings about daily life
soul	the higher self of each person which is connected to the higher power of the universe
spirit	the shared human awareness of truth, morality and wonder at all life that is beyond the material
suburbs	areas spread around cities where people live, in individual and communal homes, lifestyles built around neighbourhoods and local services
walkabout	when people take time to leave their daily round of activities and connect with their dreaming, that part of their lives which links with the higher power in the universe, as well as with ancestors, the spirit of nature, creation stories and powers beyond the material
Western	a perspective among occidental developed nations, which includes capitalist values that are expressed in societies where freedom means the right to vote, and lifestyle is an experience of transglobal consumer capitalism
will	the part of each person that represents their intention, desire and motivation for life
wisdom	the ability to apply discerning judgement to life circumstances, in the light of experience and knowledge gained in life through the mind and the spirit

Chapter Notes

1. D. Bridie, *Photograph*, Mushroom Music Publishers, performed by C. Anu, *Stylin' Up*, Festival/Mushroom Records
2. N. Murray, *Love That Heals*, Universal Music Publishers, performed by C. Anu, *Stylin' Up*, Festival/Mushroom Records

Chapter One – Introduction

1. A. Toynbee, *Civilization on Trial*, Oxford University Press, London, 1948, p. 3.
2. A. Toynbee, *The World and the West*, BBC Reith Lectures, Oxford University Press, London, 1952, pp. 10-11.
3. R. Williams, *The Long Revolution*, Pelican, London 1965, pp. 117-118.
4. M. Berman, 'Why Modernism Still Matters', in *Modernity and Identity*, S. Lash and J. Friedman (eds), pp. 35-58, Oxford, 1991, pp. 47-48.
5. R. Williams, *The Long Revolution*, Pelican, London, 1965, p. 30.
6. M. Pusey, *Jurgen Habermas*, Key Sociologists Series, ed. P. Hamilton, Ellis Horwood, Chichester, Tavistock, London, & Methuen, NY, 1987, p. 122.
7. M. Pusey, ibid, p. 121.

8. ibid, p. 117.
9. ibid, p. 117.
10. ibid, pp. 117-8.
11. A. Giddens, *Sociology*, W.W. Norton, New York, 1991.
12. ibid.
13. ibid.
14. *The Truman Show*, movie (starring Jim Carrey – where Truman Burbank's life is turned into a daily 24 hour soap opera, but he does not know his life circumstances are being continuously manipulated and filmed for others' entertainment).
    S. Rudin, A. Schroeder et al (Producers), P. Weir (Director). 1998. USA. Paramount Pictures.
15. M. Pusey, op. cit., pp. 107-110.
16. M. Pusey, ibid, p. 58.
17. ibid, p. 35.
18. ibid, p. 109.
19. ibid, p. 73.
20. ibid, p. 107.
21. ibid.
22. ibid.
23. ibid, p. 58.
24. ibid.
25. ibid.
26. M. Berman, op. cit.
27. A. Giddens, op. cit.

Chapter Two – Community, Consciousness and the Common Good

1. A. Giddens, op. cit.
2. M. Pusey, ibid, p. 40.

3. ibid, p. 48.
4. D. Tacey, *Re-enchantment*, Harper Collins, Sydney, 2000.
5. R. Williams, *Culture and Society*, Hogarth Press ed., London, 1987.
6. R. Williams, *The Fight For Manod*, Hogarth Press, London, 1988, pp. 153-4.
7. G. Robertson, *Penguin New English Dictionary*, ed. Robert Allen, New Delhi, 2000, p. 370.
8. ibid.
9. J. Habermas, *The Theory of Communicative Action Vols I-II*, Heinemann, London, 1984.
10. M. Pusey, op. cit., p. 48.
11. M. Pusey, *Economic Rationalism In Canberra*, Cambridge University Press, Cambridge, 1991.
12. M. Pusey, ibid, pp. 236-7.
13. ibid.
14. R. Williams, *Border Country*, Penguin, 1961, p. 276.
15. R. Williams, ibid, p. 277.
16. ibid.
17. ibid, p. 271.
18. R. Williams, *Second Generation*, Chatto & Windus, London, 1978, pp. 137-8.
19. ibid.
20. ibid.
21. R. Williams, *Border Country*, p. 277.
22. ibid.
23. R. Williams, *Second Generation*, pp. 233-4.
24. J. Lusseyran, *And Then There Was Light*, Floris Books, Edinburgh, 1999, pp. 18-19.
25. M. Pusey, *Economic Rationalism In Canberra*, op.cit., pp. 236-7.

Chapter Three – Travelling our Border Country of the Structure of Feeling

1. B. Smith, *European Vision And The South Pacific 1758-1850: A Study in the History of Art and Ideas*, Oxford University Press, London, 1960, p. 242.
2. ibid.
3. ibid.
4. ibid.
5. R. Williams, *Culture and Society*, Hogarth Press 1987 ed. New Foreword p. 4.
6. ibid.
7. F. Inglis, *Raymond Williams*, Routledge, London, 1995, pp. 298-9.
8. R. Williams, *The Long Revolution*, Pelican, London, 1965, p. 136.
9. ibid, p. 131.
10. ibid, pp. 131-2.
11. ibid.
12. T. Zeldin, *Conversation*, Harvill, London, 1998, p. 27.
13. ibid, p. 21.
14. R. Williams, *Culture and Society*, op. cit., pp. 68-69.
15. ibid, pp. 24-25.
16. ibid, p. 76.
17. ibid, p. 109.
18. ibid, p. 114.
19. ibid, p. 29.
20. ibid.
21. ibid, pp. 60-62.
22. ibid.
23. ibid, pp. 73-74.
24. ibid, p. 125.

25. ibid, pp. 58-59.

26. ibid, p. 82.

27. ibid.

28. ibid, p. 138.

29. ibid, p. 140.

30. ibid, p. 211.

31. ibid, p. 225.

32. J. Habermas, quoted in Michael Pusey, *Jurgen Habermas*, op. cit., p. 121.

33. R. Williams, *Culture and Society*, op. cit., p. 237.

34. ibid.

35. ibid, pp. 241-2.

36. R. Williams, *Communications*, Pelican 3rd ed. 1976, pp. 138-9.

37. ibid, pp.125-7.

38. ibid.

39. ibid.

40. ibid, p.112.

41. ibid.

42. ibid, pp. 83-4.

43. ibid, p. 103.

44. ibid, p.10.

45. ibid.

46. ibid, pp. 10-11.

47. ibid, p.11.

48. ibid.

49. ibid.

50. R. Williams, *Culture and Society*, op. cit., p. 256.

51. ibid, p. 253.

52. ibid, pp. 253-4.

53. ibid.

54. ibid, p. 266.
55. ibid, p. 274.
56. ibid, p. 291.
57. ibid.
58. ibid, pp. 292-3.
59. ibid, p. 295.
60. ibid, pp. 299-300.
61. ibid, p. 330.
62. ibid, pp. 325-6.

Chapter Four – Finding Perspective on Life by Listening for Echo-logy

1. B. Smith, *The Boy Adeodatus*, Penguin, Melbourne, 1984, p. 267.
2. B. Smith, quoted in P. Beilharz, *Imagining The Antipodes*, Cambridge University Press, Cambridge, 1997, p. 9.
3. B. Smith, op. cit., p. 266.
4. ibid, p. 267.
5. B. Smith, writing in the 'Foreword' to P. Fuller, *The Australian Scapegoat*, University of Western Australia Press, Perth, 1986, pp. xii.
6. ibid, p. xiii.
7. C. Belsey, (Chair of Centre for Critical and Cultural Theory, University of Wales, Cardiff), contributing to the *New Penguin English Dictionary*, ed. Robert Allen, Penguin Books, New Delhi, 2000, p. 362.
8. B. Smith quoted in P. Beilharz, *Imagining The Antipodes*, op. cit.

Chapter Five – People Living with Mental Illness

1. L. Bacall, quoted in A. Wilson Schaef, *Meditations For Women Who Do Too Much*, Harper Collins, San Francisco, 1990.
2. R. Johnson, Owning Your Own Shadow, Harper, San Francisco, 1991, p. 52.
3. A. Wilson Schaef, *Native Wisdom For White Minds*, Random House Australia, Sydney, 1995.
4. *New Penguin English Dictionary*, ed. Robert Allen, New Delhi, 2000, p.1235.
5. ibid, p. 1235.
6. R. Johnson, op. cit.
7. ibid.
8. ibid.
9. ibid.
10. ibid.
11. R. Steiner, *Education For Special Needs*, RS Press, London 1998, p. 43.
12. ibid.
13. A. Wilson Schaef, *Native Wisdom For White Minds*, Random House, Sydney, 1995.
14. B. Paris, *Karen Horney: A Psychoanalyst's Search*, Yale UP, New Haven, 1994, pp. xv-xvi.
15. ibid.
16. J. Rubin & S. Steinfeld, (American Institute for Psychoanalysis), writing in their Foreword to Karen Horney, *Neurosis and Human Growth*, Norton 1991, p. 4.
17. K. Horney, ibid.
18. B. Paris, op. cit., pp. 216-7.
19. ibid, p. 218.

20. J. Rubin & S. Steinfeld, in the Foreword to, K. Horney, *Neurosis and Human Growth*, op. cit., p. 5.
21. K. Horney, *Our Inner Conflicts*, Norton, NY, 1992, p. 32.
22. M. Vonnegut, *The Eden Express*, Praeger, NY, 1975, Preface, p. ix.
23. ibid, p. 85.
24. ibid, p. 81.
25. ibid, pp. 84-6.
26. J. Rubin & S. Steinfeld, op. cit., p. 2.
27. B. Paris, op. cit., p. 220.
28. K. Horney, *Our Inner Conflicts*, op. cit., pp. 42-3.
29. B. Keeney, *Everyday Soul*, Riverhead, NY, 1997, p. 10.
30. ibid, p. 11.
31. B. Keeney, *Shaking Out The Spirits*, Station Hill Press/Barrytown, 1994, p. 15-16.
32. ibid, p. 22.
33. ibid, p. 43.
34. ibid.
35. ibid, pp. 80-1.
36. B. Keeney, *Everyday Soul*, op. cit., p. 75.
37. ibid, pp. 101-2.
38. M. Vonnegut, *The Eden Express*, op. cit., p. 214.
39. ibid, p. 194.
40. ibid, pp. 190-1.

Chapter Six – People Living with Intellectual Disability

1. *New Penguin English Dictionary*, ed. Robert Allen, New Delhi, 2000, p. 729.
2. ibid, p. 729.

3. ibid, p. 278.
4. H. Nouwen, *The Road To Peace*, John Garratt, Melbourne, 1998, p. 153.
5. ibid.
6. T. Zeldin, *An Intimate History Of Humanity*, Vintage, London, 1998, p. 440.
7. ibid, p. 444.
8. ibid, p. 466-7.
9. T. Zeldin, *Conversation*, Harvill, London, 1999, p. 57.
10. ibid.
11. ibid.
12. D.H. Lawrence, *Fantasia of the Unconscious*, Penguin, 1971, p. 68.
13. ibid, pp. 68-9.
14. ibid, p. 76.
15. H. Nouwen, *The Wounded Healer*, Image Books, Doubleday, NY, 1979.
16. R. Theobald, *We DO Have Future Choices*, Southern Cross University Press, Lismore, 1999.
17. H. Nouwen, *With Open Hands*, Ballantine Books, NY, 1992, p. 25.
18. J. Vanier, *Community And Growth*, St Paul, Homebush, 1979, p. 75.
19. ibid, p. 88.
20. ibid, p. 115.
21. ibid, p. 138.
22. J. Vanier, *From Brokenness To Community*, Paulist Press, Mahway, NJ, 1992, p.14.
23. ibid, p. 16.
24. ibid, p. 34.
25. H. Nouwen, *The Road To Peace*, op. cit., p. 159.
26. ibid, pp. 167-8.

27. J. Vanier, *A Door Of Hope: The Transformation of Pain*, Hodder & Stoughton, London, 1996, p. 60.
28. ibid, p. 16.
29. ibid, p. 15.
30. ibid, p. 52.
31. ibid, p. 59.
32. J. Vanier, *Lightning Conductors of Grace*, St Paul 1979, p. 78.
33. ibid, p. 99.
34. ibid, p. 97-115.
35. T. Zeldin, *Conversation*, Harvill, London, 1999, p. 57.

Chapter Seven - Finding Others on Suburban Walkabout - Indigenous and Addicted

1. A. Wilson Schaef, *Native Wisdom For White Minds*, op. cit.
2. D. Reanney, *The Death Of Forever*, Longman Cheshire, Melbourne, 1991, p. 251.
3. ibid, p. 244.
4. M. Jackson, *At Home In The World*, Duke, Durham, 1995, p. ix.
5. J. Clifford, *The Predicament of Culture*, Harvard University Press, Cambridge, Mass. 1988, pp. 340-1.
6. J. Cowan, *Mysteries Of The Dreaming*, Brandl and Schlesinger, Melbourne, 2001, p. 9.
7. M. Jackson, op. cit., p. 26.
8. ibid.
9. J. Cowan, op. cit., pp. 12-13.
10. M. Jackson, op. cit., pp. 38-9.
11. ibid., p. 35.

12. M. L. von Franz, *The Interpretation Of Fairy Tales*, Shambhala, Boston, 1996, p. 95.

13. J. Cowan, *Letters From A Wild State*, Element Books, London, 1991, p. 75.

14. ibid, pp. 78-9.

15. M. Jackson, op. cit., p.117.

16. ibid, p. 118.

17. ibid.

18. ibid, p. 120.

19. ibid, p. 40.

20. A. Wilson Schaef, *Meditations For Women Who Do Too Much*, op. cit.

21. ibid.

22. ibid.

23. ibid.

24. A. Wilson Schaef, *Native Wisdom For White Minds*, op. cit.

25. A. Wilson Schaef, *When Society Becomes An Addict*, Harper Row, San Francisco,1987, p. 67.

26. A. Wilson Schaef, *Meditations For Women Who Do Too Much*, op. cit.

27. A. Wilson Schaef, *When Society Becomes An Addict*, op. cit. p. 61.

28. A. Wilson Schaef, *Beyond Therapy Beyond Science*, p. 12.

29. A. Wilson Schaef, ibid, p. 114.

30. A. Wilson Schaef, *Living In Process*, Random House Australia, Sydney, 1998, p. 360.

31. G. Simmel, *The Philosophy Of Money*, ed. D. Frisby, Routledge, London 1990, p. 485.

32. ibid, p. 65.

33. ibid, p. 128.

34. ibid, p. 129.
35. A. Wilson Schaef, *Living In Process*, op. cit., p. 63.
36. ibid, p. 64.
37. A. Wilson Schaef, *When Society Becomes An Addict*, op. cit., p. 126.
38. ibid, p. 108.

Chapter Eight - Suburbs

1. R. Ardery, *The Social Contract*, Collins, London, 1970, p. 219.
2. ibid, pp. 219-220.
3. ibid, pp. 220-226.
4. D. Morris, *Intimate Behaviour*, Jonathan Cape, 1971, Triad Grafton ed, London, 1979, p. 126.
5. ibid, p. 212.
6. ibid, pp. 212-213.
7. H. Stretton, *Ideas For Australian Cities*, 3rd ed, Transit Australia, Sydney, 1993, pp. 10-11.
8. ibid, p. 18.
9. A. S. Neill, *Summerhill*, Penguin, Harmondsmith, 1973, p. 13.
10. S. Schama, *Landscape and Memory*, Vintage Books, London, 1996, p. 16.
11. ibid, pp. 10, 16.
12. ibid, pp. 17-18.
13. ibid, p. 18.
14. ibid, p. 14.
15. ibid, p. 12.
16. T. Zeldin, *Paradise*, Collins Harvill, London, 1988, pp. 15-17.
17. ibid, pp. 17-19.

18. ibid, p. 30.
19. M. Bracewell, *England Is Mine*, Flamingo, London, 1997, pp. 176-177.
20. ibid, pp. 177-179.
21. ibid, pp. 178-179.
22. ibid, p. 198.
23. ibid, p. 199.
24. E. Eisenberg, *The Ecology of Eden*, Picador, London, 2000, pp. 152-153.
25. ibid, pp. 154-155.
26. ibid, pp. 158-163.
27. ibid, pp. 430-433.
28. A.S. Neill, op. cit., pp. 11-12.
29. R. B. Fuller, *Your Private Sky: The Art of Design Science*, compilation ed. J. Krausse, C. Lichtenstein, Lars Muller Publishers, and CargoLifter AG, Germany, 2002, p. 17.
30. ibid, p. 485.
31. ibid, p. 407-408.
32. ibid, p. 402.
33. ibid, p. 500-521.
34. S. Rushdie, *Imaginary Homelands: Essays 1981-1991*, Granta/Penguin, London, 1992, pp. 94-99.
35. ibid, pp. 10-12.
36. ibid, p. 19.
37. R. Critchfield, *The Villagers: Changed Values, Altered Lives - The Closing of the Urban-Rural Gap*, Anchor Doubleday, NY, 1994, p. 5.
38. ibid, pp. 8-9.
39. ibid, p. 18.

Chapter Nine - Mandorla: The Overlap of Opposites

1. M. Foucault, *The Order Of Things*, Tavistock,
    London, 1970, p. 326, quoted in Footnote 26,
    Chap 3 in M. Jackson, *At Home In The World*, Duke
    University Press, Durham, 1995, p. 179.
2. M. Jackson, Michael, op. cit. p. 167.
3. op. cit., pp. 169-172.
4. op. cit., pp. 171-172.
5. R. Johnson, *Owning Your Own Shadow*, Harper San
    Francisco, 1991, p. 92.
6. C. Trungpa, *The Secret Path of the Warrior*, ed.
    Gimian, Carolyn Rose,
    Shambhala Books, Boston, 1995, p. 75.
7. T. Singh, *Dialogues On A Course in Miracles*, Life
    Action Press, Foundation For Inner Peace, Los
    Angeles, 1995, p. 208.
8. R. M. Rilke, *Letters To A Young Poet*, Norton, NY,
    1994, p. 65.
9. A. Locey, quoted in A.W. Schaef, *Native Wisdom for
    White Minds*, Random House, NY, 1995.
10. R. M. Rilke, op. cit., p. 65.
11. op. cit., pp. 65-66.
12. J. Cowan, *Mysteries of the Dreaming*, Brandl and
    Schlesinger,
    Melbourne, 2001, pp. 51-52.
13. ibid. p. 9.
14. M.J. Christie, B. Perrett, 'Negotiating resources:
    language, knowledge and the search for 'secret
    English' in northeast Arnhem Land', Chapter 4 in
    R. Howitt, J. Connell P. Hirsch, eds, *Resources,
    Nations and Indigenous Peoples: Case Studies from*

Australasia, Melanesia and Southeast Asia, Oxford University Press, Melbourne, 1996, p. 61.

15. ibid, p. 61.
16. D. Mowaljarli, quoted in P. Collins, 'Prophets vs Profits: The gift of Australia's Indigenous People', article in *Conscious Living,* Issue 34, pp. 5-8.
17. ibid.
18. ibid.
19. R. Williams, *Culture,* Fontana, Glasgow, 1981, pp. 216-217.
20. ibid.
21. ibid.
22. J. Lauck, *The Voice of the Infinite in the Small,* Swan Raven & Co, Mill Spring NC, 1998, pp. xxi-xxii.
23. ibid, p. xxii.
24. ibid, pp. 231-232.
25. ibid, p. 232.
26. ibid, pp. 232-234.
27. T. Winton, *Dirt Music,* Picador Pan Macmillan, Sydney, 2001, p. 451.

Chapter Ten - Diamonds and Dust

1. M. Berman, 'Why Modernism Still Matters', in *Modernity & Identity,*
   op. cit., p. 41.
2. *New Penguin English Dictionary,* op. cit., p. 871.
3. M. Berman, op. cit., p. 41.
4. *New Penguin English Dictionary,* op. cit., p. 501.
5. ibid, p. 499.
6. ibid, p. 772.
7. ibid, p. 239.

8. ibid, p. 506.

9. ibid, p. 439.

10. R. B. Fuller, *Your Private Sky*, compilation ed. J. Krausse & C. Lichtenstein, Lars Muller Publishers, and CargoLifter AG, Germany, 2002, pp. 17-19, 407-8.

11. ibid, p. 485.

12. ibid, p. 407.

13. R. Williams, *The Long Revolution*, op. cit., p. 136.

14. M. Berman, op. cit., p. 40.

15. R. B. Fuller, op. cit., p. 521.

Index

N

S

OTHER BEST SELLING SID HARTA TITLES CAN BE FOUND AT

http://www.sidharta.com.au   http://Anzac.sidharta.com

***

HAVE YOU WRITTEN A STORY?
http://www.publisher-guidelines.com

Best-selling titles by Kerry B. Collison

Readers are invited to visit our publishing websites at:
http://www.sidharta.com.au
http://www.publisher-guidelines.com/
http://temple-house.com/

Kerry B. Collison's home pages:
http://www.authorsden.com/visit/author.asp?AuthorID=2239
http://www.expat.or.id/sponsors/collison.html
http://clubs.yahoo.com/clubs/asianintelligencesresources
email: author@sidharta.com.au